D0893672

APOCALYPSIS
MYSTERIORUM CYBELES.

Das ist

Eine Schnakische

Wochen-Comedie

Oder

verplauderte

Stroh-Hochzeit.

Und

Wasch-haffte

KInDeLeIns KerMsse.

Im Jahre

SeChs Gänß IM Haberstroh/
DIe KLatzgen VVahren froh!

Oder

QVanDo CoMbLaterant sVsanna, sabIna, rosIna,
serMones repLICant & ab hoC, VeL ab haC, VeL ab ILLaC.

AUTORE

VVIGANDO SEXVVOCHIO,

Bojemo.

MOTHERING BABY: ON BEING A WOMAN IN EARLY MODERN GERMANY

Johannes Praetorius's *Apocalypsis Mysteriorum Cybeles. Das ist Eine Schnakische Wochen-Comedie* (1662)

MEDIEVAL AND RENAISSANCE
TEXTS AND STUDIES
VOLUME 371

MOTHERING BABY: ON BEING A WOMAN IN EARLY MODERN GERMANY

Johannes Praetorius's *Apocalypsis Mysteriorum Cybeles. Das ist Eine Schnakische Wochen-Comedie* (1662)

Edited and translated by
GERHILD SCHOLZ WILLIAMS

ACMRS
(Arizona Center for Medieval and Renaissance Studies)
Tempe, Arizona
2010

Published by ACMRS (Arizona Center for Medieval and Renaissance Studies)
Tempe, Arizona
© 2010 Arizona Board of Regents for Arizona State University.
All Rights Reserved.

Library of Congress Cataloging-in-Publication Data

Praetorius, Johannes, 1630-1680.
  [Apocalypsis mysteriorum cybeles. English & German]
  Mothering baby : on being a woman in early modern Germany : Johannes
Praetorius's Apocalypsis mysteriorum cybeles, Das ist eine schnakische wochen-
comedie (1662) / edited and translated by Gerhild Scholz Williams.
    p. cm. -- (Medieval and Renaissance texts and studies ; v. 371)
  Includes bibliographical references and index.
  ISBN 978-0-86698-419-5 (alk. paper)
  1. Motherhood--Poetry. 2. Childbirth--Poetry. 3. Women--Poetry.
  4. Women--Germany--History--17th century. 5. Motherhood in literature.
  6. Childbirth in literature. 7. Women in literature. I. Scholz Williams, Gerhild,
1976- II. Title.
  PT1757.P786A6613 2010
  831'.5--dc22
                                                                    2010011108

Frontispiece:
With permission of the Herzog August Bibliothek,
Wolfenbüttel, Germany

∞
This book is made to last. It is set in Adobe Caslon Pro,
smyth-sewn and printed on acid-free paper to library specifications.
Printed in the United States of America

TABLE OF CONTENTS

ACKNOWLEDGEMENTS

When working on a book about the seventeenth-century journalist and writer Johannes Praetorius (1630–1680), one small tract caught my sustained attention, the *Apocalypsis Mysteriorum Cybeles* (1662). This tongue-firmly-in-cheek commentary on women, virginity, marriage, and motherhood tells about "lying-in," the six-week-period immediately following childbirth, when the new mother had to remain confined in the conjugal bedroom (also called confinement room) resting from the rigors of childbirth. During this period, only women relatives and female friends were allowed to visit with her. With them she exchanged gossip and news about family, children, husbands, maids, housekeeping, and community affairs. Praetorius's brief tract represents a man's surreptitious look into what is decidedly a woman's world, into the secrets women shared mostly with each other. The text is available in digitized form, no edition or translation had ever been done up of this time, which seems a pity because this tract is not only funny but exceedingly informative on many aspects of early modern gender, sexuality, and early modern urban culture.

In spite of its brevity, the *Apocalypsis* presented me with many linguistic and cultural challenges. This meant that, along the way, I incurred much editorial debt, most of it with Elaine Tennant, my colleague and friend from the German Department at the University of California, Berkeley. Her detailed critique of the introduction and translation provided invaluable corrections and suggestions for improvements. Moreover, her profound knowledge of early modern literature and culture immensely benefitted this volume. As did her sense of humor!

I also wish to express my gratitude and appreciation to Amy Cislo, (Washington University) who produced a first transcript of the German text. I am grateful to the graduate students in the WU German Department who, in a seminar on early modern German literature and culture (F 07), read through the transcription and translation and made helpful suggestions. The Herzog August Bibliothek at Wolfenbüttel (Germany), provided a copy of the original; as with many of my projects, the professional library staff was unfailingly helpful and supportive. I thank Washington University for providing the resources for research assistance and incidental expenses. And last, but certainly not least, I want to express my most sincere appreciation to the excellent anonymous editor whose careful review of the manuscript made this project conform to the high standards of the MRTS Press and to Todd Halvorsen who accompanied the project to completion.

Gerhild Scholz Williams
St. Louis, May 2009

ABOUT THE TRANSLATION

The casually colloquial, often coarse, use of early modern German in this tract presents a challenge for any translator. I decided to stay as close to the text as possible having made the decision that it would be more important to capture the meaning of the narrative while still bringing across some of the early modern humorous take on the lives of mothers and wives. I did not attempt to imitate in English the rhyme and rhythm of the poems interspersed in the prose text. They are quite artful and accomplished and add enjoyment for the reader of German. Moreover, the text conveys much of local and contemporary culture that may be unfamiliar to the modern reader. To aid the reader's understanding of the more obscure allusions, jokes, and sayings, I have added explanatory footnotes. For some of the proverbs, sayings, and coarse language I have provided English equivalents. However, when the occasional opacity of meaning simply could not be dispelled, I have indicated this in the notes. In the end, it was my aim to produce a readable document all the while preserving some of the language that was clearly intended to amuse the reader, and, occasionally, make her laugh.

GSW

Introduction*

"Always news, rarely good news," writes Johannes Praetorius, "but if things always remained the same, God would not need to send us so many unheard-of warning prophets in all the elements." This statement very effectively illustrates Praetorius's conception of himself as a writer and interpreter of his times. His vast output in print indeed begins and ends with his self-assigned task of informing, teaching, cajoling, and amusing his readership.[1] Commenting on contemporary culture, on issues of gender and class, and on the political and intellectual concerns of his day, he constructs a panorama in print in which wonders, the occult, the emerging scientific way of thinking, family, and social mores are recurrent themes. For Praetorius, as for many writers of the seventeenth century, knowledge, the question of who knows what and how well, was as much a social issue as an intellectual challenge. The various "ways of knowing,"[2] these types of knowledge that tell us how realities were constructed and events reported, lead

---

* The text used for this transcription and translation comes from the collection of the HAB = Herzog August Bibliothek, Wolfenbüttel, Germany, as do several other texts mentioned in this introduction. I wish to thank the HAB, as well as Ashgate Publishing for permission to use part of the introduction and chapter 4 of G. S. Williams, *Ways of Knowing in Early Modern Germany: Johannes Praetorius as a Witness to His Time* (Aldershot: Ashgate, 2006), as the basis for this introduction. HAB M: Lo 7169. The text has been digitized: http://diglib.hab.de/drucke/lo-7169/start.htm.

[1] "Immer was neues—Selten was gutes . . . [D]enn bliebe man bey dem Alten/ so würde der eyverende Gott iezt wohl nicht so viel unerhörte Straff-Propheten zu uns senden/ aus allen Elementen." He goes on: "Nehmlich/ hat man nicht von dem grausamen Erdbeben im Welschlande etc. gehöret? Seynd nicht Feuer-Kugeln und andere brennende Prodigia gewesen? Ist nicht das Wasser an etlichen Orthen in Bluth verwandelt worden?" ([H]ave we not heard about the horrible earthquake in Italy, etc.? Have there not been balls of fire and other fiery wonders? Has not water been changed into blood in several places?) (A ij). Johannes Praetorius, *Sacra Filamenta Divæ Virginis, oder Naumburgsche Plumerant-farbene Faden, daß ist/ Unerhörtes Prodigium, Von der Hoch-blauen Seide/ So bey Laucha um Naumburg/ unlängst . . . gefallen gewesen* (Halle in Sachsen: Gedruckt Melchior Oelschlegeln, 1665),1 [HAB 180.21 (6) Quod].

[2] Taken from the title of John V. Pickstone, *Ways of Knowing: A New History of Science, Technology, and Medicine* (Chicago: University of Chicago Press, 2001).

to forms of inquiry and confirmation, "ways of telling," that provided writers like Praetorius many ways of making events, however implausible, decipherable.[3]

Praetorius witnessed an age that, more than most before or since, was marked by an intensely productive, and sometimes hostile, intertwining of old and new. Shaken by seemingly interminable wars, changing political alliances, and undulating military fronts, the seventeenth century continues, to this day, to frustrate all but the most detail-oriented historians. People were stricken with illness and hunger and frightened by rapidly declining fertility rates that, along with countless war-related deaths, depleted the continent of its population by the hundreds of thousands.[4] Non-scientist and non-expert though he was, Praetorius observed with great acuity and sensitivity the political and military conflicts, the economic and social forces that pitted in ever-changing alliances the great European powers against each other. Moreover, he reacted with acerbic criticism to what he saw and what he read about the relations between the social classes and the sexes, noting the sharp contrast between the miseries of the times and the much-ridiculed interest in and passion for elaborate and costly *alamode*, meaning French, fashion. The end of days surely was near when men wore tights and *Pluderhosen*. There were other signs. Contemporaries believed that this century, more than any previous one, was marked by the appearance of uncounted prodigies and wonders, by comets and celestial portents. Either predicative or explicative, these comets and wonders accompanied the course of world events like an endless, if confusing, conversation between mankind and the divine, assiduously elucidated in print for all who wanted to understand.[5] Natural history, a relatively

---

[3] Andrew Barnaby and Lisa J. Schnell, introduction to *Literate Experience: The Work of Knowing in Seventeenth-Century English Writing* (New York: Palgrave, 2002).

[4] While Praetorius frequently refers to a population decimated by illness and death, and while the loss of life from many causes was significant, newer research has shown that the actual decline in population numbers was not uniformly spread across the continent. See Heinz Schilling, *Die neue Zeit: Vom Christenheitseuropa zum Europa der Staaten, 1250–1750*, Siedlers Geschichte Europas (Munich: Siedler Verlag, 1999), 265; see also the bibliographic information in *Zwischen Alltag und Katastrophe: Der Dreissigjährige Krieg aus der Nähe*, ed. Benigna von Krusenstjern and Hans Medick, Veröffentlichungen des Max-Planck-Instituts für Geschichte 148 (Göttingen: Vandenhoeck & Ruprecht, 1999), "Einleitung," note 4; Benigna von Krusenstjern, "Seliges Sterben und böser Tod: Tod und Sterben in der Zeit des Dreißigjährigen Krieges," in eadem and Medick, eds., *Zwischen Alltag und Katastrophe*, 469–97; Julius R. Ruff, *Violence in Early Modern Europe, 1500–1750*, New Approaches to European History (Cambridge: Cambridge University Press, 2001), 60–61, 207.

[5] Sara J. Schechner, *Comets, Popular Culture, and the Birth of Modern Cosmology* (Princeton: Princeton University Press, 1997); Christina Hofmann-Randall, *Monster, Wunder und Kometen: Sensationsberichte aus Flugblättern des 16. bis 17. Jahrhunderts* (Erlangen: Universitätsbibliothek, 1999); Franz Mauelshagen, "Illustrierte Kometenflugblätter in wahrnehmungsgeschichtlicher Perspektive," in *Das illustrierte Flugblatt in der*

recent addition to the forms of knowledge production of the seventeenth century, introduced a plethora of new information as a result of explorations abroad and experimentation at home.[6]

Still, in spite of terror, moral outrage, religious fervor, social prejudice, lax morals, and the century's seemingly perpetual wars and skirmishes, Praetorius occasionally lightens the burden for his readers by letting them laugh. This is the side of him we will see reflected in the tract transcribed and translated below. We will encounter this sense of seventeenth-century laughter — in this case laughter related to sexuality and gender — that is also Praetorius's, a socially prejudiced, xenophobic, and misogynist laughter, but it is laughter nonetheless.

Like many of his contemporaries, Praetorius recognized that he lived in an era of great change. The Neapolitan writer and philanthropist Giovan Battista Manso (1560–1645) hailed the seventeenth century for its discoveries of new and hitherto unknown worlds, in which, in its own way, it rivaled the momentous sixteenth century.[7] Praetorius anticipated comparably rapid advances in all areas of knowledge for his century, spurred on by the invention of wondrous machines like the telescope and the microscope that opened outward and inward horizons. The study of human physiology was leading to a better understanding of the workings of the human body, and research in chemical processes was creating more efficacious medicines. Writers, artists, and scientists probed the physicality and psychology of men and women in learned tracts, in dramas, novels, and poetry and virulent attacks against the supposed impulse to witchcraft and devil worship.[8] Praetorius and his contemporaries felt that their century would be the envy of ensuing generations. At its close, the German philosopher and mathematician Gottfried Wilhelm Leibniz (1646–1716) concurred that it indeed had

---

Kultur der Frühen Neuzeit: Wolfenbütteler Arbeitsgespräche 1997, ed. Wolfgang Harms and Michael Schilling, Mikrokosmos: Beiträge zur Literaturwissenschaft und Bedeutungsforschung (Frankfurt am Main: Peter Lang, 1998), 101–35.

    [6] On the singularity of the Scientific Revolution of the seventeenth century, see Brian Vickers, ed., introduction to *Occult and Scientific Mentalities in the Renaissance* (Cambridge, MA: Harvard University Press, 1984); for the more recent modifications of this view see Paula Findlen, "Francis Bacon and the Reform of Natural History in the Seventeenth Century," in *History and the Disciplines: The Reclassification of Knowledge in Early Modern Europe*, ed. R. Donald Kelley (Rochester: Rochester University Press, 1997), 240–60, here 247–48.

    [7] "[Ich glaube] dem Allerhöchsten danken zu müssen, der mich in dieses glückliche Jahrhundert treten ließ" [I have to thank the Most High that he allowed me to be born into this fortunate century]: Giovan Battista Manso in a letter to Paolo Beni of Padua, Naples, March 1610, cited by Wolfgang Schmale, "Das 17. Jahrhundert und die neuere europäische Geschichte," *Historische Zeitschrift* 264 (1997): 587–612, here 587.

    [8] Anne Llewellyn Barstow, *Witchcraze: A New History of the European Witch Hunts* (San Francisco: Pandora, 1994), Stuart Clark, *Thinking with Demons: The Idea of Witchcraft in Early Modern Europe* (New York: Oxford University Press, 1997).

been a century of transformations brought about by the emergence of many significant inventions and ideas, including his own.[9]

Succeeding generations have alternately admired, pitied, and scorned the seventeenth century's purported love of exaggerated forms in literature, its visual and architectural excesses, as well as its fascination with the occult and its passion for collecting. Frequently, students of literature, unfamiliar with the period's aesthetic apirations and linguistic inventions, have tended to turn away from Baroque narrative, bored by protagonists who wander, fight, love, and suffer through interminable sequels. Some observers smile in admiration, while others tartly dismiss as verbose their predecessors' efforts at joining natural philosophy, history, mathematics, rhetoric, and theology in a universal science of knowing. Some disparage the century's eagerness to collect, order, and categorize diverse specimens in its overflowing chambers of wonders (*Wunderkammern*), early ancestors of our museums. Even as later generations of writers and philosophers made use of the information gathered in the century's vast encyclopedias and memory books, literary scholars and historians tended to view these versions of early-modern databases—endless lists of disparate items arranged alphabetically or numerically, commentaries, and quotations taken from authorities—with only mild interest, bordering on condescension. Only of late have the efforts of these early workers in the production lines of knowledge, these constructors of huge compendia variously called *Collectanea, Theatrum* literature, or commonplace books, received the attention they deserve. These treasure troves of knowledge represent a paradigm of the depth and breadth of knowing that moves beyond narrowly focused areas of specialization.[10]

Praetorius's substantial and varied print productions are an excellent guide to this century's diversity of knowing and telling. His European outlook and his reflections on the increasing political, social, and cultural heterogeneity of his world offer fascinating insights into minds that are discovering new worlds around the globe, in the sky, and, turning to gaze at the heretofore invisibly small through the new invention, the microscope, in realms hitherto unseen. The multiversity of genres, chaos even, Praetorius's "ways of telling," are as varied and challenging to

---

[9] Schmale, "Das 17. Jahrhundert und die neuere europäische Geschichte," 587: "Finis saeculi novam rerum faciem aperuit." On Leibniz see G. MacDonald Ross, *Leibniz* (Oxford: Oxford University Press, 1984).

[10] Helmut Zedelmaier, *Bibliotheca universalis und Bibliotheca selecta: Das Problem der Ordnung des gelehrten Wissens in der frühen Neuzeit* (Cologne: Böhlau Verlag, 1992); idem, "Von den Wundermännern des Gedächtnisses: Begriffsgeschichtliche Anmerkungen zu 'Polyhistor' und 'Polyhistorie'," in *Die Enzyklopädie im Wandel vom Hochmittelalter bis zur Frühen Neuzeit*, ed. Christel Meier-Staubach (Munich: Fink, 2002), 421–45; Ann Blair, *The Theater of Nature: Jean Bodin and Renaissance Science* (Princeton: Princeton University Press, 1997), 4–5. I am grateful to Dr. Zedelmaier (Munich and Wolfenbüttel) for providing me with a copy of his essay in advance of its publication.

the modern reader as his expansive "ways of knowing" must have been to his contemporary audience. He mixes Latin and German and constructs endless acrostics using letters and numbers; he combines comic verse and theatrical prose dialogue, science and wonder, serious social invectives about the behavior of men and women and thoughtful comments on the state of women and girls.

The audience for whom he writes is, for the most part, urban, literate, and, judging by some of his Latin tracts, even learned. He writes for men and women whose ability to read he champions, even praises, while he is considerably less enthusiastic about writing women, finding that they waste too much time on writing specious love letters. Praetorius is ultimately revealed as an author who, like his readers, is able to accommodate assumptions and expectations that we find fascinating, in part because they seem to us mutually exclusive: magic appears next to science; astronomical phenomena are as carefully researched and explicated as wondrous divine messages; scathing social anger appears next to compassionate commentary about the harsh life of the less privileged; sardonic comments on marriage accompany the affirmation of familial loyalty.

Praetorius's Life

For most of his life, Praetorius lived and worked as a writer in the city of Leipzig. Born in 1630 in the small Brandenburg town of Zethlingen, he came of age during the Thirty Years War (1618–1648), the defining geopolitical event of the seventeenth century.[11] As the fortunes of the "Great War" (or the "German War," as Praetorius also calls it) waxed and waned, Praetorius's family was repeatedly forced to flee into the surrounding woods from the plundering and marauding foreign and domestic troops.[12] His family appears to have inherited rights to the local inn (*Krug*) and, possibly, to the office of mayor. His father and stepfather enjoyed a level of education and prosperity that placed them among the leading citizens of Zethlingen. Prior to his enrolment at the University of Leipzig at the age of twenty-two, Praetorius attended the Lutheran Gymnasium in Halle, where Christian Friedrich Franckenstein (1621–1679) was headmaster. Praetorius's mention of Franckenstein in the *Anthropodemus plutonic* (1666) suggests that his historical interests may have first been awakened by this teacher,

---

[11] Johannes Burckhardt, *Der Dreissigjährige Krieg* (Frankfurt am Main: Suhrkamp, 1992); for details of the war's unfolding, an extensive chronology, and a bibliography, see Klaus Bussmann and Heinz Schilling, eds., *1648: Krieg und Frieden in Europa: Politik, Religion, Recht und Gesellschaft* (Münster: Veranstaltungsgesellschaft 350 Jahre Westfälischer Frieden mbH., 1998).

[12] Volker Press, *Kriege und Krisen: Deutschland 1600–1715*, Die Neue Deutsche Geschichte 5 (Munich: Beck, 1991); note especially the chapter on "Die Krise des Reiches und Dreißigjähriger Krieg," 5:161–258.

who, in 1652, was appointed professor of Latin and history at Leipzig University.[13] Also important in this context is Praetorius's association with Christian Daum (1612–1687), principal at Zwickau Gymnasium, with whom he corresponded until 1671. As one of the famous universal intellects of the day, Daum assembled a large library (7,680 volumes), which became a source of distinction for the City of Zwickau even during his lifetime. Daum provided printed resources for many of his humanist colleagues, among them Jacob Thomasius (d. 1684), rector of the Leipzig Nicolaischule and father of the more famous critic of the witch persecutions, Christian Thomasius (1655–1728). He may have provided printed resources for Praetorius as well.

In recognition of his publications, Praetorius was named imperial poet laureate in the year 1659, a distinction that allowed him to identify himself as such in all his publications. This honorific could be bestowed by any duke or count palatine (*Hof- und Pfalzgrafen*) so designated by the German emperor, and even Helmut Waibler, the preeminent Praetorius scholar, was unable to identify who conferred this honor on him.[14] In the same year, Praetorius married Barbara Vater of Saalfeld, and despite his inability to secure a teaching post, the couple made their home in the Leipzig Paulinum, a residence hall for students and faculty at the university. He never gave up his residence at the Paulinum, remaining in close association with the university, its faculty, its students, and presumably its library resources.

Praetorius and his wife had two daughters, one of whom died of the plague at the age of twelve. Judging by his frequent mentions of the pressing scarcity of money, the enduring difficulties in financing his print productions, and the vexing need for protection from those who would appropriate his intellectual property

---

[13] Detlef Doering, *Die Bestandsentwicklung der Bibliothek der Philosophischen Fakultät der Universität Leipzig von ihren Anfängen bis Mitte des 16. Jahrhunderts: Ein Beitrag zur Wissenschaftsgeschichte der Leipziger Universität in ihrer vorreformatorischen Zeit*, Beiheft zum Zentralblatt für Bibliothekswesen 99 (Leipzig: Bibliographisches Institut Leipzig, 1990). The University of Leipzig, founded after the German students had been driven from Prague University in 1409, was not especially distinguished at this time; while it had reached a certain level of distinction during the latter half of the sixteenth century with the thirty-three-year presence of Johannes Camerarius (1500–1574), the departure in 1656 of Samuel Pufendorf and Christian Thomasius and the devastation brought about by the Thirty Years War contributed to a prolonged decline during the seventeenth century. See Helmut Waibler, *M. Johannes Praetorius, P.L.C.: Bio-bibliographische Studien zu einem Kompilator curieuser Materien im 17. Jahrhundert*, Europäische Hochschulschriften 19, Ethnologie /Kulturanthropologie und Volkskunde (Frankfurt am Main: Peter Lang, 1979), 15, cited hereafter as *MJP*.

[14] Nothing has as yet surpassed the usefulness and accuracy of Helmut Waibler's works: Waibler, *MJP*; idem, "Johannes Praetorius (1630–1680): Ein Barockautor und seine Werke," *Archiv für die Geschichte des Buchwesens* 20 (1979): 951–1152, cited hereafter as *JP*.

without his permission, it clearly was a challenge to support himself and his family through his writing alone. On the basis of several dedicatory, occasionally pleading, prefaces directed at members of the House of Alvensleben, a prominent noble family that owned land around Praetorius's birthplace, Waibler conjectures that this family may have provided financial support for Praetorius's studies and his publications.[15] In 1680, Praetorius died of the plague at the Paulinum.

What Did Praetorius Know?

While Praetorius was not active in bringing about any of the vast changes in the thinking of his and subsequent generations, he did record and comment on many of his century's great thinkers and history-making events. He diligently noted the phenomena associated with what came to be called the Scientific Revolution, such as observations through the telescope and the microscope (even though scholars like Steven Shapin have suggested that the revolution never took place).[16] Praetorius gathered, reported, and commented on heavenly bodies observed through the telescope, or the worlds made perceptible through the microscope. When worried about intellectual property, his and others', he occasionally ranted about what went on in his vicinity and far away. He was the intermediary between the world of discoveries and the larger audience that sought explications of the phenomena and events that they lived through and that often terrified them. He was aware of the new explanatory models, but this awareness did not significantly alter his beliefs or, I presume, the beliefs of his readers. For example, in his tract on comets, the *Adunatus cometologus* (1665), Praetorius disparages Johann Hevelius (1611–1687), one of the most famous astronomers of his day. Hevelius had discovered the regular and consequently predictable appearance of comets. Praetorius does not deny the validity of this hypothesis, but he is not prepared to give it pride of place over other ways of interpreting such signs. There

---

[15] Praetorius mentions twelve members of the family in the dedication of the *Catastrophe Muhammetica: Oder das Endliche Valet/ Und/ Schändliche Nativität/ des Gantzen/ und nunmehr vergänglichen/ Türckischen Reichs/ Aus ziemlich vielen/ so wohl Geistlichen Prophezeyhungen/ als Weltlichen Weissagungen/ glaubwürdigen/ Ominibus, rathsamen Portentis, tüchtigen Astrologischen/ Muthmassungen/ Richtigen Cabalistischen Schlüssen/ Und Andern unverwerfflichen Divinatorischen Gründen mehr/ entdecket/ und unserm lieben/ jetzt sehr bestürtzten/ Vaterlande/ zum sonderlichen Trost und Erfreuung/ an den Tag Gegeben* (Leipzig: J.B. Oelers, 1664) HAB QN 174 (wrongly dated 1633: Waibler, JP, 1–19).

[16] "There was no such thing as the Scientific Revolution, and this book is about it": Steven Shapin, *The Scientific Revolution* (Chicago: University of Chicago Press, 1996), 1; Lisa Jardine, *Ingenious Pursuits: Building the Scientific Revolution* (New York: Doubleday, 1999), 1–11.

was still, he points out, another kind of knowledge to be gleaned from such observations, namely knowledge of what God intended for his people.[17]

Praetorius's world and his work were constructed of wonderment at the magical universe and of the speculations of the new science. Praetorius weaves the informational threads spun by the many news writers from great changes and persistent traditional views into a vast conceptual tapestry.[18] He lived in a world where experiences, information, and news from within and without whirled about in ways that were unsettling to him and his contemporaries. Together, old and new inspired variant explanatory patterns, different keys opening new doors to different modes of understanding and of representation. Secrets of nature and the established ways of knowing continued to exist alongside the excitement generated by all manner of scientific, geographical, and astronomical discoveries; all of these strained against linguistic, rhetorical, and categorical controls as they vied for readers' and scholars' attention and for dominance in the public consciousness.[19] These ways of knowing did not exclude or impede each other's movement toward alternative models of explanation.[20] As is apparent in Praetorius's oeuvre, new discoveries in all areas of knowledge did not consign

---

[17] "Havelius will erwiesen haben/ wie alle Cometen ihre richtige *revolutiones* wissen/ und ein jeder in künfftigen das eine auch davon wissen könne . . . Ist dir das ein neues?" (Hevelius says that he has shown how all comets know their right revolutions, and that in future everyone would know about it. Is this news to you?). Johannes Praetorius, *Adunatus Cometologus; Oder ein Geographischer Cometen Extract . . .* (Leipzig: Johann Wittigau, 1665), 59. For more on Hevelius's discovery and a mention of his wife, an accomplished astronomer in her own right who energetically supported her husband's work, see Jardine, *Ingenious Pursuits,* 28–30.

[18] Mary Baine Campbell, *Wonder and Science: Imagining Worlds in Early Modern Europe* (Ithaca: Cornell University Press, 1999), 2–9.

[19] John Henry, *The Scientific Revolution and the Origin of Modern Science*, Studies in European History (London: Palgrave Macmillan, 1997; 2nd ed., London: Palgrave Macmillan, 2001). Along with much helpful information about seventeenth-century science and culture, Henry provides a useful review of the debate among historians of the last thirty years about how revolutionary the Scientific Revolution really was.

[20] Kaspar von Greyerz, "Alchemie, Hermetismus und Magie: Zur Frage der Kontinuitäten in der wissenschaftlichen Revolution," in Hartmut Lehmann and Anne-Charlott Trepp, eds., *Im Zeichen der Krise: Religiosität im Europa des 17. Jahrhunderts*, ed. Hartmut Lehmann and Anne-Charlott Trepp, Veröffentlichungen des Max-Planck-Instituts für Geschichte 152 (Göttingen: Vandenhoeck & Ruprecht, 1999), 415–33, here 421–25. Greyerz reviews the thesis that assigns an "Abwertung der Rolle der okkulten Wissenschaften" to the Scientific Revolution. He concurs with Christoph Meinel's dictum, "die Differenz von Okkult und Exact ist [jedenfalls] nicht ein Bestandteil des Objektbereichs der Naturwissenschaften, sondern Ergebnis sozialer Prozesse der Ab- und Ausgrenzung" (the difference between occult and exact [sciences] is not their objective role in the natural sciences but a result of social processes of exclusion and marginalization): Christoph Meinel, "Okkulte und exakte Wissenschaften," in *Die okkulten Wissenschaften in der*

past ways of knowing to oblivion just yet. Whether worked out by scholars or surmised by the laity, the concept of the world as a system of signs that carried many, often conflicting meanings was captured in an explosion of writing energy that encouraged, even demanded the simultaneous beholding and understanding of dissimilar explanatory models. Order and disorder in nature kept on signaling grave future events, great misfortunes, and horrific disasters. Moreover, as natural signs of transcendent origin, they provided messages about what God had in store for his people. Even when predictions made according to these signs were not borne out by events, as happened frequently, it had to be assumed that the signs had meaning.[21] Like many of his contemporaries, Praetorius believed that the physical state of the world could be compared to the moral history of mankind; thus cosmology, history, theology, and the science of the day conjoined in imparting information about the human condition to the observant mind. Praetorius's life was spent sharing this information with his readers.[22] His oeuvre explodes with the exuberance of linguistic and generic hybridization that makes his "way of telling" a hallmark of the literary energies of his age.

Praetorius also devotes considerable energy to issues of gender and class. He criticizes fashion and the conduct of men and women, specifically young men and women of the well-to-do burgher class. He alternately ridicules and chastises married and unmarried women, damsels (upper-class young women) and maids (lower-class servant girls and women). His tracts show the misogyny of his age alongside remarkably sensitive portraits of the life of the early-modern urban woman.

Where and How Did Praetorius Get His Information?

Waibler comments on the great significance of Praetorius having spent his adult life in physical proximity to the University of Leipzig's library and the Bibliotheca Paulina (JP, 958). The monastic library of the Pauline order had been added to the university's holdings in 1543, several decades after its founding, initiating a series of acquisitions of both private and institutional libraries that significantly improved the quality of its holdings. The library's expansion was slowed by the Thirty Years War, but picked up again with the acquisition of the personal

---

Renaissance, ed. August Buck, Wolfenbütteler Abhandlungen zur Renaissanceforschung 12 (Wiesbaden: Harrassowitz, 1992), 21–43, here 43.

[21] Hermann Wellenreuther, "Gedanken zum Zusammenhang von Kommunikation und Wissen im 17. Jahrhundert," in Lehmann and Trepp, eds., *Im Zeichen der Krise*, 312–18, here 314; Thomas Klingebiel, "Apokalyptik, Prodigienglaube und Prophetismus im Alten Reich: Einführung," in Lehmann and Trepp, eds., *Im Zeichen der Krise*, 17–32, here 17, 19.

[22] Schechner, *Comets*, 150.

collection of the theology professor Johann Hülsemann (1602–1662) through the agency of the university's chancellor, Johann Adam Schertzer (1628–1683). Subsequently, Schertzer bequeathed his own collection of three thousand titles, large by the standards of the day, to the university.[23] By the time Praetorius made use of it, the library contained many important titles of the day dealing with early-modern astronomy. In addition to the holdings in the traditional fields of theology, philosophy, law, and medicine, we also find mention of an edition of Paracelsus's *Wunden- und Artzney Buch* (Cologne, 1571) and a tract by Joachim Camerarius the Elder on *Astrognosis*. In all, 165 titles have been recorded that relate to medical and astronomical knowledge so very popular during the seventeenth century.[24]

Early-modern universities, whether Catholic or Protestant, were accredited by the Holy Roman Emperor. They were devoted more to disseminating than to producing knowledge. On the whole, research as we understand it today took place elsewhere, in private laboratories at the courts of princes and in the homes of wealthy burghers. However, this situation was changing. Scholars have pointed to the increasing importance of mathematics, of experiential physiology, which was making inroads in the medical schools, and of educational reforms like those introduced by Philipp Melanchthon in Germany.[25]

Aside from housing an important library collection, Leipzig became, during Praetorius's lifetime, an important link in the transfer of European print communications. Aside from having a university that attracted young men and their teachers, whose intellectual and instructional needs, in turn, encouraged book production and consumption, the city offered the additional advantage of being located on a communications axis connecting Leipzig with important printing centers all over Europe, especially Frankfurt, Nuremberg, Strasbourg, Prague, Vienna, and Paris. Moreover, contemporaries ascribed great importance to Leipzig's biannual book fairs, which ensured the regular supply of new publications, as well as to the biennially published reports on current events, the *Messrelationen*.[26] Early in the seventeenth century, Leipzig hosted two large fairs each year, the *Ostermarkt* (spring) and *Michaelsmarkt* (fall); a few years later, a New Year's Fair was added. This meant that *Relationen* reported on events covering a

---

[23] Friedlinde Krause, ed., *Handbuch der historischen Buchbestände in Deutschland* (Hildesheim: Olms-Weidmann, 1997), 38.

[24] Krause, *Handbuch*, 77.

[25] Henry, *The Scientific Revolution and the Origin of Modern Science*, 34–36.

[26] Erich Straßner, *Zeitung*, vol. 2 (Tübingen: Niemeyer, 1997), 1–4. *Messrelationen* had been printed in book form since 1580; in October 1605 they began to appear regularly with the *Relation* produced by the Strasbourg printer Johann Carolus (1574–1634); Wolfgang Behringer, "Veränderung der Raum-Zeit-Relation," in *Zwischen Alltag und Katastrophe: Der Dreissigjährige Krieg aus der Nähe*, ed. von Krusenstjern and Medick, 39–83, here 41.

period of about four months.[27] In addition to the books available at the university, those that he could borrow from other people's libraries, and the *Messrelationen*, we will see that Praetorius also made extensive use of daily, weekly, monthly, or annual news publications, such as *Zeytungen*, local and international *Relationen*, *Diarien*, and *Avisen* that had become widely available by the middle of the century.[28] Over thirty German cities produced regular newspapers in German; some produced several.[29] The publications of various national and international learned societies also began to appear in Leipzig and other important cities during the second half of the century.[30] These journals opened windows to the world by providing reports on important world events: on politics, wars, social concerns, demographic changes, as well as on strange natural phenomena, monster births, and murders. In addition to using news publications, Praetorius employed traditional sources of information gleaned from books. It would be impossible to list all the authors, past and present, on whom he drew for his tracts. He carefully cites his sources, frequently noting the title, chapter, and page.

Thus, though he traveled little during his adult life, Praetorius surveyed a vast terrain with the help of information delivered to him in print products; knowledge that came to him in memory traded in the language of the quickly expanding periodical print trade.[31] The desire of an increasingly literate readership to be informed about social, economic, political, religious, and cultural phenomena brought forth a network of communications media in which Praetorius actively

[27] Robert E. Prutz, *Geschichte des deutschen Journalismus,* part 1 (Hanover, 1845; repr., Göttingen: Vandenhoeck & Ruprecht, 1971), 198.

[28] Karl Schottenloher, *Flugblatt und Zeitung: Ein Wegweiser durch das gedruckte Schrifttum,* vol. 1 (Munich: Klinckhardt & Biermann, 1985), 225–50; Johannes Weber, *Avisen, Relationen, Gazetten: Der Beginn des europäischen Zeitungswesens,* Bibliotheksgesellschaft Oldenburg 25 (Oldenburg: Bibliotheks- und Informationssystem der Universität Oldenburg, 1997); Straßner, *Zeitung,* lists more than thirty-one names for the new print medium.

[29] Elger Blühm, "Die ältesten Zeitungen und das Volk," in *Literatur und Volk im 17. Jahrhundert: Probleme populärer Kultur in Deutschland,* ed. Wolfgang Brückner, Peter Blickle, and Dieter Breuer, Wolfenbütteler Arbeiten zur Barockforschung 13 (Wiesbaden: Harrassowitz, 1985), 741–52, here 742.

[30] *Philosophical Transactions of the Royal Society* (from 1665); *Journal de Sçavans* (Paris, 1665–1938); *Bibliotheca de scriptoribus et scriptis Hebraicis* (1675–1693): see Krause, *Handbuch,* 18: 88, 89.

[31] "The basis for all knowledge in the 16th century is language; knowledge is *memoria* preserved and transmitted in writing" ("Wissen ist in Texten überlieferte *memoria*"): Jan-Dirk Müller, "Universalbibliothek und Gedächtnis: Aporien frühneuzeitlicher Wissenskodifikation bei Conrad Gesner (Mit einem Ausblick auf Antonio Possevino, Theodor Zwinger und Johann Fischart)," in *Erkennen und Erinnern in Kunst und Literatur: Kolloquium Reisensburg, 4.–7. Januar 1996,* ed. Dietmar Peil, Michael Schilling, and Peter Strohschneider (Tübingen: Niemeyer, 1998), 285–309, here 297.

participated. From his vantage point in Leipzig, Praetorius surveyed Saxony and the vast expanse of the German Empire. His writings also reveal an intense friendly interest in the independent Netherlands; he is much less sympathetic toward France and Spain, and his reporting on England can be termed downright hostile. His acute awareness of the importance of all of these powers to European and German affairs makes them loom large in his writings. He comments in somewhat less detail on northern and Eastern Europe. However, the Near East figures prominently as he discusses the Turkish threat to the Italian city states, especially Venice, and to the German Empire. Finally, he never moves beyond the most general remarks about the New World, the Far East, and Africa. Africa figures mainly as a source of slaves for the plantations of the emergent colonial powers of England, the Netherlands, and France, and for the war efforts of the European and non-European powers. It is difficult to conjecture about his diffidence, even lack of interest, in distant lands even though a rich travel literature was available. This attitude seems to contradict his intense engagement with the wondrous, with astronomy and the occult.

Vielschreiber and *Polyhistor?*

During the ensuing centuries, Praetorius is often described as *barocker Vielschreiber* (baroque mass writer), *Buntschriftsteller* (writer of entertainment literature), or *Polyhistor,*[32] reflecting the fact that Praetorius wrote copiously on many and disparate subjects. The first two terms are somewhat ironic and condescending, and the pejorative *Vielschreiber* especially seems unfair, since, by today's standards, most seventeenth-century writers known to us produced huge bodies of work.[33] The term reflects more the way that succeeding generations of writers and readers assessed the activities of their predecessors than any meaningful judgment on Praetorius.[34] This impulse to collect and exhibit must be understood as analogous to the impulse to provide, in writing, a mental space for such collecting activity.[35] Along with this impulse grew the need to find structures

---

[32] A person of immense knowledge and the capacity to produce many volumes disseminating this knowledge.

[33] "Einleitung: Die Nähe und Ferne des Dreissigjährigen Krieges," in von Krusenstjern and Medick, eds., *Zwischen Alltag und Katastrophe,* 25; Wilhelm Kühlmann, "Lektüre für den Bürger: Eigenart und Vermittlungsfunktion der polyhistorischen Reihenwerke Martin Zeillers," in Brückner, Blickle, and Breuer, eds., *Literatur und Volk im 17. Jahrhundert,* 2: 917–34, here 917.

[34] Müller, "Universalbibliothek und Gedächtnis," 285; see also Zedelmaier, *Bibliotheca universalis und Bibliotheca selecta*; Ann Moss, *Printed Common-Place Books and the Structuring of Renaissance Thought* (Oxford: Oxford University Press, 1993).

[35] The inveterate writer of Baroque novels Eberhard von Happel authored a book whose title beautifully captures this impulse: *Thesaurus Exoticum oder eine mit Außländischen*

and organizing principles for arranging materials rationally in linguistic order as well as in real spaces. The order and structure of books should convey the order of information they contained.[36] We will see that Praetorius delighted in using various methods of structuring a huge body of material that was always in danger of escaping his authorial control. He frequently employed acrostics, alphabetical lists, and numerical lists, or a combination of all three. The magic of the alphabet proved especially enticing to him and his contemporaries. As early-modern linguists, they were thrilled that from only twenty-three letters could be constructed endless words and works.[37] The logic of these indices brought together disparate elements of knowledge that could be arranged and rearranged at will. Indices and cross-references were favorites; "vide" ("go see") is one of Praetorius's most frequent directions to his readers. Self-citations provided user-friendliness and added to the reader's enjoyment even as he was confronted with huge volumes of often unconnected information. The writer became a repository of knowledge (*Datenspeicher*) who, as a part of an endless chain of information, reached back into the past and forward into the future.[38] Therefore, as a *Vielschreiber,* Praetorius simply embodied his century.

The term *Polyhistor* describes a scholar with "fachübergreifender Kompetenz" (competency across disciplinary boundaries),[39] whose work is characterized by universality and inclusiveness.[40] The model for such a scholar is Praetorius's contemporary Daniel Georg Morhof (1639–1691), whose magnum opus is the *Polyhistor sive De notitia et rerum commentarii* (1688) and its continuation (1708).[41]

Raritäten und Geschichten Wohlversehene Schatz-Kammer . . . (Hamburg, 1688). The same can be said of Martin Zeiller's *Reihenwerke*; Kühlmann, "Lektüre für den Bürger," 917, points to Zeiller's *Topographiae Germaniae* (1642ff.), his travelogues, and his *Episteln oder Sendschreiben von allerhand politischen historischen und anderen Sachen* (1640–47).

[36] Ann Blair, "The Practices of Erudition According to Morhof," in *Mapping the World of Learning: The Polyhistor of Daniel Georg Morhof,* ed. Françoise Waquet, Wolfenbütteler Forschungen 91 (Wiesbaden: Harrassowitz Verlag, 2000), 59–74, here 65.

[37] "Wer wolte sich wol einbilden können/ daß sich die 23. Buchstaben durch die Versetz- und Verwechslung so unumschrenckt austheilen lassen/ gestalt so viele tausend Bücher aus unterschiedlicher Zusammensetzung der Buchstaben im ABC. gemacht werden" (Who could possibly imagine that twenty-three letters, by being changed around and rearranged, would make it possible that thousands of books would be written making use of various applications of the letters of the ABC). Stanislaus Mink von Weinhausen, *Proteus: Das ist eine unglaubliche Nutznützliche Lehrart* . . . (Oldenburg, 1657), 18, cited in Stefan Rieger, *Speichern/Merken: Die künstlichen Intelligenzen des Barock* (Munich: Fink, 1997), 13.

[38] Rieger, *Speichern/Merken,* 97.

[39] Zedelmaier, *Bibliotheca universalis und Bibliotheca selecta,* 425.

[40] Herbert Jaumann, "Was ist ein Polyhistor? Gehversuche auf einem verlassenen Terrain," *Studia Leibnitiana* 22 (1990): 76–89, here 83: "Der Versuch, Wissenschaft als Erfahrung der gesamten Historie zu beschreiben."

[41] About Morhof and his *Polyhistor* see Waquet, ed., *Mapping the World of Learning.*

Intellectuals of the time dealt with knowledge that reached across disciplinary boundaries. Because of their very expansiveness and inclusiveness, however, polyhistorical writings today are often considered superficial, the work of scholars dealing with too much information to meet high standards of scientific discipline and informational depth.[42] The more positive early-modern evaluation, on the other hand, saw the *Polyhistor* as well versed in languages and literary history, employing his knowledge for the amelioration of his reader's moral character.

Characterizing Praetorius as a *Polyhistor* is somewhat problematic. As well as can be determined, his contemporaries never referred to him by that name, or portrayed him as such; the term has been ascribed to him by more recent scholarship. He does, however, frequently cite Zeiller, Harsdörffer, Fincel, Gesner, and other encyclopedists who are variously called *Polyhistor* or *Polymathus,* which caused some readers to group him under the same category. The more expert Waibler correctly describes Praetorius as being influenced by the polyhistorical temperament of his time. He wrote within the tradition of polyhistory, and he corresponded with men who were called *Polyhistor,* such as Daum or Thomasius.[43]

If order and method are the fundamental requirements for being counted as a *Polyhistor,* Praetorius does not qualify. He does, however, fit if we place greater importance on compiling and rearranging exemplary information for the improvement of knowledge, morals, and manners. In fact, only in this way can his disparate oeuvre be arranged into some kind of literary and historical logic, can historical awareness (*memoria*), the reasonable assessment of information provided, the thirst for new knowledge, for the wondrous and strange, for fashion and manners (*curiositas*), and the education of the young and great caring interest in familial relationships be accepted as and subsumed into one oeuvre. He thus represents a type of *Polyhistor,* the gatherer as opposed to the organizer personified by Morhof, whose ultimate goal is an ideal completeness that will allow access to all learning and knowledge.[44] Praetorius is conversant with wide areas of knowledge of diverse subjects; he endlessly quotes the works of famous and less famous writers. This does not mean that he "sees with alien eyes, speaks with

---

[42] Zedelmaier, "Von den Wundermännern des Gedächtnisses," 419.

[43] Waibler, *MJP,* 9; idem, *JP,* 963; Christoph Daxelmüller, *Disputationes curiosae: Zum 'volkskundlichen' Polyhistorismus an den Universitäten des 17. und 18. Jahrhunderts,* Veröffentlichungen zur Volkskunde und Kulturgeschichte 5 (Würzburg: Richard Mayer, 1979), 50–51; Zedelmaier, "Von den Wundermännern des Gedächtnisses."

[44] "[D]er Magister [bleibt] ganz dem gelehrten Kosmos verhaftet und verweist auf solche 'examplarische' Gelehrte, die sich vor allem durch ihre 'polyhistorische', das heißt *historische-philologisch orientierte Gelehrsamkeit auszeichnen*" (emphasis added) (The scholar remains very much caught in the learned cosmos; he points to such exemplary scholars who are distinguished by their polyhistorical, that is their philologically oriented learnedness): Zedelmaier, "Von den Wundermännern des Gedächtnisses," 441.

alien lips, and writes with alien pens."[45] Rather, he makes all these "aliens" his own. He fits them into his time and his world, producing an oeuvre that is less learned and scholarly than it is entertaining and informative and, to some extent, personal; in short, worthy of our attention.

Responding to the challenge that a writer like Praetorius represents to the contemporary reader, I have chosen one especially entertaining tract, the tract that is devoted to Praetorius's take on gender and class, to his observations concerning the social realities of young girls and grown women, of husbands and lovers. The themes elaborated in this tract present to us women's struggles as they navigate early-modern social conventions in the lengthy, funny, and sometimes acerbic observations at the lying-in bed of a new mother. Praetorius, in an earlier work, has described the lives of young women, who in the *Apocalypsis Cybeles* predictably become wives and mothers. We now turn to married women, specifically to a new mother's life, which Praetorius observes and satirizes in the *Apocalypsis / Mysteriorum Cybeles. / Das ist / Eine Schnakische / Wochen-Comedie* (1662) (A funny/amusing birthing chamber comedy). Praetorius constructs this gendered way of knowing employing many sources, oral and written, very current and from the past. The reader will not miss the underlying message; the gendered ways of knowing are tied to the purported need for knowledge and social discipline not only for women of all ages and classes, but for urban society in general.

Married with Children (*Apocalypsis Cybeles*)

Responding to the challenge that a writer like Praetorius represents to the modern reader, I have chosen among his works the one that speaks very effectively to his time and his culture and our own. This transcription and translation is devoted to Praetorius's understanding of gender and class, to his observations concerning the social realities of the recently married and mature women, to husbands and lovers. We will smile at the wives and mothers, at this tongue-in-cheek view of the new mother's life which Praetorius observes and satirizes in the *Apocalypsis / Mysteriorum Cybeles.* Through the eyes and ears of various male listeners hidden behind doors and bed curtains, the reader observes the interactions of several groups of women as they visit a new mother after the birth of her third child. This is the six-week-long lying-in period, a time when the husband is banned from the conjugal bedroom, a space where only women are allowed.

Though Praetorius shared the misogyny of his age, he reveals himself to be an astute observer of women's lives, of female knowledge and male desire to gain entry to that knowledge. In an original and lively fashion he explores the married life of the burgher woman. The *Apocalypsis* reviews the social pressures,

---

[45] Johann Christoph Gottsched, in Zedelmaier, "Von den Wundermännern des Gedächtnisses," 445.

superstitions, anxieties, and interactions that govern the life of early-modern women of childbearing age.[46] The *Apocalypsis* is meant both to amuse and to teach. On the one hand, the tract parodies conversations women share at the bedside of a new mother; on the other, it is a coherent narrative about two of the most important aspects of an early-modern woman's life: her mothering and the networking skills she practices in the company of other women of her community.

Published under the pseudonym Vigando Sexwochio, this tract quickly went through several editions, signaling a more than casual interest in the topic among its readership. Praetorius identified himself as the tract's author in several of his later writings.[47] The satirical male gaze and the use of a male narrator and several male personae notwithstanding, the *Apocalypsis* affords us a fascinating glimpse at an aspect of early-modern domesticity that is governed equally by practicality and superstition.

Praetorius's treatment of women and gender in this tract is complicated by the presence of several different male voices belonging to the omniscient first person narrator—an implied author not to be confused with Praetorius—and its several male personae. Moreover, the narrative "I" is given various accomplices that support him in his attempts to gain access to and information about the women's chamber. One of the most fully developed among these personae is the tutor, the *praeceptor*, who might be a semiautobiographical character.[48] Inserted into three poems contained in the narrative elaborating on the lying-in theme are several additional snooping male characters. Like the actors in a multileveled *mis-en-abîme*,[49] their presence apparently going unnoticed, these male characters are versions of fictionalized authors who write about the women whom they furtively observe in the lying-in chamber. In each instance of this supposedly

---

[46] Johannes Praetorius, *Apocalypsis Mysteriorum Cybeles. Das ist Eine Schnakische Wochen-Comedie Oder verplauderte Stroh-Hochzeit* (Bojemo, 1662) [HAB La 7169].

[47] Waibler, JP.

[48] As a student in Leipzig, Praetorius was himself a tutor; he alludes to this clearly not very happy experience in the *Philosophia colus*: "Wie Spinne feind ich mein lebetage den Teufflischen Aberglauben der Weiber gewesen und werden sich zum theil guter massen zu entsinnen wissen/ die jenigen Leute/ bey welchen ich mein *Hospitium* vor Jahren gehabt/ und mich in meinem studiren auff gehalten" (All my life I have despised women's evil superstitions [and the reader] and those people with whom I did my practicum will remember that I was always keeping to my studies) (Aii): Johannes Praetorius, *Philosophia Colus, Oder, Pfy Lose Vieh Der Weiber: Darinnen Gleich Hundert Allerhand Gewohnliche Aberglauben Des Gemeinen Mannes Lacherig Wahr Gemachet Werden* (Leipzig: Johann Barthol Oehlers, 1662) lists a number of such superstitions; e.g., Canon I: "Es ist nicht gut/ wenn ihrer zwey ein Kind wiegen"; Canon XXXIX: "Wenn man ein Kind zweymahl gewehnet: oder nach deme man es einmahl gewehnet hat/ zum anderenmahl anleget; so kan es im Grabe hernach nicht faulen."

[49] Story within a story.

unobserved observation of the gossip shared among the women in the lying-in chamber, the texts reveal the most intimate experiences of a woman's life in the form of a wedding poem.[50]

The narrative and the interspersed poems of the *Apocalypsis* aim at the life of the married woman who has just become a mother. The mother in this text is not new to the experience: she is recovering from the birth of her third child. The tracts make clear that motherhood is the most important stage of an early-modern woman's life.[51] The association of the Greek goddess Cybele with a gossipy and comic tract about birth, baptisms, and lying-in, as well as the association of apocalypse and comedy, once again highlight Praetorius's ability to meld early-modern misogynist humor with serious social commentary.[52]

As was the custom in the early-modern period, the new mother remained confined to the lying-in chamber, the conjugal bedroom, for the six weeks following the birth of the child. However, the new mother could, in fact was obliged to, entertain female family members, friends, and acquaintances.[53] During this time, the husband had to keep his distance; physical intimacy was frowned upon. This conjugal banishment reminded him that, even though he was the father of the new baby, the very early mothering was taking place outside of his purview.[54] As the child grew older, full familial authority was restored to the father, who became the more substantial educational influence—influence that was often expressed, as we read in the tract, in merciless physical punishment. If men wished to be privy to the conversations that took place in the chamber, they had to find some way either to eavesdrop or to gain the confidence of intermediaries such as lying-in maids, who might be persuaded to share gossip generally

---

[50] Karma Lochrie, *Covert Operations: The Medieval Uses of Secrecy* (Philadelphia: University of Pennsylvania Press, 1999), 78, 123, 135.

[51] Merry E. Wiesner, *Women and Gender in Early Modern Europe* (Cambridge: Cambridge University Press, 2000), 51–101; Richard van Dülmen, *Kultur und Alltag in der Frühen Neuzeit: Das Haus und seine Menschen, 16.–18. Jahrhundert* (Munich: Beck, 1990), 80–101, 134–57; Heide Wunder, *"Er ist die Sonn', sie ist der Mond": Frauen in der Frühen Neuzeit* (Munich: Beck, 1992), 42–47.

[52] Cybele = Rhea: ancient goddess of the earth; daughter of Uranus and Ge, wife of Cronos, mother of Hestia, Demeter, Hera, Hades, Poseidon, and Zeus; she is associated with birth and sexuality. See William Smith, *Smaller Classical Dictionary* (New York: Dutton, n.d.), 247; David Brumble, *Classical Myths and Legends in the Middle Ages and Renaissance* (Westport, CT: Greenwood Press, 1998), 85–87.

[53] For a wealth of beautifully reproduced and expertly reviewed images of childbirth and lying-in, here called confinement room, see Jacqueline Marie Musacchio, *The Art and Ritual of Childbirth in Renaissance Italy* (New Haven: Yale University Press, 1999).

[54] Caroline Bicks, "Midwiving Virility in Early Modern England," in *Maternal Measures*, ed. Naomi Miller and Naomi Yavneh (Burlington, VT: Ashgate, 2000), 46–65.

intended to stay within the chamber. Or they concocted their own version of the women's realm, as does Praetorius, who, after all, conceived the tract.

Excluded from this space of such intense male and, in the case of Praetorius, writerly scrutiny, the authors/eavesdroppers remain twice removed from the scene: they cannot enter the room, nor are they truly privy to the conversations between the women. In her study of the early-modern French stories of "cackling women," Domna Stanton argues that the intruding male figure takes revenge for this exclusion by disclosing in his writing the secrets of what goes on in this supposedly privileged space.[55] In seventeenth-century German literature, the hidden male listener frequently appears in similar fashion as a popular object of amusement. This motif is found in Christian Weise's *Die drei ärgsten Erznarren* (1676), where a man listens in on women's conversations from behind a hedge, and in Beer's *Weiberhechel* (1681), where Sambelle and his servant Nebulo eavesdrop on women in a lying-in chamber and at a baptism.[56] Also worth noting is the presence of this theme in Madame de la Fayette's novel *La princesse de Clèves* (1678), where the husband spies on his wife, whom he suspects of unfaithfulness. The spying manservant at the door of the lying-in chamber is also the topic of a seventeenth-century broadsheet, *Der holdseligen Frauenzimmer Kindbeth-Gespräch* (The damsels' gentle conversation in the birthing room).[57] One of the three lying-in poems incorporated into the *Apocalypsis* also bears this title. It is a copy of this very text that was supposedly given to one of the women visitors by her husband who had bought it at Nuremberg (40–44). In the poem, a servant listens behind the door and notes for others what he has heard, excluding those topics that are not fit for the ears of bachelors (*Junggesell*). One after the other, the visitors share with one another experiences of marriage, childbirth, household finances, and the sexual prowess of their husbands until the baby's crying interrupts the comfortable conversation. The eavesdropper hurries off to write down what he has heard: "Drum machet er sich fort / und zeichnet fleissig auff / des lieben Weiber

---

[55] Donna Stanton, "Recuperating Women and the Man Behind the Screen," in *Sexuality and Gender in Early Modern Europe: Institutions, Texts, Images*, ed. James Grantham Turner (Cambridge: Cambridge University Press, 1993), 246–65. Note also Édouard Fournier, ed., *Les Caquets de l'accouchée* (1622) (Paris: P. Jannet, 1855). Unlike the *Apocalypsis*, which remains within the confines of narrowly "female" topics, *Les Caquets* is a collection of conversations among several politically and socially sophisticated women associated with the French court. The gossip turns not only on issues related to gender but, significantly, also on power politics. The eavesdropper, hidden behind a window curtain, is a cousin of the new mother, who gave him permission to listen to the lying-in chamber conversations.

[56] I am grateful to Barbara Becker-Cantarino for this information.

[57] Nuremberg, Germanisches Nationalmuseum 2099/1293. I am grateful to Michael Schilling for providing me with a copy.

Volcks Kindbeth-Gesprächs Verlauff" (Thus he hurries away to write down with care the gist of the conversation among the dear womenfolk).

The listening (and writing) men appear in multiple personae: the narrative "I," fictionalized as a tutor, and the male observers featured in the interjected poems. The tutor's maleness is neutralized by the dismissive treatment he receives from his employer, the new mother Margarete. The very fact that he is allowed to enter the confinement room in spite of the women-only rule sufficiently signals that his masculinity counts for very little. From behind the door he records the complaints, secrets, and confidences—the gossip—exchanged between the *Wöchnerin* and the women who come to keep her company.[58] These are her friends, her acquaintances, and the *Gevatterinnen*, the baby's godmothers. The surreptitiously listening tutor is occasionally aided by an old lying-in maid, the *Muhme*, who, as one who has access to the confinement chamber, helps him record the gossip shared among the women.[59] The forced absence from the lying-in chamber of the male persona, who wants to be privy to the birthing-room gossip, presents an intriguing challenge to any male author. He could, as did most early-modern writers on women's issues—such as the authors of midwifery and conduct books—go to his learned predecessors or contemporaries. He could also make use of the information from those men who were allowed access to the women's chamber: physicians, lawyers, and priests. During the seventeenth century, midwives began to be displaced as university-trained male doctors moved into the woman's chamber. Arguing that their medical education ensured greater competence and professionalism, physicians maintained that the authority conferred by their academic training made them a safer choice when it came to rendering assistance to the mother during and after birth. Perceived male professionalism trumped the women's need for privacy. Moreover, even before this change in birthing attendance became the rule, the early-modern imbalance between female and male literacy and learning meant that most birthing aids were written by men for women. Thus the same men who ostensibly had to

---

[58] The new mother repeatedly instructs one of her maids to check behind the door for eavesdroppers.

[59] Stanton, "Recuperating Women and the Man Behind the Screen," 250–51, reviews "cacket" (gossip, tittle-tattle) and its early-modern French derivatives: "*caqueteux* for boring, backbiting"; "le caquet" is given in the *Dictionnaire de l'Academie Française* (1694) as "the discussion of trifles that usually occurs at the home of women in childbed." In sixteenth-century England, gossip and the birthing room were joined so inextricably that *gossip* became a term for a female birth attendant and a female tattler. See Bicks, "Midwiving Virility in Early Modern England," 50. I am also indebted to Karma Lochrie's thoughts on secrecy and gossip in medieval texts. In German, the word is *Klatsch*, etymologically related to the noise made by washerwomen beating the laundry: Markus Fauser, "Klatschrelationen im 17. Jahrhundert," in *Geselligkeit und Gesellschaft im Barockzeitalter*, ed. Wolfgang Adam (Wiesbaden: Harrassowitz, 1997), 391–99, here 391. However, at no point does Praetorius designate the women's conversations as *Klatsch*.

remain outside of the space they wrote about were compelled to "ventriloquize the voice of the birthroom women."[60]

Margarete's confinement room remains free from any physician's intrusion. She relies on the help and advice of a competent midwife, a lying-in maid, the *Muhme*, and her visitors. The omniscient observer, one of several incarnations of the authorial "I," in turn observes the tutor spying on the women and interrupts the narrative not only with the *Muhme's* lullabies, but also with several lengthy poems on the topic of women in the birthing room. The lullabies will seem familiar to the modern reader, as they are occasionally still sung for babies today. The longer poems constitute yet another refraction of the conversations taking place at Margarete's bedside. Of the four poems interjected into the narrative, three, including the Nuremberg broadsheet, present lighthearted treatments of the lying-in theme, while the fourth satirizes the ill effects of smoking on health and romance. While the tobacco poem does not discuss childbirth, it is introduced by one of the women visitors. In a jocular way it ponders one of the important conversational topics: marital (un)happiness. Taken together, the four poems amplify the message of the tract, its facetious as well as its more serious moods.

The *Apocalypsis* opens with the first of these lying-in-poems. A hapless young bride queries three matrons about how to become a good wife, mother, and housekeeper now that the wedding is over and the *feuchte Brautsuppe* (moist bridal soup = semen) has been "eaten."[61] The appropriate number of months for the digestion of the bridal soup has passed (*3. viertel Jahres Frist* = three-quarters of a year); now it is time to fluff the pillows and prepare the lying-in chamber so that the guests can visit and enjoy the pancakes[62] customarily offered by the new mother. Along with dispensing much folksy wisdom about babies, child-rearing, and domestic life in general, the more experienced women of this first poem are eagerly, albeit covertly, making fun of the young bride. Rather than seriously discussing the young woman's very real anxieties about household duties and children, they regale her and each other with sexual innuendos and mock counsel.[63]

---

[60] So described by Caroline Bicks in reference to the 1612 English translation from the French of the tract *Childe-Birth, or the Happy Deliverie of Women* ("Midwiving Virility," 55). For an exception see Lynne Tatlock, trans. and ed., *Justine Siegemund: The Court Midwife*, The Other Voice in Early Modern Europe (Chicago: University of Chicago Press, 2005).

[61] 1. bridal soup served to guests; 2. "wet" bridal soup = semen.

[62] These are called *Pfannkuchen* in the conduct books. They may have been *Krapfen*, a baked good more like a doughnut without the hole.

[63] "Wenn die Braut zur ersten Nacht/ Voll den Laugentopff gemacht/ Soll es deuten auff gut Stillen/ Eben nach der Kinder Willen/ Auch wenn sich vom Schuch ein Band/ Hat zum andern hin gewandt/ Soll es nicht alß Lust gedeuten/ Bey den neuen Eheleuten" (If on the wedding night / The bride fills the chamberpot, / This predicts good nursing / Just the way babies like it. / And when one shoelace / Turns toward the other, / This means nothing but delight / For the newlyweds) (first poem).

They do allow that the baby must be frequently changed; the fireplace poker must be turned the right way to ensure good fortune for mother and child; the bride's beer is not to be forgotten, for it aids the milk production. Still more important and eminently practical is the advice to the new mother that she ask well-to-do friends or neighbors to stand as godparents for her newborn child or else risk unforeseen expense.[64]

The prohibitions, superstitions, and rituals associated with pregnancy, birthing, and lying-in had been gathered over generations into a body of knowledge that was shared in the birthing room, passed from mother to daughter, from woman to woman. Transmitted mostly orally, this knowledge provided advice for the care of newborns and assistance and comfort to the mother as she adapted to her new responsibilities. In due time, it also facilitated her reentry into the community beyond the household. Confinement after childbirth helped the mother to recover from the stresses and strains of pregnancy and birth, while keeping her sheltered from the day-to-day challenges of domestic duties and conjugal obligations.[65] At the end of this period, the new mother left the no-man's-land of the lying-in chamber to be reintegrated into the life of the community. This return to public life took place through the ritual of "churching," which removed the "contamination" brought about by the birthing process. It strengthened the new mother against the wiles of Satan and freed her once again to engage in sexual relations with her husband.[66]

Birthing and the period immediately thereafter posed significant perils for mother and child. Death from childbed fever or other infectious diseases was a constant threat to the mother in her weakened state. Problems with the milk, the baby's ability to nurse, or overanxious caretakers compromised the life of

---

[64] "Auch soll man solche Leut/ Welches auch sehr wohl zu wissen/ Die das Geld nicht borgen müssen/ Zu Gefattern lesen auß:/ Den sonst soll es hoff und hauß/ Eßen/ Trincken/ müssen borgen/ Und stets leben in viel sorgen" (It is best to choose for godparents / People who do not have to borrow money, / Otherwise you have to borrow for / House and yard, for eating and drinking, / And live constantly in great distress) (first poem).

[65] Lyndal Roper, "Witchcraft and Fantasy in Early Modern Germany," in *Oedipus and the Devil: Witchcraft, Sexuality, and Religion in Early Modern Europe* (London: Routledge, 1994), 199–226; Susan Karant-Nunn, *The Reformation of Ritual: An Interpretation of Early Modern Germany* (London: Routledge, 1997), esp. the chapter "Churching, a Woman's Rite," 72–91; Eva Labouvie, *Andere Umstände: Eine Kulturgeschichte der Geburt*, 2nd ed. (Cologne: Böhlau, 2000), 198–260.

[66] Roper, "Witchcraft and Fantasy in Early Modern Germany," 211, notes the continuing importance of "churching" in spite of the Reformers' attempts to do away with this essentially Catholic ritual of cleansing women of the contamination brought about by the birthing process; also Susan Karant-Nunn, "The Woman's Rite: Churching and the Lutheran Reformation," in *Problems of the Historical Anthropology of Early Modern Europe*, ed. R. Po-Chia Hsia and R. W. Scribner (Wiesbaden: Harrassowitz, 1997), 111–39.

the newborn. Superstitious prohibitions were plentiful. While confined to the house and resting on her bed, the new mother was forbidden to step beyond the door frame lest she fall victim to headaches, stomach aches, or painful breasts ("Hauptweh / Bocken / Oder ein böse Brust").[67] Moreover, the fear of bewitchment, of dangerously incapacitating attacks of melancholy, was never very far from the mother's and her attendants' minds. Witch writings of the period repeatedly speak of the susceptibility of women to satanic assaults during their lying-in. David Meder, whose *Acht Hexenpredigten* Praetorius quotes in his witch tract *Blockes-Berges Verrichtung*, reminds his audience that the devil pursues women with particular vigor during times when, for reasons of sadness, despair, or physical weakness, they are especially vulnerable.[68] As he puts it, women are especially endangered "during the time of their lying-in or birthing, when they are weak and depressed" ("sonderlich die armen Weiber zu zeit jrer sechswochen oder Kindbett / mit blödigkeit des heupts pflegen beladen zu sein").[69] To make matters worse, the one woman on whom the *Kindbetterin* depends most of all, the midwife, the *Wehemutter*, may turn out to be her worst enemy.[70] The anonymous *Newe Tractat von der Verführten Kinder-Zauberey* (The new tract on the witchcraft by children led astray [= by Satan] [1629]) reviews at length the reputedly close association between the midwife and the predatory devil, identifying the time of birth as especially precarious. Here, the author advises fathers to invite to the wife's bedside several devout matrons along with the midwife, so that they can be privy to what happens in the chamber during the delivery. He warns that, under the guise of helping the child, the midwife could strangle and kill the baby ("dasselbige erwürgen unnd umbbringen") (*Newe Tractat*, 21).[71] Under no circumstances should the midwife be allowed to baptize a weak or sick infant, for she might, even inadvertently, change and thus falsify the words of the

---

[67] *Apocalypsis*, introductory poem.

[68] Johannes Praetorius, *Blockes-Berges Verrichtung, Oder, Ausführlicher Geographischer Bericht Von Den Hohen Trefflich Alt- Und Berühmten Blockes-Berge; Ingleichen Von Der Hexenfahrt, Und Zauber-Sabbathe* (Leipzig: Johann Scheiben/ Friedrich Arnsten, 1668).

[69] *Acht Hexenpredigten darinnen von des Teuffels Mordkindern, der Hexen, Unholden . . . Bericht . . .* (Leipzig: David Meder, 1605), 35v (HAB QuN 169 (6)).

[70] A correction of Waibler's biography of Praetorius should be noted here. He mistakes as autobiographical a remark that Praetorius makes in the *Abentheuerliche Glückstopf* about rapacious and stingy *Wehemütter*. Waibler believes that this refers to Praetorius's own mother. *Wehemutter*, however, means midwife, not mother.

[71] This association of Satan with midwifery is a commonplace in witch literature since Heinrich Institoris's *Malleus maleficarum* identified midwives as a potentially very evil sort of witch (1487).

sacramental ritual and thereby endanger the spiritual health of the baby.[72] If the child were to die under such circumstances, its eternal salvation could be lost.[73]

Both the new mother and her visitors repeatedly refer to the many prohibitions customarily associated with childbirth and baptism. The women are to sit down so as not to "carry away peace and quiet" ("die Ruhe wegtragen"); the baby is not to be carried through the door for fear it might get heart pain ("Herzspannen") (18); to calm it down, the crying child is to be smeared with deer fat or red butter (18), or a little sack filled with bread, salt, and a penny is to be tied around its neck (19).[74] In an effort to assuage the mother's fears of demons that might harm the baby, one of the visitors, Frau Judith, advises the *Muhme* to swaddle the child carefully so that a demon might not swaddle it again, that is, strangle it ("[D]amit es der Alp nicht noch einmal wickelte") (17).[75] Another guest, Frau Christin, counsels the *Muhme* not to leave the *Wöchnerin* alone during the noon hour, for this time was considered every bit as much a witching hour and as dangerous as midnight (cf. Psalm 91:6, the *daemonium meridianum*). At both times the devil might harm the mother if he found her alone: "[L]asset sie nicht allein in der Steuben / und bleibet bey ihr zur Gesellschaft / daß der Nicker nicht komme" (Do not leave her alone in her bedroom; keep her company, so that the devil will not come in) (36). On the more mundane matter of correct nourishment, the mother was advised to eat six times a day, fish now and again, and chicken variously prepared; she should sleep three times and not forget to drink two measures of beer or a bit of wine.[76] One of the visitors suggests that the *Muhme*

---

[72] "[D]ie Materi/ oder Form deß Sacraments verändern oder verfälschen/ daß also die rechte Tauffe außbleibt" (*Newe Tractat*, 22).

[73] This tract and the sources cited by Praetorius indicate, however, that midwives indeed were authorized to baptize children when survival seemed at stake: Merry E. Wiesner, "The Midwives of South Germany and the Public/Private Dichotomy," in *The Art of Midwifery: Early Modern Midwives in Europe*, ed. Hilary Marland (London: Routledge, 1993), 77–94.

[74] Before the reader accepts this advice as genuine, it should be pointed out that in the *Philosophia Colus* Praetorius holds up the same superstitions and customs for ridicule, noting that women and the uneducated readily fall victim to what he dismisses as the silliest of superstitions.

[75] In the *Anthropodemus plutonic*, Praetorius describes in detail creatures he calls *Alps*. He writes that they fly about at night, wishing to satisfy their lust for blood with children who do not have midwives. They attack them and weaken their little bodies with their furious (blood)lust ("Sie fliegen bey Nacht/ und dencken sich zu laben/ Bey denen Kinderlein/ die keine Ammen haben;/ Denn auff die fallen sie/ und schwächen insgemein/ Mit jhrem Grimme-wüst/ die armen Cörperlein") (16). On *Alps* see the chapter "Von Alpmännrigen," *Anthropodemus plutonic*, 11–41.

[76] "Auch muß sich ein Weib bequemen/ Wie sie fleissig achtung geb/ Daß sie nicht zu kärglich leb/ Dreymahl schlaffen/ sechsmal essen/ Und das trincken nicht vergessen/ Bey zwey Stiebken Bier ist recht/ Wein ein Trüncklein auf den Hecht" (Moreover, the

should prepare wine broth and a bit of bland chicken for the *Wöchnerin,* lest spicy and heavy food make her ill and melancholy. The new mother is reminded, as well, not to get too excited and upset, for this might affect the quality of her milk and hurt the baby (19).

The conversations recorded by the spying men reveal many of the women's everyday vexations, frequently going beyond concerns about childbirth. Foremost among them are complaints about maids, whose character, temperament, and sexual predilections give rise to endless and often angry commentary. Moreover, the women gossip about other women in the community, scrutinizing husbands, household finances, personal conduct, and housewifely prowess. While the older women routinely deplore the burdens of marriage and household, they are not beyond dismissing with tart condescension the young women who, though inexperienced in the trials of both, seem to have no other ambition than to rush headlong into matrimony, longing to become members of the sisterhood of wives and mothers. Not surprisingly, considering the spatial confinement and familial closeness of the early-modern household and the smallness of most early-modern towns, little escapes the eyes and ears of those present in the *Wochenstube.* Always very near the surface of the conversational banter hover the fears, tensions, jealousies, and anguish that were the stuff of early-modern womanhood. This seems especially true for the women who, like those appearing in this tract, are comfortably *bürgerlich,* that is, middle-class, and whose secrets the male listener is eager to know.

As the visitors come and go throughout the morning and afternoon, one of the topics raised in the conversation is the baby's baptism, which has taken place the previous day. The exchange between Margarete, the new mother, and her first set of visitors, the ladies Käte, Margarita, Ursel, and Suse, signals the stresses that accompany these social and religious rituals.[77] Announcing her arrival, one of the early visitors notes with some consternation that by rights she should not have come at all, because she had been omitted from the list of invited guests to the baptismal *Kirchgang* the day before. The *Wöchnerin* expresses distress and anger at this unintended slight; she blames the *Bittfrau,* who should have delivered the invitations since the new mother had to remain in bed, incapacitated by

---

new mother has to pay attention / That she does not / Live too frugally. / Sleeping three times, / Eating six times, / And not forgetting to drink; / Two measures of beer is just about right, / And a drink of wine after fish) (first poem).

[77] An excellent example of such urban rules of behavior can be found in Joseph Baader, ed., *Nürnberger Polizeiordnungen aus dem XIII. bis XV. Jahrhundert* (Stuttgart: Bibliothek des Litterarischen Vereins, 1861): "Ain jegkliche frow mag die anndern inn irer kynndtpet vor oder nach mittag oder tischzeyt wol haymsuchen und besehen" (Any woman can visit another who is recovering from childbirth in either morning or afternoon or at dinnertime) (70).

the rigors of the delivery.[78] Nonetheless, as propriety demands, the new mother insists that she will once again offer *Pfannkuchen* (pancakes), the traditional treat served with sweetened wine ("einen gantzen Hutzucker hette [sie] zerreiben lassen") (2). Seeking her companions' approval, the *Wöchnerin* describes her efforts to please the baptismal guests who had visited the previous day. She angrily denounces an absent woman named Taudel, whom she maligns as a *schind weib* (bitch). Taudel had evidently complained about receiving only one instead of the two baptismal pancakes customarily served. The new mother anxiously reassures her guests that it was not a lack of money that had prompted this seeming infraction, but rather the *Kleiderordnungen* that prescribe the rules for such celebratory distribution.[79] Reviewing the events of the days past, the new mother caustically denounces two other visitors as *Seichfotze* and *Schurmutze*[80] for insinuating that other women's baptismal meals had been more generous than hers, because they offered greater quantities of alcohol to swill ("zu sauffen").[81] All this griping affects the new mother quite negatively; in fact, she notes that her ire had risen to such an extent that she felt like throwing the *Wochen Kanne* (lying-in pitcher) at the offending woman.[82] Offering sympathy, Frau Käte reports that even the

---

[78] "[W]as wil man machen/ wenn man da auff den Bette lieget/ und das lose Gesinde gehet so falsch mit einem umb" ([W]hat can you do if you're confined to bed and the stupid servants don't do anything right?) (9).

[79] "[I]ch hätte gerne lassen zwey außtheilen/ wenn es die Kleider Ordnung hätte wollen zu geben" (I would have liked to distribute two if the sumptuary laws had allowed it) (2). The *Nürnberger Polizeiordnung* states that on such a visit the guest could only receive one cake and a little Frankish wine or another wine at the same price: "Doch zu der kynndttawff mag man die frowen, die mit dem kynde von der tawff zu der kyndtpetterin haym geen, und derselben frowen mayde eren mit ainem leckuchen und franckenwein oder annderm wein inn demselben ungelt oder mit medt ungevarlich" (70). Women who appear at mealtime must not be offered "dann ain essen unverbottner speysse zymlich, und darzu rohe obs unnd kess und prot unnd franckenwein oder wein inn demselben ungelte" (a meal of food that is not prohibited, raw fruit and cheese, bread and Frankish wine). (71). On excessive drinking in general and during lying-in (*Kindbettzechen*) in particular, as well as on increasing criticism directed at celebratory excesses, see Karl Haerter, "Fastnachtslustbarkeiten, Hochzeitsfeiern, Musikantenhalten und Kirchweih: Policey und Festkultur im Frühneuzeitlichen Kurmainz," *Mainzer Zeitschrift: Mittelrheinisches Jahrbuch für Archäologie, Kunst und Geschichte* 92/93 (1997/98): 57–87, here 65–69; see also Labouvie, *Andere Umstände*.

[80] Variations of "cunt."

[81] The women's language is remarkably coarse, reflecting not only the linguistic habits of the time but the male writer's projection of women conversing freely in their private space.

[82] "[I]ch war so gifftig in meinem Sinn/ daß ich ihr meine Wochen Kanne bald in die Fresse geworffen" (I was so furious that I felt like hitting her in the trap with my birthing-room pitcher) (3).

marzipan[83] she had had prepared for her baptismal guests caused complaints. Yet another visitor, Frau Margarita, expresses displeasure at one of the godparents' apparent disregard for the proper way of handling the baptized baby. She had reportedly returned the baby to the young mother without the customary pronouncement about the baby's changed spiritual state. It was important to accompany the gesture by saying that a little pagan had been carried to church who was now returning a Christian.[84] Another guest supposedly neglected to wish the *Wöchnerin* good luck.

Turning to those not present, the guests discuss a woman named the Pfeifferin, who had not yet borne a child ("ist noch nie in die Wochen gekommen"), although she seems to be pregnant now. Her rumored pregnancy prompts an animated discussion about the difficulties that finding a competent lying-in maid presents to any inexperienced prospective mother. Although much of the bedside conversation centers on the lying-in maid, little concrete information can be found in contemporary literature about her and her special relationship to her mistress. Most frequently, her role appears to be subsumed under that of the midwife and the visiting matrons.[85] Nevertheless, the spirited conversation on this topic highlights the importance of lying-in maids for new mothers; it points as well to the maids' dependence on a respectable work history and on a good reputation if they wanted to be assured of steady employment. This mutual need is aggravated by the fact that the period of engagement as a lying-in maid was relatively brief, and the community whose new mothers provided maids with a living was geographically, economically, and socially quite limited. The conversations reveal that there exists little solidarity of gender among the women. The division by class, urban middle-class women interacting with the lower class of servant women, shapes the tone of the conversations. The tales told about well-to-do women falling on hard times signal to the reader the harsh reality that inclusion in this class could be as tenuous as one's marital (mis)fortune or a woman's ability to keep and manage her family's property and wealth.[86]

Apparently the subject of the women's attention, the young Pfeifferin, had not hired well when she was trying to fill the position of lying-in maid. This new maid, her inferior social station notwithstanding, dominates the conversation in the birthing room for a considerable length of time. Hired to provide help and comfort to the pregnant Pfeifferin, this maid, disparagingly called "das dicke

---

[83] A confection made from honey and almonds.

[84] "[V]orher einen Heyden weggetragen/ und nun . . . einen Christen wieder [bringen]" (3).

[85] Wiesner, *Women and Gender in Early Modern Europe*, bibliography, 113–17; Wunder, *"Er ist die Sonn', sie ist der Mond"*; Wolfgang von Hippel, *Armut, Unterschichten, Randgruppen in der Frühen Neuzeit* (Munich: Oldenbourg, 1995), 23–25; Labouvie, *Andere Umstände*, 235–39.

[86] Wiesner, *Women and Gender in Early Modern Europe*, 7.

Weib auff der Sand Gasse" (the fat woman from Sandy Lane), apparently does not pass muster with the women, while to the reader she comes across as a woman not easily cowed. It appears that she deftly exploits the temporary dependence of well-to-do ladies on her services; her reported brashness casts light on the evident power struggle between maid and mistress. She is said to be fickle and, for a woman of her station, to have the reputation of being an inappropriately finicky eater. She reputedly refused to eat sweet peas or drink *Rastrum,* the beer proper for people of her station.[87] Of unfittingly proud bearing, she is said to have recently married a widower with children. The women in the chamber predict an unhappy fate for her. They note with satisfaction that it often happens that ill-reputed and impertinent maids reduce their future chances to get a position. This is judged to be punishment for the harm they do to their female employers. But there are exceptions: the women tell of maids that could and did wilfully inflict serious damage on their mistresses without any apparent harm to their ability to find employment.[88] Frau Suse regales her compatriots with tales about one such maid who had taken extreme advantage of a well-to-do woman who did "not know a thing about keeping house" ("welche kein Teuffel von der Haußhaltung verstanden") (6). According to the gossip, this maid spent the woman's money so freely that her mistress ended up financially ruined. In the end, the lady in question had to pawn her clothes and shoes, which prevented her from attending church for a long while.[89] To add insult to injury, the same maid was heard bragging about how she had participated in the profligate spending and consequently in her mistress's ruin.

The conversations in the chamber show just how much the women know about other women in their community and about their relationships, and why this might be of great interest to the male reader. Little remains hidden from the women, and thus from the listener, as visitors and host share approbation and censure of their friends and acquaintances. Frau Suse denounces the husband of the "dicke Weib" as a good-for-nothing, violent man. He is said to have beaten his first wife almost to death ("bald todtgeschmissen") (4). She predicts that the

---

[87] "[S]o eckel im fressen wäre gewesen; Daß sie keinen Steiffmuß/ süsse Milch und Erbsen hatte essen/ noch Rastrum sauffen wollen" (She was such a picky eater that she wouldn't even have whipped cream with sweet peas, nor did she want to drink *Rastrum*) (4). *Rastrum* was a cheap beer brewed in Leipzig. Aside from determining who could eat what when, the *Kleiderordnungen* also determined which sort of beer people were allowed to drink.

[88] "[I]hren Frawen vorher alles Hertzeleyd angethan/ und darnach das liebe Brodt nicht haben zu fressen gehabt" (They did real harm to their mistresses and then she had not even a piece of bread to eat) (4).

[89] "[D]aß sie auch ihre Kleider und Schuh hette müssen versetzen und verkauffen/ und eine lange Zeit nicht können in die Kirche gehen" (That she had to pawn her dresses and her shoes; and for a long time she could not even attend church) (6).

children of the first marriage will not have it easy, at which point Frau Käte sighs about the fate suffered by many a stepchild. She tells of a malicious stepmother who is said to have caused the death of her stepdaughter, a sweet thing with yellow hair and a pale face whom the devilish stepmother delivered to the grave.[90] The child's death is common knowledge; the cause of death remains conjecture. The same is true for the paternity of a foundling recently discovered at the local cemetery. The concealed circumstances of an illegitimate birth are part of the gossip implicating parents, child, and community in a discourse of secrecy that is the subject of gossip but the truth of which remains hidden.[91]

Above all else, the women's scornful gossip accentuates the unavoidable intimacy of the lying-in chamber, which leaves the new mother vulnerable to her maid, specifically to her unwillingness to exercise discretion and keep her counsel.[92] Any hidden vice, any private sin becomes known to the observing maid and thus potentially to the whole community. One of the visitors, the wife of the apothecary, is convinced that most women are so keen on visiting the lying-in-chamber because they are eager for the gossip ("damit sie nach was neues gaffe / und hernach was außzutragen habe") (51). Frau Suse tells of her sister's maid, who gossiped to her mistress about a woman whose drinking habit made her the laughingstock of the community. A keen observer of her employer, the maid had identified the lady's disheveled clothes, discoloration of skin, and incoherence of speech as the result of *Trunckenheit* (drunkenness).[93] Female drinking was to be moderate and clearly circumscribed. It could only take place at lying-in, baptism, and Carnival in the company of women, that is, during times that were

---

[90] "[E]s ist nicht lange/ da starb ein wackers Bießgen/ mit schönen gelben Haaren und weissem Angesicht: Das hat nicht anders als die Hengrische Stieffmutter ins Grab gebracht" (It wasn't long ago that a brave little girl with beautiful blond hair and pale skin died. None other than that witch of a stepmother put the little girl into her grave) (5).

[91] Lochrie, *Covert Operations*, 41, 61: "[G]ossip is a discourse of secrecy that claims to 'speak in the world's voice'."

[92] "Da sie nemlich ziemlich alles außschwatzen soll was in vorigen Diensten/ von Herrn und Frauen gesehen und gehöret" (People say that she blabs out everything she has seen and heard in previous jobs about her previous master and mistress) (5).

[93] "Als sagte mir meine Schwester/ daß sie ihr zu Ohren gebracht hätte/ wie sie vor diesen/ bey einer Frauen gedienet/ welche trefflich hette können sauffen/ wol Bier als Brandtwein theils in der Stadt/ theils draussen auff ihrem Gute.... [S]o were ihr Gesicht davon roth geworden/ wie eines Kalkutischen Hahns-Schnabel/ sie hette auch bald wunderlich zu reden angefangen" (My sister told me that she heard from her [the maid] how at one time she had been in service with a woman. This woman really knew how to drink, both beer and brandy, here in town as well as out on her farm, where she often went on a binge.... She said that when her mistress drank even more, her face turned red like the beak of a Calcutta rooster and she started talking funny). (5).

associated with fertility and reproduction or social inversion.[94] By Praetorius's time, the custom of women drinking together on special occasions had come under increasingly negative scrutiny. Complaints about excessive consumption of alcohol and food led to restrictions and soon to edicts on the number of celebrants allowed and amount of refreshments consumed.[95]

However, the women also discuss behaviors more morally reprehensible than public drunkenness, such as the lasciviousness of a married, ostensibly respectable, burgher's wife. One of the visitors regales her listeners with tales about a woman whose fondness for student boarders reputedly had her bed them down with abandon ("auff- und abgesattelt"). She found herself denounced by her maid, who, with feigned naiveté, reported to the husband strange loud noises that issued from the mistress's room in the master's absence. Worthy of a character from a Shrovetide play and showing an enviable presence of mind, the mistress, when questioned, blamed the noise on having had to move furniture in order to search for a penny of her *Wochen-Geld* that had rolled under the bed (7).[96] The interdependence of maid (maligned as *Löffel-Magd, Lauff Petze, Seichfotze,* and *Kluncker-Mutze*) and mistress, as well as the frequent allusions to the transient life of these servant women, hint at a rootlessness that endangers as well as empowers them.[97] Maids or servant women frequently changed employment in search of positions that promised less supervision and more freedom to do as they pleased. In the minds of their employers—and, we might surmise, in the mind of the male observer—this freedom always meant freedom to have sex.[98] Nevertheless, servants and mistresses were partners in a contract that wedded

---

[94] B. Ann Tlusty, "Crossing Gender Boundaries: Women as Drunkards in Early Modern Germany," in *Ehrkonzepte in der Frühen Neuzeit: Identitäten und Abgrenzungen,* ed. S. Backmann, Hans-Jörg Künast, Sabine Ullmann, and eadem, Colloquia Augustana 8 (Berlin: Akademie Verlag, 1998), 185–98, here 189–90.

[95] Labouvie, *Andere Umstände,* 203–5.

[96] About the *Wochengeld,* we read in the *Nürnberger Polizeiordnung,* "[D]as kain gefatter noch yemant von seinen wegen einichem kyndt mer einpinden soll dann zwenunddreyssig pfenning gewonlicher werung zu Nüremberg" (No godparent should present to anyone more than thirty-two pfennig of Nuremberg currency) (70).

[97] Occasionally, such women found themselves denounced as witches, suffering the deadly outcomes we associate with such accusations. See Eveline Hasler's fictionalized novel of the trial of Anna Göldin: *Anna Göldin, Letzte Hexe* (Munich: DTV, 1982); see also the case of Anna Eberle in Roper, "Witchcraft and Fantasy," 199ff.

[98] "Ja es ist ein Ausbund aller losen Huren/ sie hat auch jederzeit diese Tugend an sich gehabt/ das sie keinmal lange an einem Orte hette können verbleiben: Sondern hat alle Viertel Jahre neue Dienste gehabt; da sie denn sonderlich solche gesucht/ wo sie frey leben/ und mit den Knechten rantzen könte" (Yes, she's a model of a whore! She is also in the habit of never remaining very long at any one place of employment. Instead, she changes jobs every three months, for she always looks for employment that will afford her a life where she is free to fuck the manservants) (6).

the poorer women's penury to the wealthier woman's dependence on servants for social representation and practical needs. Looking at it a bit differently, one might say that the wealthy woman's need of service and the competition for it contributed to the immorality of the maids.

As the conversations in the chamber move along, no names need be disclosed. The women in the lying-in chamber intimately know the subjects of their gossip, be they maids, mistresses, or spouses. When one of the women shares a story about a hapless married man who was found with his concubine, the women seem to nod knowingly. They can readily guess who the culprit might be ("Ich wollte schier errathen wer er were"). Another voices agreement, yes, "ja ich lasse es mir auch bedüncken: Der Krug gehet so lange zum Wasser / bis er einmahl bricht" (20).[99] She reminds her listeners that the whole community had shunned another woman for her alleged immoral behavior. In fact, the woman's promiscuity was so blatant that she had been excluded from the women's gatherings and thus from their gossip. The women in the chamber crassly chide her immorality by calling her a "cunt," unwilling to deny herself to any man who happened by, be he student or servant.[100] Repeatedly, the reader is reminded that the smallness of the community made privacy, in the modern sense, an impossibility.

Still, the women also know that, while reprehensible in the eyes of the community, such conduct has less dire consequences for wives than for unmarried women, young girls, or the maids themselves, who were likely to be fired if their sexual transgressions became public. When the daughters of the well-to-do trespassed and became pregnant, they either left town to deliver their babies elsewhere in secret, or they aborted them.[101] Even if, as we know, maids also would often abort or give up their newborns and middle-class adulteresses and unmarried mothers did not go entirely uncensored, Praetorius signals that the consequences of such actions seem much more dire for the poor than for the well-to-do. If the maid were caught, her honor would be permanently damaged and her chances to marry well or to marry at all would be seriously compromised. Even lower-class men tended to shun women who had been publicly censored for premarital sex.[102] Not surprisingly, the wife of the apothecary is the woman in the know about such missteps among her compatriots. She tells of one of the town's

---

[99] German proverb: the jug goes to the water until it finally breaks.

[100] "[S]oll doch das leichtfertige Aaß es keinem Kerl versagen/ es mag ihr Praeceptor ein Pennal/ ein Stutzer/ oder ein Kramer-Diener seyn" (This easy piece doesn't deny [herself] to any man, whether it is a teacher or student, townsman, or salesclerk) (7).

[101] On pregnancy and legitimacy see Ulinka Rublack, *The Crimes of Women in Early Modern Germany*, Oxford Studies in Social History (Oxford: Clarendon Press, 1999).

[102] Renate Duerr, "Die Ehre der Mägde zwischen Selbstdefinition und Fremdbestimmung," in Backmann et al., eds., *Ehrkonzepte der frühen Neuzeit: Identitäten und Abgrenzungen*, 148–79.

mothers aborting her daughter's fetus with a concoction of pepper and saffron.[103] It is clear that the women knew and shared such knowledge in the confinement room. By contrast, the excluded (eavesdropping) men wanted to find out what men are always eager to know, namely the most coveted of secrets, the secrets of lost virginity, pregnancy, fatherhood, and abortion; the secrets at the site of "the intersection between the social and the individual."[104]

Whatever the success or failure of maid-mistress relationships, whatever the potential damage when secrets were involuntarily and inadvertently shared, the fact remained that the new mother's household could not function without the help of these servant women, nor could the gossip caused by this relationship ever be quelled. One visitor, Frau Christine, comments with resignation that, in reality, the maids are in such demand that the mothers must be grateful for the ones they can employ.[105] She alludes to a potential imbalance in the relationship: the mistress has the money, but the maid has the service that she can render or withhold. A contemporary broadsheet explores this popular topic in image and text.[106] Maid, cook, nursemaid, housemaid, farm maid, and, highest in the order of maids, the household manager, the keeper of the keys (*Beschließerin*), each makes clear that she well knows her station but also her worth. While the counsel is meant in jest, the complaints about the stinginess, foolishness, and vanity of their mistresses reverberate through the whole document. The *Zeitung* reads like a draft for Praetorius's tract, closing with the caveat that the good maid is, of course, not addressed by this disrespectful tract ("die Frommen / so treu und fleissig dienen / hierunter nit gemeinet").

The women in Margarita's confinement room know all about the predicament of needing maids and being dependent on those they are able to hire. One, Frau Liese, concurs with clear distress, adding that she, for one, had to depend on rural wetnurses in order to feed her babies because she found nursing too painful (38). Weighing maternal breastfeeding against wetnursing, she addresses the pervasive early-modern anxiety over the possible transmission of

---

[103] "O/ da ist der lange Pfeffer und ungestossene Saffran wieder gut zu. . . . Auff diese Weise auch Frau Annen ihr niedlichs Bißgen/ das rantzige Muster/ ihre Frucht abgetrieben" [Oh, dear, and then the long pepper and unground saffron will be needed for that [to abort]. . . . It has been said that Frau Anna's sweet young thing, the spoiled little bitch, aborted her "fruit" this way) (51). Günter Jerouschek, *Lebensschutz und Lebensbeginn: Kulturgeschichte des Abtreibungsverbots* (Stuttgart: Enke, 1988), 128–29.

[104] Lochrie, *Covert Operations*, 61.

[105] "Man muß doch Gott dancken/ daß man Gesinde haben kan: Wird doch die Welt so böse/ als sie noch nie gewesen ist" (We actually should be grateful even to have servants; the world is getting more corrupt than it has ever been) (21).

[106] "Neue Zeitung: Ein Rathschluß der Dienst-Mägde" (Nuremberg, 1652), in *Deutsche illustrierte Flugblätter I*, 147. Schilling, "Das Flugblatt als Instrument gesellschaftlicher Anpassung."

questionable character traits from nursemaid to baby: "Die lieben Kinder saugen manchemal / ich weiß nicht was / von den Vetteln hinein" (Sometimes, when nursing, the dear children pick up Lord knows what from their wetnurses) (38). Dejectedly, she compares herself unfavorably to a female dog, complaining that a bitch never lacks sufficient milk for her pups. In this it resembles the peasant women, who are always ready and able to nurse the additional young. Not in the least disturbed about such misgivings, Frau Liese consoles her compatriot by pointing to the divinely ordained social difference between rich and poor. She, for one, is confident that it is part of God's plan that those born to wealth should hire the less fortunate, in this case the nursemaids.[107] It appears that, in the mind of these women, one can fall socially but not climb.

At one point, the new mother acknowledges that her husband, a "Magister auf dem Collegio" (master at the college), is an impressive specimen, a *tausend-Kerl* (a real man). Aside from his great learning and many other talents, he is able to read people's lives and characters from their palms and the lines in their faces. Those familiar with Praetorius's biography will recognize that through Margarita's comments he is advertising himself as the author of a tract on chiromancy, which he had published in 1661.[108] The science of *chiromantia*, of gaining insight into people's character, temperament, and moods from interpreting the lines in their palms and their faces, dates back to Greek and Roman antiquity, when it was used for soothsaying practices.[109] Along with other ancient texts on magic and the occult, tracts on chiromancy enjoyed a significant reception between 1500 and 1700 (and beyond), and hundreds of them survive today.[110] Praetorius's

---

[107] "Dessentwegen hat uns Gott mehr Geld bescheret/ als die Dorffleutgen haben/ daß wir Ammen halten können" (That is why God has given us more money than the peasants, so we can hire nursemaids) (38). Naomi Miller, "Mothering Others: Caregiving as Spectrum and Spectacle in the Early Modern Period," in Miller and Yavneh, eds., *Maternal Measures,* 1–29, here 5; Rachel Trubowitz, "'But Blood Whitened': Nursing Mothers and Others in Early Modern Britain," in Miller and Yavneh, eds., *Maternal Measures,* 82–101, here 83–84.

[108] *LVDICRVM/ CHIROMANTICUM/ PRAETORII:/ seu THESAURUS/ CHIROMANTIAE* . . . (Jena, 1661). The work is dedicated to the young Elector of Saxony Johann Georg III (1647–1691). It shows the influences of Hermes Trismegistus, Johannes ab Indagine, and Rudolph Goclenius: Waibler, *JP,* 990–98.

[109] Brian P. Copenhaver mentions Praetorius's tract on chiromancy: "A Show of Hands," in *Writing on Hands: Memory and Knowledge in Early Modern Europe,* ed. Claire Richter Sherman, catalogue of an exhibit by the Trout Gallery at Dickinson College with the participation of the Folger Shakespeare Library (Seattle: University of Washington Press, 2000), 46–59, here 51–52.

[110] I am grateful for some of this information to Sven Lembke, University of Freiburg, Germany, who presented a paper on this topic at the Sixteenth Century Studies Conference (October 2001): "Physiognomics, *Astrologia naturalis* and the Anatomical Decipherment of Man in the 16th Century."

obvious contempt for female superstitions and gossipy conjectures notwithstanding, he clearly considered chiromancy a reliable source of information for the learned practitioner. However, while this art disclosed the secrets of human nature and disposition to the inquiring male gaze (chiromancy was considered a science), the practice never completely shed its somewhat shady reputation and checkered past, which often brought it into uncomfortable proximity to satanic superstitions and the practices of forbidden magic.[111] Frau Suse notes that the *Magister auff dem Collegio* (apparently referring to Praetorius and his *Ludicrum chiromanticum*)[112] could have read from the palms of one of her maids about her sexual high-jinks had the maid, aware of the potential disclosure of the secrets of her personal life, not prevented him from doing so.[113] Johannes ab Indagine, one of Praetorius's sources, mentions that a woman's "libidinous and immoral" character could be easily discerned by looking at her hand for "a cross . . . about the upper corner proceeding to the line of life."[114] The *Magister* might have disclosed Frau Suse's maid's sexual improprieties (*Hurerey*), possibly even with him.[115]

In spite of her husband's scholarly and scientific expertise, the *Wöchnerin* is far from pleased with him; she is vexed because she would like him to buy her a *Puselmütze* (fashionable hat) and a nice green skirt instead of wasting his money on *Teuffels-Geschmeisse*[116] (devil's excrement), that is, the books he buys in such quantities that they could fill many carriages ("wol etliche Wagen damit beladen") (12). Alluding to the inability of scholars and pastors (which in Protestant Leipzig often were one and the same) to accumulate wealth, she notes with resignation that her husband will never change, because "preachers never leave anything but books and children for their inheritance" ("Pfaffen (verlassen) nichts anders als Bücher und Kinder zur Erbschaft") (12). To her chagrin, the guests do not share her jaundiced assessment of her husband's liberality. Commenting on the new baby's light complexion, Frau Christine speculates that its

---

[111] William Eamon, *Science and the Secrets of Nature: Books of Secrets in Medieval and Early Modern Culture* (Princeton: Princeton University Press, 1994), 214; Copenhaver, "Show of Hands."

[112] See note 103.

[113] "[A]lleine das verschlagene Raben-Aaß mag den Braten mercken: Drumb sie vergangen nicht gewolt hat/ wie es die Gelegenheit darzu gegeben" (Only the bitch can smell the roast: that's why she did not want to do it when the occasion arose) (7).

[114] Copenhaver, "Show of Hands," 52.

[115] "Er sagte vergangen meiner Magd ein Stückgen auß der Faust/ die er doch kaum in der quer angeblicket hatte . . . und sie gantz Schamroth drüber ward" (Just the other day, though he had hardly ever looked at her, he read such interesting information from my maid's hand that her face turned purple) (7). That the Magister might have known these facts from sources other than chiromancy is insinuated but not said.

[116] It is difficult to conjecture why this expletive was used relating to books. Maybe it refers to the type of books the *Magister* purchases if we remember that Praetorius (= the *Magister*) did write on witches and magic.

mother must have either eaten a lot of almonds or had much brandy (*Brandtwein*) to drink during her pregnancy, suggestions that the young mother emphatically rejects. She assures her guests that her husband would sooner beat her with "unburnt ash" (i.e., an ash rod) then give her a jigger of "burnt wine" (i.e., brandy) ("ungebrante Asche . . . über den Buckel / als ein Nösel Brandwein") (20).[117] But the new mother's ill-tempered outbursts are to no avail; the *Magister's* reputation among the women present seems to be better than his wife wants to admit. The reader remembers, of course, that the *Magister* is the tract's author, which surely accounts for the mocking praise Frau Christine heaps upon him. She calls him a sweet master who could not hurt a fly ("einen lieben frommen Herrn / der kein Wasser betrübet"), even while the *Wöchnerin* insinuates that her life is much harder than her naive friend surmises: "you don't know much about where the shoe pinches me" ("ir wüßt viel drumb wo mich der Schuch drücket") (20).

If the new mother's marriage is not ideal, for Frau Anna, another visitor, matrimony is hell. She favors the *Wöchnerin* and her guests with a tirade about her husband's penchant for alcohol and tobacco. Smoking slowly made inroads into early-modern German urban communities after tobacco found its way to Europe from America.[118] In his world chronicles, Praetorius comments on the economic benefits of growing and selling tobacco, especially for the Netherlands and England. But contemporary broadsheets and pamphlets also satirize the habit of "drinking tobacco," linking it to the purported German love for French fashions.[119] Introduced from the Americas as early as the second half of the sixteenth century, tobacco was credited with many beneficial effects, among them powers as an aphrodisiac. The poem notes that tobacco strengthens manhood (sexual prowess), something the wife is favored to experience every night ("hat diese Eygenschafft / die Mannheit thut er stärcken / wie ihr nächten im

---

[117] A play on words involving *Mandel* [almond] and *Mangel* [a huge wooden roll used for pressing sheets] makes the same point: "Ja/ mein Mann würde mir *Mandeln* kauffen; *Mangel* werdet ihr meinen/ oder *Mangelhöltzer*: Damit solte er mich wol eher abspeisen" (My husband buying almonds for me? I am sure you mean wooden *Mangeln*) (12).

[118] On the medicinal virtues of tobacco, one example among many: "Nicotiane, although it has only been known in France for a short time, yet holds the first place among medicinal plants": Sarah Augusta Dickson, *Panacea or Precious Bane: Tobacco in Sixteenth-Century Literature* (New York: New York Public Library, 1954), 43, 70, 72; on tobacco's introduction into England and the changing views of the weed in the sixteenth and seventeenth centuries, from divine herb with magical potential to tobacco smoked by those who could afford its high price, see Jeffrey Knapp, "Elizabethan Tobacco," *Representations* 21 (1988): 27–66.

[119] "Der teutsche Taback-trincker," Augsburg 1630, in Harms, *Illustrierte Flugblatt*, 1: 83 [HAB IE 90]. Three modishly dressed men are seen smoking. On the right side, a fool holds a very big pipe, indicating the foolishness of this habit. Smoking is also denounced for offending nonsmokers; the broadsheet recommends drinking beer rather than smoking tobacco.

Bett / von mir erfahren hätt") (13). Such testimony appears in the *Liedlein von Toback*, purchased by Frau Anna's wayward husband from a itinerant merchant, a *Trödel* (peddler), and brought home for her to read. In twenty-three verses with which Anna proceeds to regale her friends, this *Liedlein* stages a mock exchange between a man and his wife about the virtues (his side) and vices (her side) of tobacco. The husband in the song likes tobacco because smoking the herb suppresses his appetite and makes him smarter, more virile, and stronger; it is said to purge liver and lungs and thus improve his health ("und thut die Gesundheit mehren"). Moreover, tobacco is presented as a social equalizer. While initially only available to princes and lords ("Fürsten und Herren"), it is now smoked by rich and poor alike. Even gender matters are affected by it; smoking, it turns out, affirms that the man is "Herr im Hauß." Conversely, the poem's female voice inveighs against the *Schand-Kraut* in ways that sound much like modern opinions on smoking. She complains that her husband's tobacco habit is wasting the money that she had brought into the marriage, that it makes them poor, stinks up the air, increases the consumption of alcohol, soils clothing and furnishings, and, most significantly, damages the health of the smoker, shortening his life.[120] The rhymed dispute escalates to the point of physical abuse, in the course of which the husband grabs his wife by the neck and soundly thrashes her. She, in turn, pulls his hair and beard. Not surprisingly, the man is victorious and remains the lord and master ("Herr im Hauß / da wird nichts anders drauß") (14).

After deploring her husband's passion for tobacco, Anna says that she married him when he did not have a penny to his name ("er kam ja / so zu sagen / zu mir ohne Schuhe und Hembde") (15) and laments the fact that after the wedding he took control of her dowry. She presents herself as an example of the sad truth that a woman should never marry a man who is unable to provide at least six gold pieces (*Thaler*) a week to spend at the market. Frau Judith, another guest, concurs. While her husband's frugality has brought the couple modest wealth, it also presents a vexing problem for her. Rather than letting his wife enjoy some of their monetary blessing, he forbids her to wear attire appropriate for her station. Instead of fur, she owns only cloth; instead of pretty and dainty shoes, she has to go about in unsightly peasant clogs ("ungeheure Bauern-Schuh"). She has to warm her hands in a plain old muff instead of a fur muff decorated with ribbons.[121] This turns the purpose of the sumptuary laws on its head. While authorized to wear certain clothes and prohibited from wearing others, the laws apparently did not empower women in their daily lives to lay claim to the money that

---

[120] "[D]u kanst nicht werden alt/ der Toback thut dich verderben/ wirfft schon die Lunge auß/ und Leber auch mit Grauß/ zehn Jahr mustu eh sterben" (You won't get old; tobacco will kill you. You already spit out your lungs and your liver, and in ten years you will be dead) (14).

[121] The rules for clothing were strict, although difficult to enforce. See "Regulation of Clothing," in "Sumptuary Law in Nuremberg," 106–26; Eisenbart, *Kleiderordnungen*.

would allow them to wear what, according to the *Kleiderordnungen*, their social station entitled them to wear.

The guests' attention eventually turns to household items. They review where the best bargains could be obtained to furnish the lying-in chamber. The curtains of the new baby's cradle are admired in great detail, and the reader senses an intense, if submerged, competition among the women. One woman trumps the other, not with how much has been spent for each item mentioned but rather with how little, showing off her frugality in spite of her bourgeois affluence. The women note with pride how cleverly they profit from the misfortune and economic foolishness of women who have fallen on bad times and are forced to sell their possessions to the more fortunate. The triumph at getting a bargain, and, conversely, the shame implicit in reversals of fortune that force women to sell their family's belongings, are clearly audible in the self-satisfied report of the *Wöchnerin* as she muses about having purchased her cradle for a mere pittance from some poor woman down on her luck.[122] Commenting on the waxing and waning of fortunes, Frau Judith boasts that she could tell who had previously owned the clothing purchased just by looking at the way it had been sewn ("ich soll es fast an den Säumen und Nähten kennen / wer es vorhin gehabt"). With obvious *Schadenfreude,* she ridicules the fate of one woman who, formerly indulging in wine and fine beer, now is so destitute that she has to content herself with the cheapest of beers, the Leipzig *Rastrum* (10).

Time and again, as the visitors exchange their confidences, criticisms, and gossip, the social differences that divide the community are revealed. Aside from the most obvious social chasm between the ladies and their maids, or between the well-off ladies and those who have lost their place in the social hierarchy owing to financial or personal setbacks, a third division emerges toward the end of the tract. At this point, we glimpse the separation between the wives of the town's leading citizens and the women in the birthing room. When the members of this last group come to pay a visit to the new mother—Frau Apothekerin, Frau Pfarrerin, Frau Secretarien, and Frau Magister—they are identified not by their names but by their husbands' standing in the town. At their arrival, the tone in the chamber and the demeanor of the *Wöchnerin* change markedly. Apologies are exchanged—the new arrivals apologize for the lateness of their visit, and the new mother, for the messiness of her bedroom. Asked who the *Wehe-Mutter* (midwife) was, the mother says it was Frau Dorthen and praises her. The pastor's wife concurs, describing Frau Dorthen as having almost a physician's skills, judging by the success of her cures (50). As visitors and hostess exchange

---

[122] "[I]ch erschacherte es von einer Trödel Frauen/ so in der Peterstrasse . . . sitzet/ es muste wol eine sehr vornehme Frau gehabt haben/ die es aus Noth zu verstossen" (I haggled over it with the peddler woman who always sits in Peter Street by the College of St. Peter. It must have belonged to a really wealthy woman at one time who was forced to sell it because of hard times) (10).

pleasantries, a child's loud wailing is heard outside the bedroom door. This elicits caustic comments about husbands' habits of disciplining their children by beating them like so many sacks of flour. The women deride their husbands' annoying tendency to forget their own wild childhoods and youths when taking out their frustrations on their offspring and their wives. The women maintain that all this domestic strife could be avoided if men kept to their duties and left the raising of children and training of maids to the women.[123]

Moving from marital discord to larger community concerns, the *Apothekerin* reports with dismay that wedding celebrations have become increasingly sumptuous and lavish, even for the less well-to-do. Furthermore, the wealthiest families have taken to celebrating weddings at ten in the morning. The reasons given for these changes reflect an interesting blend of social, economic, moral, and sexual concerns. The visitors offer a number of serious and not-so-serious arguments in support of the announced changes. First of all, a ceremony before noon would limit the number of candles and torches needed and prevent the ladies' dresses from being soiled by candle wax or soot. Young, pimply boys ("Pusenickligte Jungen") would not sneak off to get drunk under the cover of darkness; food would be less costly because the guests would not have starved themselves all day in anticipation of the banquet; people would not be disturbed by loud music in the middle of the night; eager young women would not surreptitiously slip out of doors to meet potential lovers under the cover of darkness. Thus the virtue of young virgins would be protected more effectively and pregnancies averted if daylight prevented young men from grabbing the girls and lying with them in the dark. The dancers' dexterity and practiced steps could be more readily appreciated in daylight. Finally, the bride and groom would get to be alone earlier, giving the groom a chance to enjoy his bride throughout the night. The quality of the bridal soup (*Brautsuppe*)[124] most assuredly is better earlier in the day. Another advantage of morning weddings would be the equalizing effect of such social arrangements: everyone would celebrate the same way. The last reason brings us back to the first: the dresses of the women, and presumably their virtue, would not be as easily stained (55–57). The women jokingly comment on these new wedding rules, but extensive lists of rules and prohibitions do appear in various *Polizeiordnungen* and *Kleiderordnungen* from about this time. These include rules

---

[123] "Wenn die Männer ihres Thuns warteten/ und überliessen den Weibern die Kinder und Gesinde zu ziehen; so bliebe mancher Hauß Krieg nach" (If men would just mind their own business and leave the children and servants to us women, many a household war would be avoided) (52).

[124] *Feuchte Brautsuppe* (moist bridal soup) also appears as a metaphor for semen and pregnancy in the first poem and in the prologue: "[Die Braut] muß sich nothwendig erst vor ein 3. viertel Jahres Frist der feuchten Braut-Suppen bedienet/ und selbige wohl verdauet haben" (Nine months before, [the bride must have] partaken of the wet bridal soup and digested it well) (Prologue).

about when and how weddings could be celebrated, what and how many guests were to be invited, what the guests were to wear, and what kinds of presents they were allowed to purchase. A specific time of day for the wedding feast, however, is rarely mentioned.

The fact that the women had read about these changes makes it clear, once again, that all the women in this tract, whether maids, damsels, or married women, are literate; they read for instruction and enjoyment, and many are able to write. A good deal of the laughter generated in the confinement room is related to reading, and reading aloud is equated here with sharing gossip, love talk, and lascivious advice. This is brought to the fore especially in the four poems interjected into the tract, which are severally described as being given to the women by their husbands with the instruction to read them carefully. Frau Anna's husband brings home the tobacco poem, the theme of which is marital discord. The three additional poems interspersed in the *Apocalypsis*, devoted to weddings, to lying-in, and to hidden men observing gossiping women, have reportedly been presented at recent weddings, to the great amusement of all those present. One of Margarita's visitors reports how she and her husband enjoyed reading one of the poems at night in their conjugal bedroom. It is entitled "Geheimer-Stul/ welcher der Jungfer Braut in künfftige Haußhaltung zum freundlichen Ange-dencken/ verehret" (Secret chair given to the bride with wishes for happy future housekeeping). This poem talks of an elaborate dream vision about a husband who, with the help of Venus's son Amor, listens, unseen and unheard, to the intimate conversations in a lying-in chamber. The author is identified as yet another male persona, Frau Regina's secretary (*Schreiber*), who supposedly made common cause with the maids who are privy to their mistress's conversations.[125] A copy has been delivered to the *Wöchnerin*, who heard her husband laughing when he read it. This both chagrins the women (about the indiscretion of the conversations) and amuses them (because of the humorous treatment). The lengthy poem (22–29) is an elaborate joke about Venus cuckolding her husband Vulcan. Amor offers to lead the secretary into the *Wochenstube* after the baptism. The secretary resists in mock fear, exclaiming that under no circumstances would he be persuaded to enter the birthing chamber, even if he had to lose his hat ("Ich geh dir nicht hinein; es kostet meinen Hut"). When he finally relents, he is overcome by the luxury of the room and its furnishings ("was man sah / das ware nett und schön"). Moreover, the beauty of the female visitors soon captivates his voyeuristic gaze, and the young mother's exposed white breasts are instantly arousing to

---

[125] "Da hat mir das Gottlosen Stück alle Reden auffgeschnappet/ welche die Weibrichten in meiner Stuben fürm Kindelbett gehalten: Und hat solche Heimlichkeiten hernach dem Schreiber offenbahret/ der es auff Herr Licentiatens Hochzeit mit in ein Carmen gebracht" (The godless cunt listened to all the confidences that my women friends and I exchanged. And then she blabbed about it to the tutor, who made a song of it, which he brought along to the recent wedding of one of the lawyers) (22).

him.[126] It should be noted here that for fear of spoiling the milk, sexual inter-course was forbidden to the nursing mother. Since nursing mothers were also less likely to conceive, the image of a woman who was exposed but sexually unavail-able makes this a scene of unfulfilled, comic sexual desire.[127]

The poem returns to the semiserious theme of the man looking in on the doings in the women's room, conveying, once again, his anxiety about women sharing language and tales that are hidden from men. Having control over birth-ing and lying-in might also indicate secrets concerning conception: "Und [ich] hörte fein was hier die Weiber für die Wochen Gantz in geheim geredt" (And I heard quite well what the women talk about in secret concerning lying-in) (28).[128] When, still in his dream, the authorial "I" is discovered by the *Muhme*, who forc-es him to swear, hand on the birthing stool[129] and standing in front of the lying-in bed, not to tell what he had seen and heard.[130] Venus is so pleased with the poem that she promotes the hapless *Schreiber* to the position of privy secretary of secrets of the women in general ("geheimer Secretar / Der Weiber insgesambt") (23), at which point he wakes up and immediately writes down the tract.

The second poem returns to Frau Margarita's chamber and to her hapless tutor (*praeceptor*), who is found hiding behind the closed door of Frau Marga-rita's chamber. Wise to male subterfuge, Margarita sends a maid to the door to find out who might be listening; it is the *Muhme* and the tutor, who is obviously disdained by the children and despised by their mother (29–31). She calls him a *Blut-Aeser* and *Hungerleider* (pathetic starving fool), whose duties in the house-holds of the well-to-do are described as an endless series of humiliations. It is a clear sign of the tutor's emasculation in the early-modern household in general, and in Margarita's in particular, that he is expected to do housewifely chores such as laying the table and carrying the candle for the man of the house (34). Moreover, in the fictional world of the poem, he is the only man allowed to enter the *Wochenstube*. Scorned for being ungrateful for employment, room, and board, even though the women insist that he is treated better than he deserves,[131] he

---

[126] "Die Weiber saßen dort man kriegte gar ein Lüstgen/ Und wusten sich so viel mit den geklarten Brüstgen" (The women sat around, / And showed off those beautiful little breasts / So that one could get quite excited) (25).

[127] Margaret L. King, *Women of the Renaissance* (Chicago: University of Chicago Press, 1991), 16–19.

[128] Bicks, "Midwiving Virility," 50.

[129] "[B]ey allen Wochen-Stühlen."

[130] "[D]aß keinem ich hinfort/ Davon nicht sagen soll/ nicht das geringste Wort."

[131] "[G]ab ihm zu Fressen/ so gut als es mein Gesinde selber frißt: Und warff ihme auch hernach etliche Lümpgen zu: weil er gantz nackicht war/ und ihn die Läuse ihn bald hetten fressen mögen" ([I]gave him food to eat that was as good as what I feed my servants. And I threw him a few rags because he was almost naked; the lice had all but devoured him) (34).

makes common cause with the *Muhme* in an attempt to avenge the humiliations he has to suffer in his hardscrabble existence. He eavesdrops holding a writing tablet in his hand, pressing his ear to the door and whispering with the old lying-in maid.[132] The abuse ("Hundsfutt, Galgendieb") heaped on the tutor by the new mother prompts a marginal note by an unknown early-modern reader, who, obviously sympathetic, calls this section of the tract "des Praeceptors Klage" (the tutor's complaint). In spite of the tutor's privileged knowledge, he is, after all, only an academic. His marginalized position makes him less of a person than the woman whose family he serves; he is socially and sexually neutered, bereft of any authority at all.

The third and last poem, entitled "Des holdseligen Frauenzimmers Kindbet-Gespräch" (40–44) (The lovely women's childbed conversation), had come to one of the women by way of her brother-in-law from Nuremberg, who found it very amusing (39). This is, in fact, a copy of a broadsheet of the same title printed in Nuremberg.[133] While the provenance of the tobacco poem is not clear, the two remaining lying-in poems might implicate the new father, Praetorius's persona, Margarita's husband, as the writer. He is the one who has surreptitiously spied on the women's conversations, secretly looking in, hiding behind the gossiping maid and the snooping tutor. Praetorius employs these different masks as he ridicules male curiosity and female gossip with equal tartness. Still, the hidden observer's amusing experiences and his slapstick reports cannot hide the fact that women share with each other information kept secret from men, information not always complimentary to them. Now the narrator has heard it all: who among the women of the town keeps lovers by the dozen; who wishes her husband dead; who would just as soon marry rich; who has found out about her husband's infidelity but was forced to keep quiet. And the eavesdropping man, the narrator as well as Praetorius, the writer, himself a father of daughters, heard the women brag that they surely planned to teach their daughters all they knew.[134] The listening men and the reader also learn that when a maid gets pregnant, she loses her job; if the same happens to the damsel, she goes out of town or has an abortion. If a married woman has dalliances, with or without consequences, it is for her or her maids (and friends) to know. The husband would be the last to find out were it not for the gossip he might be able to overhear. Small wonder that he goes to great lengths to take his position behind the door or the stove or under the bed, or wherever he might hide, so he can listen to the gossip that would disclose what

---

[132] "[H]alt eine Schreibe-Tafel in der Hand/ und horchte so leise mit der Muhmen zu/ was ihr hie schwatzet" ([H]e was carrying a little slate tablet in his hand. With the *Muhme* he listened behind the door to hear what you all said in here) (44).

[133] See note 53.

[134] "Die schneidet tapffer auff/ wie sie bey ihrem Leben/ Nur alls zu dutzenden den Töchtern mitgegeben" (This one boasts about how much [money] / She had given for her daughters' dowries) (27).

he is most anxious to know: who does what with whom, and whether he really is the father of the child that has just been born.

The women's voices in the lying-in chamber form a veritable chorus whose comments help the young mother keep in touch with her friends and give and take advice. While she remains physically confined to this small space, these visits help her cross the boundaries into the community. The women's chorus enables the new mother to participate in town life even during her prolonged physical absence; it also eases her reentry into the community once the six weeks of semi-isolation are officially declared over with the ceremony of churching, the *Kirchgang*. The conversations produce a symbiosis between the small private room and the larger public space, as the visitors assess, judge, praise, or condemn the conduct of the town's women and their families. The visits to this confined space bring the larger and the smaller world into the contact necessary for the women to continue to function as the community's arbiters of moral, social, and economic judgment. The challenges of childrearing and household management provide the entry ticket into the company of married women, who, as they come and go during the lying-in period, pass judgment on the community and each other.

Bibliography

Baader, Joseph, ed. *Nürnberger Polizeiordnungen aus dem XII. bis XV. Jahrhundert.* Stuttgart: Bibliothek des Litterarischen Vereins, 1861.

Backmann, Sybille, Hans-Jörg Künast, Sabine Ullmann, and B. Ann Tlusty, eds. *Ehrkonzepte in der Frühen Neuzeit: Identiäten und Abgrenzungen.* Colloquia Augustana 8. Berlin: Akademie Verlag, 1998.

Banks, Amanda Carson. *Birth Chairs, Midwives, and Medicine.* Jackson: University Press of Mississippi, 1999.

Barnaby, Andrew, and Lisa J. Schnell. *Literate Experience: The Work of Knowing in Seventeenth-Century English Writing.* New York: Palgrave, 2002.

Barstow, Anne Llewellyn. *Witchcraze: A New History of the European Witch Hunts.* San Francisco: Pandora, 1994.

Behringer, Wolfgang. "Veränderung der Raum-Zeit-Relation: Zur Bedeutung des Zeitungs- und Nachrichtenwesens während der Zeit des Dreissigjährigen Krieges." In *Zwischen Alltag und Katastrophe: Der Dreissigjährige Krieg aus der Nähe*, ed. Benigna von Krusenstjern and Hans Medick, 39–83. Göttingen: Vandenhoeck & Ruprecht, 1999.

Bicks, Caroline. "Midwiving Virility in Early Modern England." In *Maternal Measures: Figuring Caregiving in the Early Modern Period*, ed. Naomi Miller and Naomi Yavneh, 46–65. Burlington, VT: Ashgate, 2000.

Blair, Ann. *The Theater of Nature: Jean Bodin and Renaissance Science.* Princeton: Princeton University Press, 1997.

————. "The Practices of Erudition According to Morhof." In *Mapping the World of Learning: The Polyhistor of Daniel Georg Morhof*, ed. Françoise Waquet, 59–74. Wolfenbütteler Forschungen 91. Wiesbaden: Harrassowitz, 2000.

Blühm, Elger. "Die Ältesten Zeitungen und das Volk." In *Literatur und Volk im 17. Jahrhundert*, ed. Brückner et al., 741–52.

Brückner, Wolfgang, Peter Blickle, and Dieter Breuer, eds. *Literatur und Volk im 17. Jahrhundert: Probleme Populärer Kultur in Deutschland, Teil I*. Wolfenbütteler Arbeiten zur Barockforschung 13. Wiesbaden: Harrassowitz, 1985.

Brumble, David. *Classical Myths and Legends in the Middle Ages and Renaissance*. Westport, CT: Greenwood Press, 1998.

Burckhardt, Johannes. *Der Dreissigjäehrige Krieg*. Edition Suhrkamp 542. Frankfurt am Main: Suhrkamp, 1992.

Burghartz, Susanna. "Rechte Jungfrauen oder unverschämte Töchter? Zur weiblichen Ehre im 16. Jahrhundert." In *Frauengeschichte—Geschlechtergeschichte*, ed. Karin Hausen and Heide Wunder, 173–83. Frankfurt am Main: Campus, 1992.

Bussmann, Klaus, and Heinz Schilling, eds. *1648: Krieg und Frieden in Europa. Politik, Religion, Recht und Gesellschaft. Textband 1*. Münster: Veranstaltungsgesellschaft 350 Jahre Westfälischer Frieden mbH., 1998.

Campbell, Mary Baine. *Wonder and Science: Imagining Worlds in Early Modern Europe*. Ithaca, NY: Cornell University Press, 1999.

Clark, Stuart. *Thinking with Demons: The Idea of Witchcraft in Early Modern Europe*. New York: Oxford University Press, 1997.

Copenhaver, Brian P. "A Show of Hands." In *Writing on Hands: Memory and Knowledge in Early Modern Europe*, ed. C. R. Sherman, 46–59. Seattle: University of Washington Press, 2000.

Daston, Lorraine. "The Nature of Nature in Early Modern Europe." *Configurations* 6 (1998): 149–72.

Döring, Detlef. *Die Bestandsentwicklung der Bibliothek der Philosophischen Fakultät der Universität Leipzig von ihren Anfängen bis Mitte des 16. Jahrhunderts: Ein Beitrag zur Wissenschaftsgeschichte der Leipziger Universität in ihrer vorreformatorischen Zeit*. Beiheft zum Zentralblatt für Bibliothekswesen 99. Leipzig: Bibliographisches Institut Leipzig, 1990.

Dülmen, Richard van. *Kultur und Alltag in der Frühen Neuzeit: Das Haus und seine Menschen, 16.–18. Jahrhundert*. Munich: Beck, 1990.

Duerr, Renate. "Die Ehre der Mägde zwischen Selbstdefinition und Fremdbestimmung." In *Ehrkonzepte der Frühen Neuzeit: Identitäten und Abgrenzungen*, ed. Backmann et al., 148–79.

Eisenbart, Liselotte C. *Kleiderordnungen der deutschen Städte zwischen 1350 und 1700. Ein Beitrag zur Kulturgeschichte des deutschen Bürgertums, Göttinger Bausteine zur Geschichtswissenschaft 32*. Göttingen, 1962.

Faulstich, Werner. *Medien zwischen Herrschaft und Revolte.* Göttingen: Vanden-hoeck & Ruprecht, 1998.

Fauser, Markus. "Klatschrelationen im 17. Jahrhundert." In *Geselligkeit und Ge-sellschaft im Barockzeitalter,* ed. Wolfgang Adam, 391–99. Wiesbaden: Har-rassowitz, 1997.

Findlen, Paula. "Francis Bacon and the Reform of Natural History in the Seventeenth Century." In *History and the Disciplines: The Reclassification of Knowledge in Early Modern Europe,* ed. R. Donald Kelley, 240–60. Roches-ter: Rochester University Press, 1997.

Gloning, Thomas. "Zur Vorgeschichte von Darstellungsformen und Textmerk-malen der ersten Wochenzeitungen." In *Die Sprache der ersten deutschen Wochenzeitungen im 17. Jahrhundert,* ed. Gert and Erich Strassner Fritz, 196–256. Tübingen: Niemeyer, 1996.

Greenfield, Kent Roberts. *Simptuary Law in Nürnberg: A Study in Paternal Gov-ernment.* Baltimore: Johns Hopkins Press, 1918.

Greyerz, Kaspar von. "Alchemie, Hermetismus und Magie: Zur Frage der Kon-tunitäten in der wissenschaftlichen Revolution." In *Im Zeichen der Krise,* ed. Lehmann and Trepp, 415–33.

Haerter, Karl. "Fastnachtslustbarkeiten, Hochzeitsfeiern, Musikantenhalten und Kirchweih: Policey und Festkultur im frühneuzeitlichen Kurmainz." *Mainzer Zeitschrift: Mittelrheinisches Jahrbuch für Archaeologie, Kunst und Geschichte* 92/93 (1997/98): 57–87.

———. "Sicherheit und Frieden im frühneuzeitlichen Alten Reich. Zur Funktion der Reichsverfassung als Sicherheits- und Friedensordnung 1648–1806." *Zeitschrift für historische Forschung* 30 (2003): 413–31.

Harms, Wolfgang, and Michael Schilling, eds. *Das illustrierte Flugblatt in der Kultur der Frühen Neuzeit: Wolfenbütteler Arbeitsgespräche.* Mikrokosmos: Beiträge zur Literaturwissenschaft und Bedeutungsforschung. Frankfurt am Main: Peter Lang, 1998.

Henry, John. *The Scientific Revolution and the Origins of Modern Science,* ed. Richard Overy. Studies in European History. London: Macmillan Press, 1997.

Hofmann-Randall, Christina. *Monster, Wunder und Kometen: Sensationsberichte auf Flugblättern des 16. bis 17. Jahrhunderts.* Erlangen: Universitätsbiblio-thek, 1999.

Jardine, Lisa. *Ingenious Pursuits: Building the Scientific Revolution.* New York: Doubleday, 1999.

Jaumann, Herbert. "Öffentlichkeit und Verlegenheit: Frühe Spuren eines Konzepts öffentlicher Kritik in der Theorie des *Plagium Extrajudiciale* von Jakob Thomasius (1673)." *Scientia Poetica: Jahrbuch für die Geschichte der Lit-eratur und der Wissenschaften* 4 (2000): 62–82.

———. "Was ist ein Polyhistor? Gehversuche auf einem verlassenen Terrain." *Studia Leibnitiana* 22 (1990): 76–89.

Kaiser, Michael. "'Excidium Magdeburgense': Beobachtungen zur Wahrnehmung und Darstellung von Gewalt im Dreissigjährigen Krieg." In *Ein Schauplatz herber Angst: Wahrnehmung und Darstellung von Gewalt im 17. Jahrhundert*, ed. Markus Meumann and Dirk Niefanger, 43–65. Göttingen: Wallstein, 1997.

Karant-Nunn, Susan. *The Reformation of Ritual: An Interpretation of Early Modern Germany*. London: Routledge, 1997.

———. "The Woman's Rite: Churching and the Lutheran Reformation." In *Problems of the Historical Anthropology of Early Modern Europe*, ed. R. Po-Chia Hsia and R. W. Scribner, 111–39. Wiesbaden: Harrassowitz, 1997.

King, Margaret L. *Women of the Renaissance*. Chicago: University of Chicago Press, 1991.

Klingebiel, Thomas. "Apokalyptik, Prodigienglaube und Prophetismus im Alten Reich: Ginführung." In *Im Zeichen der Krise*, ed. Lehmann and Trepp, 17–32.

Knapp, Jeffrey. "Elizabethan Tobacco." *Representations* 21 (1988): 27–66.

Krause, Friedlinde, ed. *Handbuch der historischen Buchbestände in Deutschland*, ed. Dietmar Deben and Waltraut Guth. Vol. 18. Hildesheim: Olms-Weidmann, 1997.

Krusenstjern, Benigna. *Selbstzeugnisse der Zeit des Dreissigjährigen Krieges: Beschreibendes Verzeichnis*. Selbstzeugnisse der Neuzeit 6. Berlin: Akademie, 1997.

Kühlmann, Wilhelm. "Lektüre für den Bürger: Eigenart und Vermittlungsfunktion der Polyhistorischen Reihenwerke Martin Zeillers." In *Literatur und Volk*, ed. Brückner et al., 2: 917–34.

Labouvie, Eva. *Andere Umstände: Eine Kulturgeschichte der Geburt*. Cologne: Böhlau, 2000.

Lehmann, Hartmut. "Die Kometenflugschriften des 17. Jahrhunderts als historische Quelle." In *Literatur und Volk im 17. Jahrhundert*, ed. Brückner et al., 683–700.

———, and Anne-Charlott Trepp, eds. *Im Zeichen der Krise: Religiosität im Europa des 17. Jahrhunderts*. Veröffentlichungen des Max-Planck-Instituts für Geschichte 152. Göttingen: Vandenhoeck & Ruprecht, 1999.

Lochrie, Karma. *Covert Operations: The Medieval Uses of Secrecy*. Philadelphia: University of Pennsylvania Press, 1999.

Manko-Matysiak, Anna. *Das Teufelsmotiv in der Schlesischen Wunderzeichenliteratur der Frühen Neuzeit*, ed. Heike Muens. Schriftenreihe der Kommission für Deutsche und Osteuropäische Volkskunde in der Deutschen Gesellschaft für Volkskunde E.V. 79. Marburg: Elwert Verlag, 1999.

Mauelshagen, Franz. "Illustrierte Kometenflugblätter in Wahrnehmungsgeschichtlicher Perspektive." In *Das Illustrierte Flugblatt in der Kultur der Frühen Neuzeit*, ed. Harms and Schilling, 101–36.

Medick, Hans. "Historisches Ereignis und zeitgenössische Erfahrung: Die Eroberung und Zerstörung Magdeburgs 1631." In *Zwischen Alltag und Katastrophe: Der Dreissigjährige Krieg aus der Nähe*, ed. von Krusenstjern and idem, 377–409.

——, and Benigna von Krusenstjern. "Einleitung: Die Nähe und Ferne des Dreissigjährigen Krieges." In *Zwischen Alltag und Katastrophe: Der Dreissigjährige Krieg aus der Nähe*, ed. eidem, 13–36.

Meinel, Christof. "Okkulte und exakte Wissenschaften." In *Die okkulten Wissenschaften in der Renaissance*, ed. August Buck, 21–43. Wiesbaden: Harrassowitz, 1992.

Miller, Naomi. "Mothering Others: Caregiving as Spectrum and Spectacle in the Early Modern Period." Introduction to *Maternal Measures: Figuring Caregiving in the Early Modern Period*, ed. eadem and Naomi Yavneh, 1–29.

Müller, Jan-Dirk. "Universalbibliothek und Gedächtnis: Aporien frühneuzeitlicher Wissenskodifikation bei Conrad Gesner (Mit einem Ausblick auf Antonio Possevino, Theodor Zwinger und Johann Fischart." In *Erkennen und Erinnern in Kunst und Literatur: Kolloquium Reisensburg, 4.–7. Januar 1996*, ed. Dietmar Peil, Michael Schilling, and Peter Strohschneider, 285–309. Tübingen: Niemeyer, 1998.

Musacchio, Jacqueline Marie. *The Art and Ritual of Childbirth in Renaissance Italy*. New Haven: Yale University Press, 1999.

Pickstone, John V. *Ways of Knowing: A New History of Science, Technology, and Medicine*. Chicago: University of Chicago Press, 2001.

Praetorius, Johannes. *Blockes-Berges Verrichtung, oder, Ausführlicher geographischer Bericht von den hohen trefflich alt- und berühmten Blockes-Berge; Ingleichen von der Hexenfahrt, und Zauber-Sabbathe*. Leipzig: Johann Scheiben; Frankfurt am Main: Friedrich Arnsten, 1668.

——. *Catastrophe Muhammetica: oder das Endliche Valet, und Schändliche Nativität des gantzen, und nunmehr vergänglichen Türckischen Reichs, aus ziemlich vielen, so wohl geistlichen Prophezeyhungen. tügtigen astrologischen Muthmassungen, richtigen Cabalistischen Schlüssen, und andern, divinatorischen Gründen mehr, entdecket, und sunserm. Vaterlande. an den Tag gegeben*. Leipzig: J. B. Oelers, 1663.

——. *Daemonologia Rubinzalii Silesii: das ist, Ein ausfurlicher Bericht von dem wunderbarlichen sehr alten und weitbeschrienen Gespenste dem Rubezahl*. Leipzig: Johann Barthol Oehlers, 1662.

——. *Dulc-Amarus Ancillariolus, das ist, Der süsz-wurtzligte und saur-ampferigte Mägde-Tröster erzwingend, Dasz die Mägde bessere Thiere seyn, als die so genanten Jungfern; Item, Dasz sie einen angenehmlichen Nahmen führen. Denn eine jedwede Jungfer wildoch gerne eine Magd hinter sich her-gezottelt haben*. Leipzig: H. Grosse(?), 1663.

————. *Philosophia Colus, oder, Pfy lose Vieh der Weiber: Darinnen gleich hundert allerhand gewöhnliche Aberglauben des gemeinen Mannes lacherig wahr gemachet werden.* Leipzig: Johann Barthol Oehlers, 1662.

Press, Volker. *Kriege und Krisen: Deutschland 1600–1715.* Die Neue Deutsche Geschichte 5. Munich: Beck, 1991.

Prutz, Robert E. *Geschichte des deutschen Journalismus. 1. Teil.* 1845. Repr. Göttingen: Vandenhoeck & Ruprecht, 1971.

Roeck, Bernd. "Der Dreissigjährige Krieg und die Menschen im Reich: Überlegungen zu den Formen psychischer Krisenbewältigung in der ersten Hälfte des 17. Jahrhunderts." In *Krieg und Frieden: Militär und Gesellschaft in der Frühen Neuzeit*, ed. Bernhard Kroener, 265–79. Paderborn: Schöningh, 1996.

Roper, Lyndal. "Witchcraft and Fantasy in Early Modern Germany." In *Oedipus and the Devil: Witchcraft, Sexuality, and Religion in Early Modern Europe*, 119–226. London: Routledge, 1994.

Rublack, Ulinka. *The Crimes of Women in Early Modern Germany.* Oxford Studies in Social History. Oxford: Clarendon Press, 1999.

Ruff, Julius R. *Violence in Early Modern Europe, 1500–1750.* New Approaches to European History. Cambridge: Cambridge University Press, 2001.

Schilling, Michael. *Bildpublizistik der Frühen Neuzeit: Aufgaben und Leistungen des illustrierten Flugblatts in Deutschland bis um 1700.* Tübingen: Niemeyer, 1990.

————. "Das Flugblatt als Instrument gesellschaftlicher Anpassung." In *Literatur und Volk im 17. Jahrhundert*, ed. Brückner et al., 601–19.

————. "Flugblatt und Krise in der Frühen Neuzeit." In *Wahrnehmungsgeschichte und Wissensdiskurs im illustrierten Flugblatt der Frühen Neuzeit (1450–1700)*, ed. Wolfgang Harms and Alfred Messerli, 33–60. Basel: Schwabe & Co AG Verlag, 2002.

Schmale, Wolfgang. "Das 17. Jahrhundert und die neuere europäische Geschichte." *Historische Zeitschrift* 264 (1997): 587–612.

Schottenloher, Karl. *Flugblatt und Zeitung: Ein Wegweiser durch das gedruckte Schrifttum.* Vol. 1, *Von den Anfängen bis zum Jahre 1848.* 1922. Repr. Munich: Klinckhardt & Biermann, 1985.

Schroeder, Thomas. *Die ersten Zeitungen: Textgestaltung und Nachrichtenauswahl.* Tübingen: Narr, 1995..

Shapin, Steven. *The Scientific Revolution.* Chicago: University of Chicago Press, 1996.

Stanton, Donna. "Recuperating Women and the Man Behind the Screen." In *Sexuality and Gender in Early Modern Europe*, ed. J. G. Turner, 246–65. Cambridge: Cambridge University Press, 1993.

Strassner, Erich. *Zeitung.* Vol. 2, *Grundlagen der Medienkommunikation.* Tübingen: Niemeyer, 1997.

Tatlock, Lynne, trans. and ed. *The Court Midwife, by Justine Siegemund*. The Other Voice in Early Modern Europe. Chicago: University of Chicago Press, 2005.

Tlusty, B. Ann. "Crossing Gender Boundaries: Women as Drunkards in Early Modern German." In *Ehrkonzepte in der Frühen Neuzeit: Identitäten und Abgrenzungen*, ed. Backmann et al., 185–98.

Vickers, Brian, ed. *Occult and Scientific Mentalities in the Renaissance*. Cambridge, MA: Harvard University Press, 1984.

Waibler, Helmut. *Johannes Praetorius (1630–1680): Ein Barockautor und seine Werke*. Frankfurt am Main: Buchhändler-Vereinigung GMBH, 1979.

Weber, Johannes. *Avisen, Relationen, Gazetten: Der Beginn des europäischen Zeitungswesens*. Oldenburg: Bibliotheks- und Informationssystem der Universität Oldenburg, 1997.

Wellenreuther, Hermann. "Gedanken zum Zusammenhang von Kommunikation und Wissen im 17. Jahrhundert." In *Im Zeichen der Krise*, ed. Lehmann and Trepp, 312–18.

Wiesner, Merry E. "The Midwives of South Germany and the Public/Private Dichotomy." In *The Art of Midwifery: Early Modern Midwives in Europe*, ed. Hilary Marland, 77–94. London: Routledge, 1993.

Wilke, Juergen. *Grundzüge der Medien- und Kommunikationsgeschichte: Von den Anfängen bis ins 20. Jahrhundert*. Cologne: Böhlau, 2000.

Williams, Gerhild Scholz. *Ways of Knowing in Early Modern Germany: Johannes Praetorius as a Witness to his Time*. Aldershot: Ashgate, 2006.

Zedelmaier, Helmut. *Bibliotheca Universalis und Bibliotheca Selecta: Das Problem der Ordnung des gelehrten Wissens in der Frühen Neuzeit*. Cologne: Böhlau, 1992.

———. "Von den Wundermännern des Gedächtnisses: Begriffsgeschichtliche Anmerkungen zu 'Polyhistor' und 'Polyhistorie'." In *Die Enzyklopädie im Wandel vom Hochmittelalter bis zur Frühen Neuzeit*, ed. Christel Meier-Hambach, 419–49. Munich: Fink, 2002.

Johannes Praetorius

Apocalypsis
Mysteriorum Cybeles
Das ist
Eine Schnakische
Wochen -Comedie
Oder
verplauderte
Stroh-Hochzeit
Und
WasCh-haffte
KinDeLeIns KerMsse
Im Jahre

SeCHs Gänß IM Haberstroh/
DIe Klatzgen VVahren froh
Oder
QVanDo CcMbLaterantsVsanna, sabIna, RosIna,
serMones repLICant& ab hoC, VeL ab haC, VeL ab ILLaC,

AUTORE
VVIGANDO SEXVVOCHIO
Bojemo

[1662]

Johannes Praetorius
Celebrating the Mysteries of
Motherhood
That is:
A Chatty Comedy
About the Birthing Room
And
A Little Children's Laundry
Festival
In the Year
****

Six Geese in the Straw
The Gossip goes
Happily about . . .
THE AUTHOR
WIGAND SIXWEEKS
Bojemo

[1662]

Prologus

Weil schwerlich ein Weib schlechter dings mit der Thür ins Wochen-Hauß fället/ oder der treugen Pfannen-Kuchen gewürdiget wird: Sondern muß sich nothwendig erst vorein 3. virtel Jahrers Frist der feuchten Braut-Suppen bedienet/ und selbige wohl verdauet haben. So halte ich es auch nicht für rathsam/ das ich meinen klatzsch-hafften Hummeln flugs die Polster auff den Wochen-Stüelen weich klopfe; Sondern ich muß sie zuvorderst ans Braut-Bette führen/ allda zu Rede setzen/ und den nachfolgenden drey-Bletterigen Weiber-Rath vortragen; welchen/ vor etlichen Jahren E.F. kein geringer *Practicus*, so die Kacristey (sic) der Frauen mehrmahlen besuchet hat/ als vorweilen *Cato* thun können/ aus dermassen wohl registriren/ und domahlen denen neuen Hochzeitern/ als Hn. A.W. und Fr. M.E.C. widmen wollen/ also:

F. Braut

Prologue

Because a woman hardly ever gets pregnant unexpectedly,[1] nor is she found worthy of a dry pancake[2] unless, nine months before, [she] has partaken of the wet bridal soup[3] and digested it well—I don't find it advisable to fluff up too quickly the pillows on the birthing-room chairs for my gossipy ladies.[4] Rather, first I must lead them to the bridal bed, talk to them there, and then present them with the following clover-leafed women's council which, several years ago, E.F.—not a bad practitioner himself, who has visited the women's inner sanctum several times, as before him Cato[5] was able to do—wanted to report [about] and at that time dedicate to the newlyweds, A.W. and M.E.C., therefore:

Frau Bride

---

[1] The original refers to a proverbial phrase: "Mit der Tür ins Haus fallen," to arrive without warning.

[2] Pancakes were traditionally served to visitors in the birthing room during the six-week lying-in period.

[3] Semen.

[4] "Klatzsch-hafften Hummeln." The German *klatschen* can be understood as an endearment: cute, gossipy young women.

[5] Cato the Younger (95–46 B.C.), Stoic philosopher. The allusion is probably to P. Clodius Pulcher's notorious attempt to infiltrate the festival of the Bona Dea in 62 B.C.

Fr. Braut
Nun ich in den Weiber Orden/
Heinte bin versetzet worden;
Und auch kommen bin zur Lust/
Die mir sonst war unbewust: 5
Muß ich gleichfals/ sol ich alten/
Wissen/ wie ich mich soll halten;
Was man vornimmt/ was man thut/
Mit der lieben kleinen Bruth.
Was man habe für Gelücke   10
Mit der alten Ofen-Krücke;
Mit dem Knecht und mit der Magd/
Wo und wie und was man sagt/
Wann das kleine Kindgen lachet.
Oder gar was anders machet   15
Was bedeute/ wenn der Hahn seiner Henne gut gethan/
Auch wenn offt die Hüner krehen
Wie es mit ihnen stehen.
Nun ihr Weiber gebt Bericht
Was man doch zu allem spricht/   20
Daß ich es von euch erfahre
Wie ich mich darein gebahre/
Ach was thut man/ saget an/
Wenn ein Kind nicht schlaffen kan?

Frau B.   25
Ey fürwar das macht mich lachen
Seynd das nicht wohl freye Sachen/
Daß die Braut schon wissen will
Wie man kleine Kinder still:
Ja viel mehr/ sie solte fragen   30
Was sie sonsten solte sagen/
Oder aber wie sie sich
Halten solt bescheidentlich/
Auff daß sie im Ehe-Leben
Nicht in Kummer dürffte schweben/   35
Denn sie weiß gewißlich nicht/
Was da ins gemein man spricht/
Nemblich wenn die lieben Leute/
Die so jung alß schöne Bräute/
So sie/ sag ich/ nicht geschwind   40

Frau Bride:
As of today I have joined the wives' order;
Last night I was transported
And arrived at [sexual] pleasure
Unknown to me previously: 5
Now I want to know
How I should conduct myself;
What is proper, what is fit, how do I treat the
Sweet little brood.
How best to handle the poker;[6]   10
The servant and the maid,
Where and how and what does one say
When the little baby laughs
Or when it does its business.
What it means if the rooster   15
Has pleasured his hen;
Or what it means
When the hens cackle a lot.
Now, you wives, let me know
What to say on every occasion   20
So that I might learn from you
How to now conduct myself in these matters.
And what needs to be done, tell me,
When the baby can't fall asleep?

Frau B.   25
Verily, this makes me chuckle;
Aren't these things common knowledge,
That the bride now wants to know
How one nurses [quiets][7] little babies?
Rather she should ask   30
What she otherwise might say
Or how she should modestly conduct herself;
So that in her married life
She does not come to grief;
For she surely does not know   35
What people say about this,
Which is, when good people
Who [become] beautiful brides
Don't—I say—quickly get their

---

[6] "Ofenkrücke": fireplace poker.
[7] "Stillen": to nurse.

Mit dem nehen fertig sind/
Wenn sie sich ein Hembde machen/
Oder sonsten hochzeit Sachen:
Eben traun soll auch so lang
Ihnen seyn in Wochen bang/   5
Denn es sollen grosse Schmertzen
Sehr beängsten ihre Hertzen.

Fr. L.
Wenn die Braut zur ersten Nacht
Voll den Laugentopff gemacht/   10
Soll es deuten auff gut Stillen
Eben nach der Kinder Willen
Auch wenn sich vom Schuch ein Band
Hat zum andern hin gewand/
Soll es nichts alß Lust bedeuten   15
Bey den neuen Eheleuten.

Fr. B.
Auch wenn sich der Himmel zeigt/
Und der Mond am selben leucht/
Solches weiset auff viel Kinder/   20
Auff viel Schaffe/ Genß und Rinder.
Regnets in der ersten Nacht/
Wird en Mägden erst gebracht.
Und wenn sie die Flöhe beissen/
Sollen sie sich schlagn und schmeißen: 25
Fellt denn gar das Bette ein/
Das soll gar was gutes seyn/
Dessen knacken/ dessen krachen
Soll bedeuten Lust und Lachen.
Felt ein Küssen etwa rauß   30
und beleufft es eine Mauß/
Dieses soll den guten Leuten
Mülbersbürgerey bedeuten.

Fr. B.
Nein/ so wolt ihr mir nun nicht   35

Sewing done
When they make a shirt
Or other wedding clothes,
They will for sure
Be anxious during pregnancy,[8]   5
For this predicts that great pains
Will terrify their hearts.

Frau L.
If on the wedding night
The bride fills the chamberpot,   10
This predicts good nursing
Just the way babies like it.
[iij] And when one shoelace
Turns toward the other,
This means nothing but delight[9]   15
For the newlyweds

Frau B.
And if the sky can be seen
And the moon shines brightly,
That predicts many children,   20
And many sheep and geese and cattle.
If it rains in the first night,
A girl will be the first born.
And if fleas bite the two,
They will hit and beat each other.   25
If the bed collapses in the first night,
That is certainly a good sign;
The bed's creaking and crashing
Means good sex and foretells much laughter.
Should a pillow fall off the bed   30
And a mouse run across it,
This means good fortune[10]
For the young couple.

Frau Bride:
Oh, please, don't you want to tell me   35

---

[8] "In Wochen sein": to be pregnant.

[9] "Lust": gaiety, happiness, but also sexual lust, desire.

[10] "Dieses soll den guten Leuten / *Mülbersbürgerey* bedeuten." The reference could not be identified.

Dieses sagen/ was man spricht/
Wenn das kleine schreyt und wimmert/
Und man sich sonst sehr bekümmert!

Fr. B.
Ja/ ich sag es Ihr fürwahr/   5
Ich erfuhrs für einem Jahr/
Da nam ich ein Hasenfüßgen /
Legte solches unters Küßgen/
Da schlieff er gar balden ein.

Fr. Br.   10
Dencket doch/ soll diß wahr seyn?

Fr. F.
Sonsten hab ich auch gehöret/
Wenn das Kind was hat bethöret/   15
So soll mann es also bald
Auß der Wiegen dergestalt
Mit dem einen Küssen fassen/
Und es schleunig legen lassen
Unter eine Ofenbanck/
Wehr es gleich noch eins so kranck   20
Soll es bald zu rechte kommen.

Fr. B.
Sonsten hab ich auch vernommen/
Man soll es mit Speicheling   25
Wohl beschmiern das liebe Ding/
Oder soll es gar belecken/
Es soll gar nach Saltze schmecken:
Nichts ist fast so köstlich gut/
Und ist leichte wenn mans thut: 30
Ach! Man dörffte wol sein Leben
Umb die Kinder gar hingeben/
Solt man dieses denn nicht thun?

Fr. F.
Ja fürwahr daß sie wohl ruhn.   35
Soll sich niemand in die Wiegen
Setzen/ legen/ oder schmiegen:
Auch soll man die Wiege nicht
Etwas regen/ denn man spricht: 40

What people do
When the little one cries and whines
And when I am otherwise upset?

Frau B.:
Well, I will surely tell you this,   5
I went through this a year ago.
I took a little rabbit's foot
And put it under the pillow;
He fell asleep right away.

Frau Bride: 10
Really? Is this supposed to be true?

Frau F.
Moreover, I have also heard
That if something has upset the baby,   15
You should immediately take it out of the cradle,
Swaddle it in a pillow, and
Quickly put it beneath the bench by the stove;
No matter how sick it may be,
It will soon recover.
                                                                     20

Frau Bride:
I also have heard
You should cover the sweet thing with spittle,   25
Or lick it all over.
People say it tastes like salt;
Nothing is quite so delicious
And it is easily done.
Dear, one could sacrifice one's whole life   30
For the children's sake.
Why shouldn't we do this too?

Frau F.
Yes, indeed, and so that the babies rest well,   35
No one should sit, or lie in, or cuddle up
In the cradle [with them].
No one should rock the cradle at all.
For it is said   40

Es sey gantz nichts schädlicher
Alß wenn jemand ohngefähr
Eine leere Wiege rüttelt/
Und sie so vergebens schüttelt/
Es soll offt im Schlaff geschwind   5
Sehr erschreckn das liebe Kind.

F. L.
Auch ist sonsten wohl zu wissen/
Wenn man es in einen Küssen.
Träget zu dem Fenster zu/   10
Sollen ihm in einem Nu
Alle beyde Augen schweren:
Welches denn nicht ohne Zähren
An den Kindern ist zu sehn/
Dennoch ists gar leicht geschehn.   15
Auch das spinnen gantz nicht tüget/
Wenn man noch in Wochen lieget/
Denn dasselbe kleine Kind
Das zerreisset ganz geschwind
Seine schönen neuen Kleider   20
Wenn dieselben kaum von Schneider.

E.W.
Gleichfals soll man haben acht/
Welches ich sonst nicht gedacht/   25
Wenn ich es nicht selbst erfahren/
Nicht so gar vor vielen Jahren.
Daß ja nicht die Wöchnerin
Komm auff einen solchen Sinn/
Und verändern ihre Stelle/   30
Noch betrette eine Schwelle:
Denn wie man es täglich hört/
hat es ihr gar viel bethört/
Da sie denn hernach erschrocken/
Und bekommen Hauptweh/ Bocken/   35
Oder eine böse Brust/
Welches eine schlechte Lust.

F.F.   40
Wenn zwey Wöchnerinne trincken/
Und die Kanne lassen sincken/
nicht zugleich/ so soll es dann/

That nothing does more harm
Than if someone accidentally rocks an empty cradle
And shakes it in vain.
Doing so, they say, often
Frightens the dear child in its sleep. 	5

Frau L.
In addition, it is good to know that
If you carry the baby on a pillow
To the window, 	10
Both of the baby's eyes will be afflicted in an instant.
This is often observed in children
And not without shedding tears.
Even so, it can happen very easily.
Furthermore, it does not do much good 	15
To spin when in the birthing-room.
For the same little baby
Will quickly tear its pretty new clothes
As soon as they come from the tailor's.
	20

Frau W.
You should also take note
Of something which I almost forgot 	25
Had I not experienced it myself
Not so many years back.
It is important that the new mother not get it into her head
Either to leave the chamber or step across the threshold.
For, as we all have heard, 	30
Many of them, so tempted, became startled,
Which gives then a headache, stomach aches and pains,
Or sore breasts,
Which is not a happy thing.
	35

Frau F. 	40
If two new mothers drink
From the pitcher at the same time
And they don't put it down at the same time,

Wie es leichtlich kommen kan/
Dieser ihr die Milch benehmen.
Auch muß sich ein Weib bequemen/
Wie sie fleissig achtung geb/
Daß sie nicht zu kärglich leb/ 5
Dreymahl schlaffen/ sechsmal essen/
Und das trincken nicht vergessen/
Bey zwey Stiebgen Bier ist recht/
Wein ein Trüncklein auff den Hecht.
10

F.B.
Wenn die Hunde durch
      die Wiegen
Kriechen oder drinnen liegen/
Soll der kleine Hampelmann 15
Seine Noth von Flöhen han.

F.F.
Wann die Magd die Stuben kehret/
Und des Herren Ort nicht ehret/ 20
Und daselbst nicht fänget an/
Ist es auch nicht wohl gethan/
Denn es gehet an ein beissen/
Oder auch wol gar ein schmeissen.
Wenn sie es im winckel thut/ 25
Dieses ist auch gantz nicht gut/
Denn das jüngste unter allen
Kan nicht schlaffen/ und muß fallen:
Wie mann augenscheinlich sieht/
Daß es alle Tag geschieht. 30

F.Br.
Aber was doch für Gelücke
Hat bedeut die Ofenkrücke?
35

F.S.
Dieses ich ihr sagen will:
Wen da wacklend wird der Stiel
Wird sich iemand kranck befinden.
Oder muß man selbe binden / 40
Oder felt der Stiel herauß/
So stirbt iemand in dem Hauß.
Lest die Magt die Ofengabel

It could easily happen that they lose their milk.
Moreover, the new mother has to pay attention
That she does not
Live too frugally.
Sleeping three times,   5
Eating six times,
And not forgetting to drink;
Two measures of beer is just about right,
And a drink of wine after fish.
                                                                  10

Frau B.
If dogs crawl into the cradle
Or lie in it,
The little clown will greatly suffer from the fleas.
                                                                  15

Frau F.
When the maid sweeps the room
And first cleans the space belonging to the master of the house,   20
It is not a good practice,
Because it might lead to biting or even to beating.
If she puts the baby in the corner,
That is not at all good either.
For the youngest cannot sleep because   25
It will certainly fall down.
As everyone observes,
It happens every day.

                                                                  30

Frau Bride:
But what sort of fate does the stove poker foretell?

                                                                  35

Frau S.
This I will tell you:
If the shaft gets loose,
Someone will get sick;
Or if one has to wrap it,   40
Or if the shaft falls off,
Someone in the house will die.

(Es ist glaubt mir keine Fabel)
Glüend werden eine Zeit/
Das bedeutet Zanck und Streit.
Auch noch eins hab ich gehöret/
Wie man seltzam Ding erfähret/   5
Das den Kindern auch ist gut/
Wenn mans achtet und auch thut/
Wenn mann zu Gevattern stehet/
Und die Zeit/ daß man gehet/
Soll man mit Bescheidenheit   10
Sich erleichtern ja bey zeit:
Denn wenn man sich angezogen/
Es ist/ traut mir/ nicht erlogen/
Und thut letzlich alßdenn daß/
Lieget das Kind stetig naß/   15
Und verfeulet seine Betten/
Gar gewiß ists/ ich will wetten/
Man erfährets allezeit.
Auch soll man solche Leut/
Welches auch sehr wohl zu wissen/   20
Die das Geld nicht borgen müssen/
Zu Gefattern lesen auß:
Den sonst soll es hoff und hauß
Eßen/ Trinken/ müßen borgen/
Und stets leben in viel sorgen.   25

F.F.
Sonsten auch wenn etwa steht
Eine junge Henn und kreht;
So soll man viel neues hören   30
Und die Klatzscherey vermehren.
Und noch eins/ ich lüg es nicht/
Wenn es ungefähr geschicht/
Und ich offt gemerckt vorhin/
Daß da eine Wöhnerin   35
Ihre Zäne wolten plagen/
Mit sehr großen Wehetagen/
So soll sie alßdann ihr Haupt/
Welches ihr gar wohl erlaubt/
In des Mannes Hosen stecken   40
Und sich gleichfals wohl bedecken/
Daß ihr gantz wird warm und heiß/
Biß da heuffig kommt der Schweiß/

If the maid lets the stove fork[11]
Get red hot
(Believe me, this is not a tall tale),
That means anger and discord.
And I have heard   5
Another strange tale:
That it is also good for kids
If one makes sure
That they spend time with the godparents.
And when it is time to go,   10
One should, in all modesty, relieve oneself.
For, once one is dressed,
Believe me, I am not lying, and it turns out
The child will always wet itself
And soil its bedclothes.   15
This is true, I'd bet on it;
You hear it all the time.
It is important to know that
It is best to choose for godparents
People who do not have to borrow money,   20
Otherwise you have to borrow for
House and yard, for eating and drinking,
And live constantly in great distress.

                                                         25

Frau F.
Besides, when a young hen stands and crows,
You'll hear a lot of news,
And gossip.   30
And, finally, I'm not lying,
If it happens by chance
And I have often noticed this in the past—
That a new mother's teeth are torturing her
Horribly,   35
She should put her head—which is permitted—
Into her husband's pants,
And cover herself up
So that she feels very warm and hot
Until she sweats mightily;   40

---

[11] "Ofengabel" = "Ofenkrücke," implement to stir coals in a cooking stove.

Es soll flugs in einer Stunden
Aller Schmerzen seyn verschwunden.
Ja man bildet sich nicht ein/
Wie die Hosen kräfftig seyn.

F. Br.   5
Ich bedancke mich wie sehre/
Daß ihr mir so gute Lehre/
Und so viel derselben geben/
Ich will fleißig darnach leben:
Ich will euch hinwieder dienen   10
Weil die Wälder werden grünen/
Und mich halten wie ich soll/
Großen Danck: gehabt euch wohl!

Within an hour, that quickly
All the pain will have vanished.
Truly, it is not imagination
How powerfully healthful the pants can be.

Frau Bride: 5
Thank you very much,
That you have given me such good advice,
And so much of it.
And I will eagerly live
Accordingly.   10
In turn, I promise to serve you
Until the rivers run dry [i.e., forever].
And I will conduct myself as is appropriate.
Many thanks: Good-bye.

Die erste Abhandelung/ oder Wäsche.

Frau Wöchnerinne/ Fr. Margarita/ Frau Käte/ Fr. Ursel/ Fr. Suse/ Muhme

Frau Margarita: Gott gebe euch einen guten Morgen/ Fr. Mag. Was machet ihr guts mit eurem Kindgen? Sehet/ hier komme ich mit einer ganzen Compagnie an/ euch zu besuchen. **Fr. Käte:** Ich wünsche euch auch einen guten Morgen sampt euren jungen Erben; Habt es mir doch nicht vor übel/ daß ich so grob bin. **Fr. Ursel:** Je/ einen glückseligen Morgen, Fr. Mag: seyd ihr auch noch wol auff? **Fr. Suse:** Gott grüsse euch liebe Fr. Magisterin/ nehme es doch nicht in Unwillen auff/ daß wir euch so früh überlauffen. **Fr. Wöchnerin:** Seyd doch allezumahl sehr freundlich willkommen ihr lieben Weibergen: Und setzet euch doch mit einander bey mir ein wenig nieder. Habt auch grossen fleissigen Danck/ daß ihr mir vor allen die erste Ehr anthut/ und mich flugs in meinen Zustande nach verrichter Tauffe/ besucht: Werdet ihr auch wiederumb auffs neue Pfannkuchen außtheilen lassen; So wil ich gute Abrechnung halten/ und auch nicht außbleiben. **Fr. Margarita:** Ja/ mit mir wirds nun mehr wol bleiben; ich habe meine letzte Pfannkuchen schon vertheilet; [2] Und hoffe, daß es hinführo nicht weiter geschehen soll. **Fr. Wöchn:** Ey/ ich dachte/ was mich bisse! Ihr werdet uns ja nicht außfallen zu den mehr lustigs machen; Ich wil es ja immermehr hoffen; Damit würde euer Herr nicht zu Frieden seyn/ wenn ihr so wolt kommen. **Frau Käte:** Ja ich meine es selber Frau Mag: Sie ist zur Sache nocht nicht veraltert. Ich hielte es dafür/ daß es erstlich recht mit ihr angehen dürffte. **Frau Marg:** Wenn ich in eure Haut stecke/ so wolt ich es wol glauben/ jetzund schwerlich: Denn ich weiß wie es mit mir stehet: Meine Sachen bleiben schon für alter auß/ und mein Herr befind sich auch gar schwach; Daß Gott im hohen Himmel walte. **Frau Ursel:** Ihr müsset so nicht sagen/ liebe Nachtbarin: Es hat wol eher hart gehalten/ und sind dennoch wol ein paar Söhne darauff erfolget. **Frau Suse:** Ich weiß selber die liebe Zeit/ daß wol eine ältere Frau sich vor diesen also entschuldigte: Und kam dennoch alle drey viertel Jahr in den Wochen. **Frau Wöchnerin:** Ja was kan man darwieder/ wenn es denn nicht außbleiben wil? Wenn es nur einem an allen Orten nicht so sauer gemacht würde: Ich wolte mich viel drumb scheren/ und wolte alle acht Tage ein Kind kriegen. Aber so würde es mir so gar blut verdrießlich

[1] Lying-in Comedy
First Chapter, or Washing.

The Young Mother; Frau Margarita; Frau Kate; Frau Ursel; Mistress Suse Muhme[12]

Frau Margarita: "I bid you God's good morning, Frau Mag.[13] [the young mother]. How is your baby? See, I am coming to visit with a whole group of women." **Frau Kate:** "I bid you and your young offspring a good morning; please don't be offended that I am so forward." **Frau Ursel:** "Yes, a wonderful morning, Frau Margarita. Are you feeling well?" **Frau Suse:** "God's greetings, dear Frau *Magister*; please do not be annoyed at us for barging in on you so early in the day." **The young mother:** "Let me welcome all of you most warmly, dear women; and please sit down together beside me. I thank you very much that, before anyone else, you honor me with a visit so soon after the baptism of my baby. And, once again, I intend to serve you pancakes;[14] I want to treat you generously and spare no expense." **Frau Margarita:** "Well, nothing much is going to happen with me in this regard; I am sure that I have served my last pancakes, [2] and I hope there won't be any more."[15] **The young mother:** "Oh, I can tell you I didn't know what bit me![16] You won't abandon us and miss out on this fun. I am certainly hopeful for you; your husband would not be happy with this kind of attitude." **Frau Kate:** "Yes, I agree, Frau *Magister*, she is not yet too old for such as this [pregnancy]. I would think that she's now really only getting started." **Frau Margarita:** "If I were in your place, I might think that; now, however, I can hardly believe it any more; for I know where I am. My monthlies[17] have stopped long since, and my husband is also not what he used to be, God knows." **Frau Ursel:** "You mustn't say such things, dear neighbor. It has often seemed as if it had ended, and still, several sons were born." **Frau Suse:** "I myself know of such a case, where an older woman kept excusing herself like you're doing, and still she became pregnant every nine months." **The young mother:** "Indeed, what can you do to prevent it, if the periods don't want to stop? If only everything weren't so difficult, I wouldn't care at all, and have a new baby every other week. But as it stands, it's always such a chore that I keep getting really disgusted. For, dear women, listen to me:

---

[12] *Muhme*: a Silesian term for lying-in maid, who looks after the new mother during the six weeks of her lying-in period; also an older female relative.

[13] Wife of a man who has a university degree (master).

[14] Customary for lying-in visits. See Labouvie, *Andere Umstände*.

[15] That I will not get pregnant any more.

[16] Reference to "the bite of a stork," euphemism for getting pregnant.

[17] Menstruation.

gemacht/ daß ich immer auffs höchsten zu eiffern habe. Denn hört doch ein-
mahl/ ihr hertzlieben Weibergen: Wie ich gestern/ nach meinem Vermögen/
die Kuchen außtheilen ließ: Da brumte bald hier ein Weib/ bald war es da einer
andern nicht recht gemachet. Ich kunte es gar wol hören/ daß Taudel Grite mur-
rete/ daß sie nur jetzt einen Kuchen bekäme; Da sie sonsten hätte zwey bekommen: Nun habe ich das schind Weib für die lange Weile bitten lassen; Und war
gleich wol mit meinen geneigten Willen nicht zu Frieden. Ich hätte gerne lassen
zwey außtheilen/ wenn es die Kleider Ordnung hätte wollen zu geben; Wider
welche ich nicht habe handeln können. Weiter grunssete ein ander Seichfotze
/ daß ihr der Wein nicht gnug gezuckert were/ sondern zu herbe schmeckete;
Da ich doch einen ganzen Hutzucker hatte zerreiben lassen. Von einer andern
Schurmutze kunte ich gar eigentlich vernehmen; Daß sie nicht so vielmahl zu
sauffen [3] bekäme als sie anderswo gekriegt hätte: Alldieweil/ weil die Weiber
samt den Gefattern zu früh auffstünden und sich verlieffen.

Ich war so giffig in meinem Sinn/ Daß ich ihr meine Wochen Kanne bald
in die Fresse geworffen/ wenn ich mich nicht eines andern besonnen. **Frau Margarita**: Ja liebe Fra Magist: solches darff man sich nicht befrembden lassen: Es
gieng mir vergangen noch wol viel übeler: Da ich mir nicht alleine muste wieder
vor die Ohren bringen lassen/ daß die Gefattern auff ihre Gevatterstücken gesto-
chert hatten/ weil sie waren zu viel gesaffert gewesen. **Frau Käte**: Wist ihr nicht/
daß ich wegen meinen außgeteilten Marcipan auch vergangen Händel hatte?

Frau Margarita: *pergit*: Nein höret/ lieben Weibergen/ es schmählet auch
eine von meinen besten Freundinnen drauff/ wie sie nach verrichteter Tauffe
waren auß der Kirche gekommen/ daß sie nicht hoch genug gegangen were; Da
wider ich ja leyder nicht kunte. Ebenfalß so machten auch die Paten eine Sau
über die ander/ wie sie mir das getauffe Kindgen übern Bette wieder über gaben.
Die erste ließ auß/ daß sie nicht sagte: Wir haben vorher einen Heyden wegge-
tragen/ und nun bringen wir euch einen Christen wieder. Die andere wünschte
mir gar kein Glück: Doch muß ich es ihr noch zu gute halten/ weil sie zum er-
stenmahl gestanden/ und noch sehr jung ist. Sie verstehet es nit besser; Sie wirds
noch wohl lernen. **Frau Ursel**: Liebe Frau Mag. War denn bey euren Kirchgang
gestern auch die Fr. Steinschneidern? **Frau Wöchnerin**: Ach nein; Weil sie keine
Pfankuchen mehr giebt/ so kömpt sie auch nunmehr zu keiner Kindtauffe weiter. **Frau Suse**: Wie war denn die Pfeifferin da? **Frau Wöchnerin**: Je/ ist sie doch
noch ein Pennal/ und ist noch nie in die Wochen gekommen: Wie solte sie denn
mit gangen seyn? **Frau Suse**: Ja sieh/ es ist doch war: Aber/ wenn mir recht ist/
so hat sie schon allbereit eine Paucke angehänget/ und möchte bald in die Federn kriechen.

Yesterday, when I served pancakes, as my means would allow, one of the woman grumbled; then another was displeased. I could even hear Taudel Grite mumble that she had received only one pancake where normally she had gotten two. Actually, I had invited the bitch only for diversion, even though I really didn't want to. I would have gladly served two pieces if the sumptuary rules had permitted it. I could not act against them.[18] Another cunt[19] grunted that the wine was not sweet enough for her; that it tasted too dry, even though I had had a whole sugar cone grated into it.[20] And I could hear another biddy say that because the guests as well as the godparents got up and left too early, she didn't get as much to drink [3] as she had gotten at other places.

"At this point I was so furious that I felt like hitting her in the trap with my birthing-room pitcher; but I thought better of it." **Frau Margarita:** "Yes, dear Frau *Magister*, things like that should not get you too upset; I had much worse happening to me just last time. I had to put up with being told that the godparents just nibbled at their food because they were too drunk." **Frau Kate:** "Don't you know that I got a lot of guff last time on account of the marzipan I served?"

Frau Margarita: *interrupts.* "No, no, listen, dear women, even one of my best girlfriends put me down because, when they came out of church after the baptism, she thought she wasn't treated well enough; unfortunately, there was nothing I could do about that. Moreover, the godparents messed up[21] when they returned the baptized baby to me in bed. The first omitted and neglected to say: 'We carried away a heathen, and we bring you back a Christian.' [And then] the other didn't congratulate me at all. However, I do have to forgive her because this was the first time she stood [at baptism] and she is still very young. She doesn't know any better; she will surely learn." **Frau Ursel:** "Dear Frau *Magister*, did Frau Steinschneider attend your churching[22] yesterday?" **The young mother:** "No, no; because she's not giving out pancakes anymore [i.e., she is past childbearing age], she doesn't attend any baptisms either." **Frau Suse:** "Did Frau Pfeiffer attend?" **The young mother:** "Oh, good Lord, she's [practically] still a schoolgirl[23] and has never been pregnant. How could she have joined us?" **Frau Suse:** "Sure, that's true; but if I see this right, she's pregnant and getting ready for the delivery."[24]

---

[18] *Kleiderordnung:* sumptuary laws that regulated dress codes as well as expenses for hospitality and presents: Baader, *Nuernberger Polizeiordnungen*, 70–71.

[19] "Seichfotze," from "seichen," to urinate, and "fotze," vulgar term for the female genitals.

[20] Sugar harvested from sugar cane was pressed into cones and used to sweeten wine or punch.

[21] Made one mistake after the other.

[22] Church ceremony conducted to purify the mother after childbirth. See Labouvie, *Andere Umstände*, and and Karant-Nunn, *The Reformation of Ritual.*

[23] "Pennal": school.

[24] "Eine Pauke tragen": to be pregnant; "in die Federn kriechen": to crawl into bed.

Frau Marg: Gott gebe/ daß es wol ablauffe; Ich wil es ihr von Hertzen gerne wünschen; aber sie wird einen harten Stand außstehen müssen; [4] Wie ich schon ein Vöglein davon hab singen gehört. **Fr. Käte:** Wenn sie doch nur solte eine gute Wärterin haben/ **Fr. Wöchnerin:** Ja/ da dürffte es der guten Frauen wol dran fehlen. **Fr. Ursel:** Sie wuste mir ja vergangen zusagen/ daß sie schon das dicke Weib auff der Sand Gasse gemietet hätte. **Fr. Suse:** Ey behüte Gott/ wer hat denn ihr das lose Weib zu gewiesen? Damit wird sie übel außkommen. Das Thier hat Brannskätzgen/ wie aller Teuffel; Sie krochen ihr auff die Kleider wie nichts guts herumb. Es erzehlete mir vergangen ein ander stückgen von ihr meine Schnur; Nemlich/ wie sie dieselbe hätte gemiet gehabt; Daß sie so eckel im fressen wäre gewesen; Daß sie keinen Steiffmuß/ süsse Milch und Erbsen hätte essen/ noch Rastrum sauffen wollen.

Fr. Margarita: Macht es doch unser Kinder-Magd jo so bund; Ich hatte vergangen Heydelbeer kochen lassen; so wuste das Rabenvieh nicht/ ob sie die liebe Speise fressen solte oder nicht. **Fr. Käte:** Sie mag sich wol für das schwarze Maul gefürchtet haben/ welches man in Geniessung der Heydelbeer machet; Daß es davon auffstehet/ wie ein Ofen Loch. **Fr. Margarita:** Ich bilde es mir auch ein; Zu dem weil sie schon angebrandt/ und mit einem Hauß-Knecht versprochen ist: Der sie vielleicht nicht würde gehertzet haben/ wunn er solte ihr schwarz Maul gesehen haben. **Fr. Ursel:** O Armethen! Hättestu nur künfftig solche Kost viel übrig; Ich habe wol viel glättere und stoltzere Mägde gekandt; Welche ihren Frauen vorher alles Hertzeleyd angethan/ und darnach das liebe Brodt nicht haben zu fressen gehabt: Sie dencken nur/ wenn sie nur einen Kerl haben/ so ist alles gut. Aber weit gefehlet. **Fr. Suse:** O das Mensch möchte sich wol so viel nicht einbilden: Der Mann/ welchen sie kriegt/ ist nicht fünff Pfennige wehrt: Er hat/ höre ich/ seine vorige Frau bald todt geschmissen. **Frau Wöchnerin:** Ich gläube/ der Bräutgamb hat noch ein paar Kinder von ihr übrig. **Fr. Margret:** Ja es ist gar recht: Das Schelmstück wird die armen Wayßgen wol übel mit verfahren: Es ist eine unbarmhertzige Magd. **Fr. Käte:** Ach/ höchster Gott/ wie seufftze ich/ wenn ich von einer Stieffmutter [5] sagen höre! Es ist noch nicht lange/ da starb ein wackers Biefgen/ mit schönen gelben Haaren und weissem Angesicht: Das hat nicht anders als die Hengrische Stieffmutter ins Grab gebracht; welches ihr doch nichtes zu widern gethan/ sondern mit so freundlichen Worten begegnet/ daß es einem billich das Hertze hette sollen nehmen. Wenn es ein Steck-Nädelgen gefunden hat/ so hat es mit Freuden auffgenommen/ und der Mutter gebracht/ welche ihnen dafür also angefahren: Gehe du Rabenstück/ wiltu mir nichts anders geben/ so packe dich damit hinweg. Uber solche und dergleichen unbarmhertzige Wörter und Schläge/ soll das liebe Hertzgen so traurig und tieffsinnig geworden seyn/ daß es immer nach seiner vorigen Mutter geseufftzet/ und in den Himmel zu kommen gewünschet hat/ da sie were.

Frau Margarita: "God willing, it will all work out fine; I wish her the very best with all my heart. [4] But she will have a tough row to hoe; a little bird already told me about it." Frau Kate: "If she only had a good lying-in maid." The young mother: "Yes, the young woman will probably have problems with that." Frau Ursel: "She recently told me that she had hired the fat woman from Sandy Lane." Frau Suse: "Oh, God forbid, who has sent that loose woman to her?[25] That will serve her ill! The bitch has cooties[26] like the very devil; they were crawling like crazy over her clothes. The other day I heard a tit-bit about her from my daughter-in-law,[27] who had hired the same woman. She was such a picky eater that she wouldn't even have whipped cream with sweet peas, nor did she want to drink *Rastrum*."[28]

Frau Margarita: "My children's maid is just as bad; the other day I had a dish of blueberries prepared, and the old bat[29] didn't know if she should deign to eat the fine dish or not." Frau Kate: "She may have been afraid her mouth would turn black, as happens when eating blueberries, it tends to look [black] as an open stove." Frau Margarita: "I can imagine. Besides, she's already caught fire and promised herself to a manservant who might not have wanted to embrace her, if he had seen her black trap." Frau Ursel: "Oh, the poor thing, if she only had such good food to excess [in times to come]. I have seen so many smoother and prouder maids, who treated their mistresses badly, and later did not even have bread to eat. They think that as soon as they have a man, all is well. They are so wrong!" Frau Suse: "Oh my, that bitch[30] shouldn't be so uppity! The man she's getting isn't worth a nickel. I've heard that he beat his previous wife almost to death." The young mother: "I think the groom still has a few of her kids from the first marriage." Frau Margarita: "Yes, that's right. The piece of work will surely mistreat the poor orphans; she's a hard-hearted maid." Frau Kate: "Oh, dear God, how I must sigh when I [5] hear people tell of stepmothers! It wasn't long ago that a brave little girl with beautiful blond hair and pale skin died. None other than that witch of a stepmother put the little girl into her grave, [the girl] who had done nothing against her stepmother but had rather spoken so sweetly that my heart went out to her. When the girl found a little pin, she picked it up happily and brought it to the mother, who yelled at her: 'Get out of my sight, you piece of shit;[31] if you have nothing else to give me, then get away from me with it.' People say that because of such cruel words and blows the little darling became so sad and despondent; she always sighed for her dead mother, wishing to go to

---

[25] "Das lose Weib": woman of loose morals.

[26] "Brannskätzgen" = "Wanzen": cooties, bedbugs.

[27] "Schnur."

[28] Cheap beer brewed in Leipzig.

[29] "Rabenvieh": also bitch.

[30] "Das Mensch": derogatory term for a female.

[31] "Rabenstück": piece of carrion; black bitch.

Worüber es auch endlich gestorben ist; und sich die steinerne Stieffmutter kein Gewissen drüber gemacht hat. **Fr. Ursel**: Ich solte es bald errathen/ was ihr für ein Kräutgen meynet; und wie diese es gemachet hat/ so möchte es auch leichte deß Haus Knechts seine Liebste machen. **Fr. Suse**: Ich habe mir viel von das Muster erzehlen lassen; sonderlich wegen ihrer verplauderten Gosche: Da sie nemlich alles außschwatzen soll/ was sie in vorigen Diensten/ von Herr und Frauen gesehen und gehöret. Als sagte mir meine Schwester/ daß sie ihr zu Ohren gebracht hette/ wie sie vor diesen/ bey einer Frauen gedienet/ welche trefflich hette können sauffen/ so wol Bier als Brandtwein theils hier in der Stadt/ theils auch draussen auff ihrem Gute/ wohin sie bißweilen mit Fleiß were gegangen/ ihren Muth zu kühlen. Es hette aber der zehende dem Weibe die Trunckenheit nicht anmerken können als dieses Muster/ welches es flugs verspühret/ an ihrer Pusel Mütze und Hals Kragen/ wenn solche schlimm gesessen/ und wie der Zeiger an der Uhr/ vom Mittel in solche Revier gerathen gewesen/ da es schier zwey oder drey schlagen möchte. Hette ihre Frau aber noch ein wenig mehr getruncken gehabt/ so were ihr Gesicht davon roth geworden/ wie eines Kalkutischen Hahns- Schnabel/ sie hette auch bald wunderlich zu reden angefangen/ hette sich in dem nieder gesatzt/ und auff einem Stule eine Schuhr abgeschlaffen. [6] Ferner were sie sonsten bey einer vornehmen Frauen gewesen/ welche kein Teuffel von der Haußhaltung verstanden: Die hette im Hause alles kunterbund lassen gehen/ wie es selber gewolt; Drüber die Mägde es getrieben wie sie gewolt/ sie hetten den Wein auss dem Keller geholet/ und alle Abend mit ihren Kerlen außgesoffen: Ja was das Essen beträffe/ so hätte solches ihre Frau ihr Lebe nicht besehen/ wenn es beygesetzt worden/ wie viel und was es noch were; sie hette auch niemalen darnach gefraget: Derentwegen denn das Gesinde solche Speise verschleppet/ andern Leuten außgetheilet/ und ihre Frau sich bekümmern lassen/ wo sie was weiters hernehme. Drauff es mit ihr endlich gar außgeworden/ daß sie auch ihre Kleider und Schuh hette müssen versetzen und verkauffen/ und eine lange Zeit nicht können in die Kirche gehen/ da sie doch vorher sehr wohl gestanden. Zu solcher Armuth nun/ hette sich die verzweiffelte Magd gerühmet/ daß sie tapffer geholffen hätte. **Fr. Margr.** Ja es ist ein Ausbund aller losen Huren/ sie hat auch jederzeit diese Tugend an sich gehabt/ das sie keinmal lange an einem Orte hette können verbleiben: Sondern hat alle Viertel Jahr neue Dienste gehabt; da sie denn solche sonderlich gesucht/ wo sie frey leben/ und mit den Knechten rantzen könte. Es ist eine rechte Löffel-Magd/ und Lauff Petze/ das kan ich ihr wol unerlogen nachsagen. **Fr. Käte**: So/ so! Es wird dem Schelmstükke die Büberey ihr Kerl wol eintreiben/ und nach der Schwere dafür lohnen: Sie mag sich nicht Leide dafür seyn lassen/ es wird ihr schon zu Hause kommen. **Fr. Ursel**: Weil wir also von dem losen Stücke so zu reden kommen seyn; so muß ich doch auch eines und das andere vorbringen/ was ich von ihr gehöret habe. Sie soll an einem Orte auch dieses außgeplaudert haben; daß sie bey einer andern Frauen gewesen/ welche es trefflich mit den Studenten zugehalten/ und bald diesen/ bald jenen auff- und abgesattelt habe. Sie soll einmal unten im Hause gewesen

heaven to join her. She finally died of it, and the flinty stepmother suffered no pangs of conscience at all." **Frau Ursel:** "I should guess pretty quickly just what piece of garbage you mean; and the servant's lover will do just as she did." **Frau Suse:** "I have had people tell me about this 'lady' [of Sandy Lane], particularly about her gossiping trap. People say that she blabs out everything she has seen and heard in previous jobs about her previous master and mistress. My sister told me that she heard from her how at one time she had been in service with a woman. This woman really knew how to drink, both beer and brandy, here in town as well as out on her farm, where she often went on a binge.[32] Hardly anyone would have noted her drunkenness but this bitch; the maid recognized it immediately by the way her mistress wore her hat and collar, all rumpled and messed up, like the hands of a clock gone awry from the center, so it looks like it's just about to strike two or three o'clock. She said that when her mistress drank even more, her face turned red like the beak of a Calcutta rooster and she started talking funny; then she sat down on a chair and promptly went to sleep off her buzz. [6] Furthermore, she [the maid] was, in the past, in service with a noble lady who didn't know a thing about managing a household. She [the lady] let everything in the house go as it wished; thus the maids also did whatever they wished. Every night they took wine from the cellar and drank with their boyfriends. And where food was concerned, the lady never checked on it, what she had, how much, and what was needed; she never even asked about it. Thus the servants took it from the house and distributed it among other people, leaving their mistress to fend for herself. In the end, she [the lady] fell into such destitution that she had to pawn her dresses and her shoes; and for a long time she could not even attend church, where she previously had been in very good standing. In the meantime, the miserable maid bragged that she had been a moving force in her lady's descent into poverty." **Frau Margarita:** "Yes, she's a model of a whore! She is also in the habit of never remaining very long at any one place of employment. Instead, she changes jobs every three months, for she always looks for employment that will afford her a life where she is free to fuck the manservants.[33] She really is a piece of work, and a gossipmonger, I can swear to that." **Frau Kate:** "Well, well, this floozy[34] will get her just desserts when her guy beats the tar out of her for her foolishness. She won't have to leave home for it, she'll get it there." **Frau Ursel:** "As long as we're talking about this whore, I can contribute to our conversation a few things I've heard about her. Supposedly she gossiped at some other place that she had served another mistress who had a lot of fun with students, saddling up one and then the other, if you know what I mean.[35] It's said that once, when she

---

[32] "Mut kühlen": to have fun, to go hog-wild, to cut loose.
[33] "Ran(t)zen": lewd term for sexual intercourse.
[34] "Schelm(enstück)": rotten flesh, carrion, plague, rotten person.
[35] "Auf- und absatteln": to put on and take off a saddle: sexual intercourse.

seyn/ da ein junger Bursch die Treppe hinauff zu ihr allein in die Stube gegangen: drauff sich ein sonderliches Knacken erhoben/ daß die Magd solchen Possen unten habe können hören. Weil ihr nun aber (der Magd) die Frau kurtz vorher was zuwidern gethan/ so hätte [7] sie es dem Manne so weit endecket als was sie gehöret gehabt/ nemlich/ es hette vor eine halbe Stunde oben in der Stube sehr geknacket/ als wenn eine Bancke hette wollen brechen; sie wüste aber nicht was es müste gewesen seyn. Drauff denn der Mann seine Frau gefraget/ was es gewesen wer? sie würde es ja auch gehöret haben/ weil sie nicht auß dem Hause gekommen were. Die Frau soll über diese Rede erschrocken seyn/ und leichte gemuthmasset haben/ worauff die Magd zielete: Doch damit sie nicht allerdings ohne Antwort erschiene/ hätte sie geschwind listig gesprochen: was wird es groß gewesen seyn? Ich zehlete ohngefehr das Wochen Geld/ so ich noch übrig hatte; davon fiel mir etwan ein Groschen unter die Bancke/ drüber ich den Tisch fort rückete und die Banck auffhube/ bis ich ihn wieder fand. Diese Historie und noch viel andere mehr soll sie von der gedachten Frauen an einem wohlbewusten Orte loß geschwatzet haben. **Fr. Suse:** Ich weiß gewisse/ was es für eine Frau seyn muß. Doch wer will viel sagen? Es ist gnug/ daß es Landkündig ist/ und ist zu bethauren/ daß ihr ehrlicher Mann solch Weib haben soll. Sie bildet es sich wol nicht ein/ daß es andere auch wissen: Ob es gleich dannenhero geschiehet/ daß man sie sitzen lässet/ und nicht leichtlich zu einer Versamblung bittet/ es geschehe denn gar selten von ihren Freunden. Soll doch das leichtfertige Aaß es keinem Kerl versagen/ es mag ihr *Praeceptor*/ ein Pennal/ ein Stutzer/ oder ein Kramer-Diener seyn: Man siehet es ihr leicht an den Augen; viel besser aber möchte es jener Magister auff dem Collegio auß der Hand sehen/ wenn er Gelegenheit darzu hette; alleine das verschlagene Raben-Aaß mag den Braten mercken: Drümb sie vergangen nicht gewolt hat/ wie es die Gelegenheit darzu geben. **Fr. Wöchn:** Das Schelmstücke hat gewisse gedacht/ er würde die Hurerey vermercken und auß der Karten schwatzen. Ja es mag ein tausend-Kerl seyn/ derselbige gedachter Magister auff dem Pauliner Collegio; Er sagte vergangen meiner Magd ein Stückgen auß der Faust/ die er doch kaum in der quer angeblicket hatte/ daß ich mich höchlichst drüber verwunderte/ und sie ganz Schamroth drüber ward. **Fr. Käte:** Was der Teuffel thut/ Gott gesegne das liebe Kind dem Schlaffe; [8] schlägt es doch schon achte: Ich muß/ mein Bint/ wieder gehen. **Fr. Ursel:** Wir wollen auch mit/ es ist gleich Zeit. **Fr. Wöchn:** Ey wartet doch noch ein wenig: Ihr kommet doch zeitlich gnug wieder nach Hause. **Fr. Suse:** Ey/ nein/ liebe Frau Magisterin/ wir haben gewisse Zeit zu gehen/ daß wir das liebe Kind nicht aus dem Schlaffe verstören. Zu guter Nacht also/ Hertzen Frau Magisterin: Haltet uns doch nichts vor übel. Behüte euch auch Gott ihr Muhme/ und nehmet so vor lieb. **Die Muhme:** Eyapoppause/ das Kätzgen will nicht mause: Wir wollen das Kätzgen auffm Köpffgen schlagen/ es soll uns ein

was alone at home, a young man went up to her bedroom and, once there, created such a ruckus that the maid downstairs could hear the goings-on upstairs. And because the mistress had annoyed the maid just before this incident, [7] the maid went to the husband to tell him what she had heard just half an hour before, that is, that the bedroom floor had been creaking loudly, as if a bench were breaking apart, but that she didn't know what it might have been. Whereupon the husband inquired of his wife what was going on. Surely she must have heard it, since she too had been in the house. The mistress was said to have been very startled by his question, and she easily saw through what her maid intended to convey. But slyly, in order not to appear at a loss for words, she quickly responded that surely it was nothing important: 'I was counting my lying-in money, a penny had fallen on the floor, and I had to move the table and raise the bench to look for it until I found it.' This tale and many more the shiftless maid was said to have blabbed all over town." **Frau Suse:** "I know who the woman is. Still, who's to say! It is enough that everyone knows about it, and it is sad that such a good husband has such a hussy for a wife. She could not possibly think that no one knows it: for it frequently happens that she is shunned, and that she is rarely asked to join a gathering, except for the few times when her friends ask her along. Rumor has it that this easy piece doesn't deny [herself] to any man, whether it is a teacher or student, townsman, or salesclerk. One can see it in her eyes, or, even better, a certain *Magister* at the college could read it from her hand, if he had the chance. But the shifty wretch sensed a trap when she recently refused, when the the occasion arose to have her palm read."[36] **The young mother:** "The bitch probably thought that he would detect her whoring and that he would tell on her. Yes, indeed, this fellow, this *Magister* from the College of St. Paul, is truly clever. Just the other day, though he had hardly ever looked at her, he read such interesting information from my maid's hand that her face turned purple."[37] **Frau Kate:** "What the devil! God bless the sweet baby in his sleep! [8] The clock is already sounding eight o'clock; I really have to hurry along!" **Frau Ursel:** "We'll come along; it's time for us, too." **The young mother:** "Why not stay a little while longer? You'll get home soon enough." **Frau Suse:** "Oh no, dear Frau Magister, it is time that we leave, so that we don't disturb the little one in his sleep; we bid you good night, dear Frau Magister. Don't be annoyed! May God bless you, dear *Muhme*, and have a good evening." *Muhme* [sings a lullaby]:

"Eia, popeia,
The cat does not want to hunt mice;
We want to hit the cat

---

[36] "Magister" here is a reference to Johannes Praetorius himself, who held a master's degree in the liberal arts and had written a book on chiromancy, the art of reading the character of a person and the future from the lines of the hands or face.

[37] This could also mean that the *Magister* had an affair with her, which now he "reads out of her hands."

hüpsch Mäusgen fahen; schlaff balde. Schlaff Kindgen ich wiege dich/ der liebe
Gott der behüte dich/ und auch die lieben Engelein/ so allzeit umb und bey dir
seyn; schlaff balde. Schlaff Kindgen balde/ die Vöglein fliehen im Walde/ sie
fliehen wol über Menschen und Vieh/ schlaff mein Kindgen biß morgen früh;
schlaff balde. Eya/ poppey ey/ kocht mein Kindgen ein Brey/ Brey: Thut ein paar
Pfund Butter dran/ daß es mein Kindgen essen kan; schlaff balde!

Die ander Abhandlung/ oder Klatzschung.

Fr. Wöchnerin. Fr. Anna. Fr. Juditha. Muhme

Frau Anna: Guten Morgen Fr. Magisterin/ was macht ihr mit euerm jungen
Söhnlein? **Fr. Wöchn.** Ich bedanke mich euers Fragens; Es hat die vorige Nacht
gar sanffte geruhet/ und habe es etwan nur dreymahl dörffen anlegen. **Fr. Anna:**
Nun/ Gott Lob/ das ist mir lieb: Gott helffe/ daß es lange beständig bleibe! **Fr.
Juditha:** Ich wünsche euch auch einen guten Morgen/ traute Fr. Magisterin: Ich
habe es auch nicht können unterlassen Euch zu zusprechen/ nach dem ich gehöret habe/ daß ihr gelegen seyd; ob ihr mich schon zu Kirchgange nit habt bitten lassen. **Fr. Wöchn.** Ach! [9] vergebt es mir doch/ liebe Jungefrau: Es ist fürwar meine schult nicht gewesen; Es wird es die lose Bittfrau versehen haben;
Welche nach ihrer Unachtsamkeit/ mehre gute Weibergen vorbey gegangen ist/
wie ich es leyder unlängst verstanden habe. Haltet mir doch jo diesen Streich zu
gute ihr wist ja sonsten/ wie ich iederzeit so viel von euch gehalten habe: Daß ihr
auch ja darauß werdet abnehmen können/ daß es mit meinem Willen nicht
müsse geschehen seyn/ daß ihr dieses mahl so schandloß vorbey gegangen seyd.
O verzeyht mir doch umb Gottes Willen! Ich kan sonst nicht zu gute werden.
Frau Jud: Nun/ gebt euch zu frieden/ Frau Mag: seyd ihr doch scheltiger drauff
als ich bin: Achte ich es doch nicht groß / und glaube gar leichtlich/ daß es nach

On the head,
So that she goes a-hunting for mice;
Sleep, baby, sleep; I will rock you in the cradle.
May God bless you
And may the sweet angels surround you.
Sleep, dear child, sleep now.
The birds fly in the woods; they fly over men and beasts.
Sleep, my dear child, sleep sweetly until the morning.
Eia, popeia,
I will cook some porridge for my baby
With a pound of butter,
Which my baby will eat;
Go softly to sleep."

The Second Chapter, or Gossip.

The young mother; Frau Anna; Frau Judith; *Muhme*

Frau Anna: "Good morning, Frau *Magisterin*! how is your little baby boy?" **The young mother:** "Thank you for asking. He slept really well last night; I only had to nurse him three times." **Frau Anna:** "Praise the Lord; that's really nice; may God see to it that it stays this way!" **Frau Judith:** "I, too, wish you a good morning, dear Frau *Magisterin*. I couldn't help but come by once I heard that you had a baby, even though you didn't invite me to your churching." **The young mother:** [9] "Please forgive me, dear damsel. It was truly not my fault; it was the stupid *Bittfrau*[38] who made the mistake; she neglected to invite a number of good women, as I recently was chagrined to discover. Please don't hold it against me; you know very well that I have always thought the world of you. You must know that it was not my intention that you be treated so badly. Please forgive me, for heaven's sake! Otherwise I will never feel good again." **Frau Judith:** "Now, now, calm down, Frau Margarita. You are more upset about this than I am. It is no big deal, and I readily believe that it didn't happen according to your wishes." **The**

---

[38] Woman sent around to deliver invitations.

euren Befehl nicht mag geschehen seyn. **Frau Wöchnerin:** Ja freylich nicht/ hertzliebe Jungefrau: Sehet/ was wil man machen/ wenn man da auff den Bette lieget/ und das lose Gesinde gehet so falsch mit einem umb? Ich habe der leicht-ferigen Wittfrau ihren halben Thaler so richtig gegeben/ daß kein Dreyer dran fehlet; Und dennoch hat sie es an sich müssen ermangeln lassen. Verzeihet es mir doch jo; Unnd setzt euch miteinander was nieder: Rücket doch ein wenig näher heran/ daß ich euch ansehen möge; Muhme legt doch der Frau Annen ein Küs-sen unter: Je/ nehmt doch nicht das garstige: Habet ihr denn keine Augen; und sehet das ander nicht für euch liegen? Wenn es ein Hund were/ so bisse es euch in die Nase. **Frau Anna:** Ey liebe Mag. seyd doch unbemühet/ ich sitze gar gut: Nehmt ihr/ Frau Judithe. **Frau Jud.** Ach nein/ ich bin es nicht gewohnet/ und zu dem habe ich doch schon eins/ behaltet es doch selber. **Frau Wöchnerinn:** Ja/ daß ihr euch doch so nöhtigen möget/ liebe Frau Anna/ nehmt es doch zu euch/ setzt euch drauff nieder/ und schwatzt ein bißgen mit mir. **Frau Anna:** Sind das nicht schöne Vorhänge/ Frau Mag. vergebt mir/ daß ich fragen mag; Was kom-men sie euch doch zu stehen? **Frau Wöchnerinn:** Ach liebe Jungefrau/ wenn es meinen Halß fast kosten solte/ so wißte ich es euch ietzund nicht mehr zu sagen/ zu deme wurden sie mir auch halb und halb geschencket/ von meinem Herrn Gevatter/ von welchen [10] ich sie bey guter Zeit genommen habe: Ist mir recht/ so kosten sie sonst achtehalben Gülden. **Frau Judith:** Nun/ das gehet hin: Davor weren sie nicht zu theuer: Kosten doch meine 6 Gülden; und sind elende Dinger gegen diese. **Frau Anna:** Ich sehe jetzund/ Fr. Mag. eure Wiege an; ist sie nicht so aus der massen schön gemacht: Ihr habet sie gewisse allhier in Leipzig bey einem Meister bestellet. **Frau Wöchnerin:** O JEsu/ nein: Ich kauffte sie vergan-gene Messe von einem frembden auff den Alten Neu-Marckte: Rahtet/ was sie kostet? **Frau Anna:** Zwey Gülden. **Frau Wöchnerin:** weniger 6. Pfennige; doch muste ich solche dem Träger geben/ wie er mir sie ins Haus brachte; Und habet ihr es also flugs getroffen. **Frau Jud:** O/ sie kriegt doch noch einen Rathsherren/ wenn dieser Mann wird gestorben seyn: Ich hätte bald nur auff anderthalb Gül-den gerahten. **Fr. Wöchn.** Ja/ wie wolte denn seyn können? Ist es doch ohne das schand wolfeil: Müste man doch allhier noch wol einmahl so viel darfür geben. **Fr. Anna:** Das ist fürwar gewiß; Dürfften doch die Tischer allhier wol für euer Wochen Bette sieben Gülden begehren. **Frau Wöchnerinn:** Ja/ wenn ich es hier hätte sollen kauffen; So möchte ich wol nicht viel näher davon kommen seyn. Aber nun kostet es mir von den Frembden vier Gülden/ damit ich sehr wol zu frieden seyn kan. In gleichen gerieht ich auch ungefähr zu mein ander Bett-Gerähte noch umb einen geringen Pfennig. Nemlich ich erschacherte es von einer Trödel Frauen/ so in der Peterstrasse am *Petrino Collegio* sitzet/ es muste es wol eine sehr vornehme Frau gehabt haben/ die es aus Noht zu verstossen; Daß es mir noch hat müssen zu gute werden. **Fr. Jud.** Ich soll es fast an den Säumen und Nähten kennen/ wer es vorhin gehabt. Es ist freylich bey derselben Frauen weder zu beissen noch zu brocken übrig und muß sich gar elende ietzund be-helffen; Da ihr vorher der Rheinische Wein und Zerbster Bier wol nicht allezeit

young mother: Surely not, dearest damsel. See, what can you do if you're confined to bed and the stupid servants don't do anything right? I have paid a gold
piece to the scatterbrained *Bittfrau*, not a penny was missing; and still, she didn't
do her job the way she was supposed to. Forgive me and sit down with us. Come
a little closer, so that I can look at you. *Muhme*, please hand Frau Anna a pillow
to sit on; and don't take the ugly one! Can't you see the other one right in front
of you? If it were a dog it would bite your nose." **Frau Anna:** "Oh, dear Margarita, don't make such a fuss; I am sitting just fine. You take it, Frau Judith." **Frau
Judith:** "Certainly not, I'm not used to this; besides, I already have one, just keep
yours." The young mother: "Oh, please stop fussing, just take it and sit down,
and chat with me a bit." **M. Anna:** "What nice bed curtains you have, Frau Margarita. Forgive me for asking, but how much did you pay for them?" **The young
mother:** "Oh, dear damsel, if my life depended on it, I couldn't tell you offhand.
Besides, they were almost a gift from my godfather, [10] where I picked them
up a while ago. If I remember correctly, I paid eight and a half gold pieces." **Frau
Judith:** "Well, that is tolerable; they do not seem too expensive. Mine actually
cost six gold pieces, and they're pretty chintzy compared to yours." **Frau Anna:**
"I'm just now noticing the cradle, dear Frau Margaret. How very beautifully it
is made. Surely you must have ordered it here in Leipzig from a master cradle-
maker." The young mother: "Good heavens, no. I bought it from a stranger at the
Old New-Market at the most recent fair.[39] Just guess what I paid for it!" **Frau
Anna:** "Two gold pieces." The young mother: "Six pennies less, although I had
to pay that much to the porter. Otherwise you guessed exactly right." **Frau Judith:** "Oh boy, surely she'll marry a magistrate after her current husband dies; I
would have guessed only one and a half gold pieces." The young mother: "Well,
how could that be? Without being ashamed, it is dirt cheap. Around here you
would have to pay double for it." **Frau Anna:** "Definitely; around here carpenters
want seven gold pieces for a lying-in bed." The young mother: "Certainly if I'd
bought it here, I wouldn't have gotten it under that price. But having bought it
from a stranger, I paid only four gold pieces; and that suits me just fine. Likewise, I acquired my other bedding for only a little money. I haggled over it with
the peddler woman who always sits in Peter Street by the College of St. Peter. It
must have belonged to a really wealthy woman at one time who was forced to sell
it because of hard times—which really served me well." **Frau Judith:** "I can easily tell by the seams and the hems who the former owner might have been. The
poor woman has nothing left to eat, and she is quite destitute. She has to make do
with very little, where in the past Rhine wine and Zerbst beer were not ever good
enough for her. Now she has to make do with *Rastrum*, if she can afford even

---

[39] In the mid-seventeeth century, Leipzig had two big fairs, one in the spring and
one in the fall.

zu Maule war; Da muß sie ietzund mit den Rastrum verlieb nehmen/ wenn sie
ihn nur noch allemahl haben könte. **Fr. Anna:** Ich habe auch etliche geringe
stückgen von ihr/ die ihr zwar auch ein grosses mögen gekostet haben; Doch
kam ich gar wol feiler [11] zu; In dem vor wenig Wochen ein Capittlers Weib
hausiren gieng und solches vertrödelte. Ja ich weiß auch die liebe Zeit/ da unser
einer solches Betten-Geräthe wol nicht sauer hätte dürffen ansehen/ oder mit
den eussersten Finger anrühren/ Daß man ietzund ihr wiederumb mit den Hindern nicht anschauen läst. Und dennoch wil die Teufflische Hoffart nicht auff-
hören/ Sondern pudert sich in die Grube hinein/ damit sie zu gleich ihre Eißgraue
Haar beschönen oder entschuldigen möge. Ob sie nun aber noch allemahl rechten Puder nehme/ oder dafür auch Asche gebrauche; Das lasse ich dahin gestellt
seyn: Sonsten daucht mir allezeit/ daß sie wol wenigs übrig haben möge/ den
Parrücken-machern die theure Sache abzukauffen. **Fr. Wöchnerinn:** O wie
theuer ist sie denn wol? Sie kan vielleicht grau gedorretes und zerriebenes Baum
Mooß nehmen/ oder zerstossene Bonen gebrauchen; Die ja nicht allzuviel kosten. **Fr. Jud:** Siehe/ was der Henger nicht thut! Kan man auch den Hoffart so
unmerklich umb ein kleines haben? **Frau Wöchnerinn:** Ja freylich/ wisset ihr das
noch nicht? gleichmässig kauffen die hochmütigen Matronen/ doch armsehlige
Scheißsäcke/ wol andere Sachen umb ein geringes; Die sie hernach für Gold/
Silber/ Perl/ und Edelgesteine tragen. Wisset ihr nicht/ daß man Sprichwortes
weise sagen? Es ist nicht alles Gold/ was da gläntzet. **Frau Wöchnerin.** Muhme/
wie stehet ihr denn/ und sperrt das Maul auff/ wie ein Kuhe die Augen fürs neue
Thor/ sehet ihr denn nicht/ daß sich das Kind reget? Wieget doch ein wenig ge-
schwinder fort. **Muhme.** Es ist seine Gewohnheit/ es hat es schon offte vorher
gethan/ und wachet derentwegen nicht flugs davon auff. **Frau Jud.** Es wird
gewisse durstig seyn und trincken wollen. **Frau Wöchnerinn.** Es kan viel mehr
übel gewickelt seyn; Wie ich mir einbilde: Daß das arme Püppgen so hart und
uneben lieget; Derentwegen es sich von einer stelle zur andern drehen will. **Fr.
Anna.** Je Frau Magisterin/ sihet das Kindgen nicht schön weiß auß/ und hat so
klare Haut; Gott gesegne es ihme! Ihr müsset viel Mandelkörner gegessen ha-
ben/ wie ihr mit das Kindge seyd schwanger gegangen: Sehet doch einmahl/
[12] wie das liebe Engelgen so freundlich außsiehet; Daß es einem ins Herze
hinein erfreuet. **Wöchnerinn.** Ey/ Frau Anna/ vergebe es euch der liebe GOtt/
daß ihr so reden möget: Ja/ mein Mann würde mir Mandeln kauffen; Manttel
werdet ihr meinen/ oder Mangelhöltzer: Damit solte er mich wol eher abspeisen.
Ja/ vergebe es ihme GOtt: Er würde einen Pfennig meinet wegen an solcher
Näscher-Waare legen; Er giebt es lieber für Bücher aus; und käuffet solch
Teuffels-Geschmeisse häuffig auff/ daß man wol etliche Wagen damit beladen
möchte. Ach/ wie sehe ich ihn offte/ gantze Arme/ (wie Ärmel) vol/ unter dem
Mantel ins Haus schleppen; Da mein Wundsch darbey ist; Ach/ wenn er doch
solches Geld auff hebe/ und mir eine feine Puselmütze unnd schönen grünen
Rock darfür kauffte/ wenn die Messe herbey kommet: Aber vergebens: Ich kan
ihme nicht anders einreden; Er bleibet immer bey seiner alten Weise und Geige/

that." **Frau Anna:** "I also have bought a few small items from her which probably cost her a fortune. But I got some stuff really cheap **[11]** from a woman peddler who sold these things door to door. Besides, I remember a time when none of us would have dared to look at such bedstuff very closely, let alone dared to touch it. Whereas now people won't give her the time of day.[40] Still this devilish arrogance does not stop; rather it powders itself on the way to the grave so that the gray hair might be beautiful and hidden. Whether they use real powder or apply ashes, I will leave up to you to decide. But in my opinion she might not have much left to give to the wig-maker for his expensive wares." **The young mother:** "Well, how expensive is that stuff? She could use dried moss or ground bones; those don't cost much." **Frau Judith:** "See what the devil can do; can vanity not be bought for a modest price?" **The young mother:** "Certainly, don't you know that? Conceited matrons, the pathetic shitheads, are always buying things on the cheap and wearing them as if they were pearls, silver, or diamonds. Don't you know the proverb, all that glitters is not gold?"[41] **The young mother:** "*Muhme*, why are you standing there with your mouth gaping, like a cow in front of a new gate? Don't you see that the baby is stirring? Go and rock a bit faster." *Muhme*: "This is just the way he is; he always acts like this; it doesn't mean he'll wake up." **Frau Judith:** "It must be thirsty and want to nurse." **The young mother:** "It may actually be swaddled badly. It seems to me that the little doll is lying uncomfortably in the crib; that's why it turns from one side to the other." **Frau Anna:** "Dear Frau *Magisterin*, the baby has truly lovely white and clear skin; God bless him! You must have eaten a lot of almonds during your pregnancy. **[12]** Look how sweet the little angel looks! It truly brings joy to my heart." **The young mother:** "Oh, for heaven's sake, Frau Anna, may God forgive you that you speak this way: my husband buying almonds[42] for me? I am sure you mean wooden *Mangeln*.[43] That is what he would happily let me have.[44] May God forgive him, but he would not spend a penny on sweets for me. He rather spends his money on books; he buys so much of that devil's shit that one could fill wagons with it. How often do I see him carrying armloads of books into the house hidden under his coat. All the while I wish he would save his money and buy me a hat and a pretty green skirt in time for the fair. But in vain; I cannot talk him into it. He always sticks to his old habits; in the end, we will see the truth of the old saying: 'Preachers

---

[40] "Mit dem Hintern ansehen": to turn one's behind to something (someone), dismiss, insult him/her.

[41] "Es ist nicht alles Gold, was glänzt": not everything that shines is gold, i.e., worth anything.

[42] "Mandel(n)": almond(s).

[43] A pun is being made here between "Mandeln" and "Mangeln," heavy, wooden, cylindrical bolts used for pressing sheets and large pieces of linen.

[44] I.e., he would sooner beat me with a two-by-four than buy me almonds.

und wird er dermahl eins wahr machen: Daß Pfaffen nichtes anders als Bücher und Kinder (*Libros & Liberos*) zur Erbschaffft verlassen. **Frau Anna:** Ach schweiget doch jo stille/ Frau Mag. es kan es euer Herr mit euch so arg noch nicht machen/ wie mein Kräutgen: Euer behält jo noch auff solche Weise in seinem Hause/ was er erworben: Aber meiner träget es leyder gar hinauß/ und versäufft alle seinen Vorraht: Draussen säufft er Bier und Wein/ und wenn er zu Hause kompt/ so schmeicht er mit seinem Toback mir das Hauß und die Stube so voll/ daß ich nicht weiß / wo ich bleiben soll. Rede ich etwan ein wenig umbs Kraut: So hebt er solchen Hader und Keiff an; Daß ich Gott dancke/ wenn er wieder stille schweigt. Ja wie manches unnützes Wort und Pille habe ich über den schelmischen Toback müssen einfressen. Und höret nur/ wie es mir vergangen mit ihm gienge: Da war der lose Mann auff einen Trödel gerahten/ und hatte allda ein Liedlein von Toback angetroffen/ welches er mir mit ein paar Ohrfeigen durch zulesen zustellete: Und wiewol ich es lieber in tausend stücken hätte zureissen wollen; so durffte ich es doch nicht: Und habe also den Teufflischen Pritzschmeister Gesang noch biß auff diese stunde verwahret der etwan dieser ist: [13]

1. Hört zu ein wenig hie/ an einem Morgen früh/ bin ich spazieren gegangen/ da hört ich einen Streit/ von einem Mann und Weib/ zu zancken sie angefangen.

2. Umbs Edle Kraut zu hand/ Toback wird er genand/ welchs Fürsten und Herren brauchen/ das Weib loß unverschämbt/ das Edle Kraut zunamt/ drumb der Mann sich mit ihr muß rauffen.

3. Das Weib sprach du loser Tropff/ steht dirs Bier noch im Kopff/ versäuffst das meine darneben/ alle mein Gut und Geld/ was ich hab in der Welt/ thust umb schlimmen Toback geben.

4. Der Mann spricht hör du Weib/ Toback erhält mein Leib/ stärckt mich die gantze Wochen/ erspart viel Brodt und Fleisch/ manch schönes Eylein weiß/ darffst mir schier gar nichts kochen.

5. Die Frau sprach abermals/ du leugst in deinen Hals/ du thust hie nichts ersparen/ du ja dreymal mehr frißt/ Toback der sättigt nit/ drumb laß das Schand-Kraut fahren.

[and scholars] leave nothing but books and children."[45] **Frau Anna:** "Oh, be quiet, Frau Margarita. Your husband cannot possibly treat you as badly as mine does me. At least this way your husband keeps his earnings in the house. Mine takes all his money and wastes it on drink. Away from home he swills wine and beer, and at home he fills the whole house with so much tobacco smoke that I don't know what to do. And if I mention his smoking, he starts such yelling and fighting that I thank God when he finally shuts up. How many useless words and bitter pills I have to swallow because of his horrid smoking. Listen to what happened recently: This good-for-nothing jerk happened on a street peddler who sold him a little song about tobacco. My husband handed it to me and, hitting me several times, he ordered me to read it. And though I just as soon would have torn it into many pieces, I was not allowed to do so. I have kept the devilish song[46] to this very day; **[13]** listen to it:

1. Listen to me, all of you! One recent morning early as I went for a walk, I heard a husband and wife getting into a fight

2. About the noble herb, called tobacco, used by princes and lords. The loose, shameless wife had taken the noble herb from her husband, which prompted a row between the two of them.

3. The wife said: "You good-for-nothing fool, you are [still] drunk; you guzzle away all our possessions and our money along with it. Whatever I have in the world, you spend on tobacco."

4. The husband replied: "Listen, woman, tobacco keeps me healthy and gives me strength throughout the week. It saves bread and meat, and many a pretty little white egg. You need hardly cook anything for me."

5. The wife replied: "You are lying through your teeth; far from saving money, you eat three times more. Tobacco does not fill you up [satisfy your hunger]. Do give up this this weed of shame."

---

[45] "Libros et Liberos."
[46] "Teufflischen Pritzmeister Gesang."

Der teutsche Taback trincker.

Augspurg / bey Matthei Rhembold.
1630.

6. Toback trinck ich mit Lust/ wenns mich trückt umb die Brust/ Tobacks Krafft thu ich spüren/ schnupff ihn mit grosser Freud/ Winter und Sommer Zeit/ er stärckt mir auch mein Hiren.

7. Das Weib herwieder redt/ Schnuptücher Falcenet/ erzeuchstu wie ich erfahren/ hälst dich gleich wie ein Schwein/ wischt allen Unflat drein/ kein Seiff kan ich nicht sparen.

8. Der Mann sprach Tobacks Krafft/ hat diese Eygenschafft/ die Mannheit thut er stärcken/ wie ihr nächten im Bett/ von mir erfahren hätt/ wärd ihr fromm könt ihrs mercken.

9. Ja Taback stärckt wol dich/ nur zum schlaffen mercke mich/ thust wie ein Wiedhopff stincken/ fartzt wie ein alter Gaul/ liegst wie ein Esel faul/ das macht dein Toback trinken.

10. Der Mann sprach an den Ort/ Weib du gibst böse Wort/ der Toback thut dich gheuen/ ich trinck Bier oder Wein/ muß er allzeit dabey seyn/ thut mir mein Herz erfreuen.

11. Das Weib antwort zu Hand/ die Sauff-Brüder allesampt/ [14] Tobackschnupffer und Trincker/ bey ihn kan niemand bleiben/ der Rauch thut sie vertreiben/ sind rechte Hosenstincker.

12. Toback ist mein Purgatz/ den halt ich vor meinen Schatz/ thut mir gar wol bekommen/ er purgirt mich von Leber und Lunge rein/ geht offt über die Zunge.

13. Das Weib sprach wieder bald/ du kanst nicht werden alt/ der Taback thut dich verderben/ wirffst schon die Lunge auß/ und Leber auch mit Grauß/ zehn Jahr mustu eh sterben.

14. Dem Toback bin ich hold/ dient mir besser denn Gold/ ich hab ihn auch viel lieber; /die Gesundheit thut er mehren/ drumb halt ich ihn in Ehren/ er bewahrt mich für dem Fieber.

15. Das Weib sprach Gold und Geld/ hat den Preiß in der Welt/ ist besser denn Tobacks Leben/ mit dem wolt ichs auch haben/ wenn dich fressen die Raben/ viel Geld wolt ich drumb geben.

6. "I lustily drink[47] tobacco. Especially when my chest feels tight do I appreciate its power. I snort it with gusto in winter and in summer to fortify my brain."

7. The wife once more retorts: "I am forced to notice all your ruined handkerchiefs. You act like a pig and wipe up all kinds of filth in them; I can't spare any more soap to wash them clean."

8. The husband replied: "Tobacco makes me a better man, strengthening my virility, as you would have noticed in bed at night, if you were smart enough to pay attention."

9. "Oh yes, tobacco makes you strong! It only strengthens your ability to sleep. You stink like a skunk;[48] fart like an old horse; lie around like a lazy ass: that is what smoking does to you."

10. The husband promptly replied: "Woman, you speak unkind words; tobacco makes you angry. When I drink beer and wine, I need my tobacco; that is what makes me happy."

11. The wife responds: "You are all lushes, [14] tobacco snorters and boozers. No one can live with you, the smoke will drive them away; you are true stinky-pants."

12. "Tobacco is my purgative and laxative; I hold it as my treasure. It purges my liver and my lungs, and often crosses my tongue."

13. The wife replied: "You won't get old; tobacco will kill you. You already spit out your lungs and your liver, and in ten years you will be dead."

14. "I love tobacco; it serves me better than gold; I love it even more than money. It improves my health; that is why I hold it dear; it protects me from fever."

15. The wife: "Money and gold are honored in the world; [they are] much more beneficial than tobacco. I would not mind having lots of [wealth] when you finally become food for the crows. In fact, I won't mind when you are gone."

---

[47] "Drinking" tobacco was the expression at the time, rather than "smoking."
[48] "Wiedehopf": hoopoe.

16. Der Mann sprach Weib schweig still/ mach der possen nicht zu viel/ Toback dient Armen und Reichen/ die sich Hoffmännisch stellen/ Männer und Jungen Gesellen/ wie ich und meines gleichen.

17. Ihr seyd Hofmännisch frey/ gleich wie die groben Säw/ man muß es von euch tragen/ speyt all Kübel voll/ das reucht leider nicht wol/ die Warheit muß ich euch sagen.

18. Der Mann im Zorne sprang/ erwischt ein Toback lang/ die Haselnüße tragen/ kriegt sie beym Kragen in Eyl/ versuchts mit ihr ein weil/ thät ihr die Haut voll schlagen.

19. Das Weib fiel ihm im Bart/ und räufft ihn mächtig hart/ sprach harr ich will dich lehren/ der Mann war auch nicht faul/ schlug sie vielmahl auffs Maul/ von dannen thät ich mich kehren.

20. Doch sage ich der Mann/ dißmal die Schlacht gewann/ das Weib kunt nicht entweichen/ ihr Weiber merckt mich eben/ wolt ihr ein Zanck anheben/ so last die Männer schleichen.

21. Der Mann ist Herr im Hauß/ da wird nichts anders drauß/ thut euch der Herrschaft nicht anmassen/ wenn der Mann nicht daheim/ die Weiber Herren seyn/ die Herrschafft soll man thu lassen.

[15] 22. Das Liedlein ist erdicht/ auff den Toback gericht/ all die ihn trincken zu ehren/ ob gleich die Weiberlein/ darüber schellig seyn/ trotz daß sies uns thun wehren.

23. Der das Liedlein gemacht/ den Toback nahm in acht/ tranck und schnupfft ihn gar eben/ bey Bier und kühlen Wein/ thät er praf lustig seyn/ drauff er gute Nacht gegeben.

Hört einmal/ liebe Fr. Gevatterin/ dieses unverschämbte Lied gab mir mein Kerl mit Ungestümmigkeit in die Faust/ daß ich es lesen und practiciren solte; sonderlich was den Schluß beträffe. Ey wie kräncket mich das in meinem Hertzen/ wolte Gott/ daß ich ihn nimmer genommen/ oder den nackichten Hund auff die Beine gebracht hette; Er kam ja/ so zu sagen/ zu mir ohne Schuhe und Hembde/ und hatte wenige Lumpen/ damit er sich bekleiden kunte/ biß ich ihme Vorschub thate/ und alles wohlmeynend unter die Hand gab. Ey daß ich nicht jener Frauen ihrem Sprichtwort nachkommen bin/ welche saget: daß man keinen zum Manne nehmen solle/ ehe er nicht wöchentlich sechs Thaler zum Marckt-Gelde geben könte. Ja/ Gott erbarme es/ meiner hette mir wol nicht können einen Pfennig geben/ so er es nicht vorher von mir empfangen hette.

16. The husband to his wife: "Just be quiet; don't go too far. Tobacco serves rich and poor and those who pretend to be courtiers, old men and young, just like me, and men like me."

17. "You are as much a courtier as you as a barnyard pig; you fill up whole buckets at a time with your stinking spit, and I have to put up with it; I'm sorry, I simply had to tell the truth."

18. In a fit of anger, the husband jumped up, got hold of a hazel switch, grabbed his wife by the neck, and proceeded to soundly thrash her.

19. The wife very roughly pulled his beard and said, "I'll teach you!" Not to be outdone, the husband hit her in the mouth many times, at which point I turned away,

20. But not without noting that this time the husband had won the fight. The wife could not get away. Women, remember: if you want to start a fight, let the man slink away.

21. The man is lord of the manor; nothing can change that. You must not claim dominion for yourself. When the husband is away from home, the woman can rule the house, but not when he is home.

[15] 22. This little song has been written in praise of tobacco for all those who deign to partake of it, even though it drives women crazy and makes them nag.

23. The one who made this poem smoked and snorted and drank tobacco when drinking beer and cool wine. And he was happy, and afterwards he bid a good night.

"Listen, dear Godmother, my husband had the nerve to shove this impudent little poem into my hand so that I should read it and act accordingly, especially where it concerns the conclusion. How that sickens my heart; if only I had never married him and helped the poor, naked dog back on his feet. One could say that he came to me without shoes or shirt and few rags with which to cover himself until I gave him some decent clothes and let him take charge of everything. Ah, if only I had remembered the advice for women that says never to take a man for a husband unless he can give you six gold pieces weekly to spend at market. Heaven have mercy, if I do not give it to him first, mine cannot give me a penny."

Frau Judith: "In strictest confidence, Frau Magdalena, I don't have it any better; I did not get much when I married my husband. Still, with time he

Fr. Judithe: Hier auch fünff Augen Fr. Magdal. gehet es mir doch nicht viel anders/ alldieweil ich auch anfänglich sehr wenig mit meinem Manne freyete: Doch ist er gleichwol nach der Zeit/ wie er zu mir gekommen/ fleissig gewesen; Also daß er numehr täglich einen schönen Pfennig verdienet; davon er mir alle acht Tage ein hübsches Marckt-Geld giebet/ davon ich ein merkliches erübern kan; welches ich mir auffhebe: Weil ich es nicht weiß/ worzu es mir nocht dienen möchte. Doch habe ich bey dieser meiner Schacherey auch gar sehr wohl meine Noth/ und fehlet mir an dergleichen Hauß Creutze nicht/ worüber ihr so lange geklaget: Sintemal mein Mann/ auch leider einen Kopff vor sich hat/ und mir viel Dinges zu tragen verbietet/ welches mir doch nach meinem Stande wol zukäme. Bald muß ich ihm die Schiffmütze ablegen/ und in eine Püselmütze kriechen ungeachtet daß jener reputirlicher Habit oder Schiffmütze so er mir verbietet/ [16] von keinen rechten Zobeln/ sondern nur auff die Art angefärbet ist. Bald muß ich nach seinem Kopffe die eingefaßten und gebremeten Schuhe meiden/ und ungeheure Bauren-Schuh tragen. Noch neulichst bat ich ihn/ daß er mir doch zum Jahrmarkt wolte ein rauhen Muff mit Bändern spendiren/ der etwa nur ein Thaler oder neune were zu stehen gekommen: da brachte mir der Läppisch eine kahlen Muff von Plyß/ etwan vor einen Gülden zu Hauß; und gedachte er würde mir eine trefflichen Gefallen thun. Nun ich nahm ihn hin/ und durffte nicht viel sagen; aber ich ward in meinem Sinn über den Haderlump so toll und thöricht/ daß ich mich hette zustossen mögen. Und also/ liebe Frau Mag: höret ihr nun/ daß es mir auch an Hauß-Creutze nicht ermangelt.

Fr. Wöchnerin: Muhme was macht doch das Kind? Seht doch ein Bißgen zu/ wie es sich ängstet: Es hat gewiß das Hertzgespan. **Fr. Anna:** Es ist nicht anders/ dem lieben Mäusgen muß etwas fehlen: Muhme nehmt es doch herauß und wickelts auff. **Fr. Judithe:** Komm her in meine Hand/ und werde starck und lang; Ach du liebes Hertzgen/ schweig doch ein Bißgen stille! Ach Frau Magisterin/ es muß dem lieben Kinde geholffen werden/ wer hat gewiß das Hertzgespan: Die Muhme hat es etwan durch eine Thüre getragen/ da ein Mensch sich darzwischen mit allen vieren außgestrecket gehabt.

Fr. Wöchn. Ja es kan wol seyn/ denn unsere Rangen/ als sonderlich Paul und Friedrich/ die pflegen es immer in Gewohnheit zu haben sich in die Thüre außzudehnen: da ich es doch ihnen vielmahl verboten habe. Da lauffen die Dachdiebe den ganzen Tag herumb/ und treiben lauter Schelmstücke: Der Praeceptor gehet seinen Gang/ und gibt wenig achtung auff meine Kinder/ da ich doch dem Lause Igel alle Tage muß zweymal zu fressen geben/ die Stube und Bette halten/ und auch noch wol muß seine beschißene Hembde waschen lassen. Er meynet/ daß ich nichts drumb wisse/ weil er nur der jungen Magd gibt/ die seine Liebste ist/ daß sie sein Geräthe soll heimlich mit waschen. Aber ich kam vergangen gar wacker ungefehr drüber/ und fand [17] sie auff einem faulen Pferde; Er meynet/ wenn er der Kinder 6. Stunden abgewartet/ daß es gar genug sey: Gott erbarms! **Fr. Judithe:** Ey Muhme helfft doch dem Kinde: So smieret es doch ein wenig mit rother Butter und Hirschunschlit oder Cappaunen Fett. **Fr.**

worked hard and now he makes a pretty good penny, of which he gives me a nice sum each market day. I can save a bit of it and put it aside, because one never knows what the future holds. But being so frugal has its trials; and I, too, have my troubles at home just as you complain about. Especially since my husband is rather obstinate, forbidding me to wear the things that are due me by right of my [social] standing.[49] Sometimes I have to take off my fancy hat and put on a woolen cap even though **[16]** the forbidden hat is not really made from fur but only dyed to look like it. On other occasions, he makes me wear clumsy peasant boots instead of fur-lined shoes. The other day I begged him to buy me a fur muff with ribbons for about nine gold pieces. He brought me a plain cloth one that cost less than a gold piece. And, on top of it, he thought he was doing me a big favor. Well, I had to accept it without making much of a fuss. But inside I was so furious at this jerk that I could have killed myself. So you see, dear Frau Margarita, now you know that I, too, have my cross to bear."

The young mother: "*Muhme*, what is with the child? Don't you see how upset it is? I'm sure it's colicky." **Frau Anna:** "Surely there's something wrong with the little one. *Muhme*, pick him up and change his diapers." **Frau Judith:** "Come into my arms and you will be strong and tall. You dear little baby boy, just calm down! Oh, Frau *Magisterin*, something needs to be done with the little baby; maybe he has a stomach-ache? Maybe the *Muhme* carried it under the door frame after a person had stood there with hands and feet touching [the frame] on all four sides."[50]

The young mother: "Maybe the boys, Paul and Friedrich, did that. They are always fooling around like that, stretching under the door frame even though I have forbidden them many times to do that. These little good-for-nothings run around all day, up to no good. The tutor[51] goes about his business and pays little attention to the children. That in spite of the fact that I have to provide this good-for-nothing two meals a day, room and a bed; and I have to have his soiled shirts laundered. He thinks I don't notice when he secretly gives it [his laundry] to his lover, the young maid, but just recently I surprised them in the act.[52] **[17]** He thinks it is enough to watch the children for six hours, Lord have mercy!" **Frau Judith:** "*Muhme*, why don't you look after the baby? Spread a bit of red butter or deer or capon fat on its skin." **Frau Anna:** "No, Frau *Magisterin*, listen to my advice. I usually do this with my children: before I have eaten anything [on

---

[49] Sumptuary laws prescribed for each social class the types of permissible clothing, hair length, weapons, and all manner of social interactions in the early-modern city.

[50] "[D]a ein Mensch sich dazwischen mit allen vieren ausgestrecket gehabt": superstition that, if a person stretched his/her arms and legs to fill the door frame, bad things would happen to those who go through the door.

[51] "*Praeceptor*": tutor. As a young man Praetorius was himself a tutor.

[52] I.e., having sex.

Anna: Nein Fr. Magist folget meinem Rath/ und macht es/ wie ich es mit allen meinen Kindern gemachet habe: Streichet es in den Seiten Creutzweise dreymal mit nüchtern Speichel / ich weiß für gewiße/ es wird euch helffen. **Muhme:** Ja wer doch nüchtern were! **Fr. Wöchn:** Ja freylich seyd ihrs nicht; weil ihr allbereit eine Schüssel voll Suppe außgefressen habet. **Fr. Judithe:** Wir wollen also das erste Mittel gebrauchen. Seht nu Muhme/ es läst sich schon ein bißgen besser mit dem klein Mäusigen an: Wickelts sanffte wieder ein/ und schlaget jo einen Zippel von der Windel erstlich ein; damit es der Alp nicht noch einmal wickele/ und leget es fein sanffte in die Wiege: Wir wollen hiemit auch beyde einen Abtritt nehmen/ damit das liebe Hertze sampt der Fr. Magist desto besser ruhen möge. Guten Tage Fr. Magist. schlafft fein wol/ und thut euch was zu gute/ last euch der Muhme ein Wein Süppgen machen/ und ein paar Hünichen kochen. **Fr. Wöchn.** Grossen Danck liebe Junge Frau: Grüsset doch euren Herrn meinetwegen/ und kompt doch bald unbeschwert wieder zu mir. **Fr. Anna:** Ich wünsche euch eine gute weile/ und sampt dem lieben Kinde eine sanffte Ruhe: Ich will schon umb ein paar Tage wieder kommen. **Fr. Wöchn:** Ich bedancke mich liebe Junge Frau; Eya/ kompt doch gewiß wieder/ vergesset nicht/ und besuchet mich nocht einmal/ eher ich auß den Wochen komme. Nun guten Tag Muhme/ nehmet so vor Lieb/ (sie geben ihr was bey der Wiege:) **Muhme:** Habet Danck/ ey es hette es nicht bedürffet. **Die Muhme singet:** Schlaff mein liebes Kindlein/ und thu dein Aeuglein zu: der liebe Gott will dein Wächter seyn/ drümb schlaff mit guter Ruh. Dein Wächter ist der liebe Gott/ und wils auch ewig seyn/ der dir Leib und Seel gegeben hat/ wol durch die Eltern dein. Und wie du warst in Sünden gebohrn/ wie Menschen Kinder all: und lagst darzu [18] in Gottes Zorn/ durch Adams Sünd und Fall. Da schenckt er dir seinen lieben Sohn/ etc.

Die dritte Abhandlung/ oder Dröschung.

Frau Wöchnerinne. Fr. Christina. Fr. Justina. Fr. Regina. Friederich. Muhme

Fr. Christin: Guten Tag Fr. Magisterin/ Wie befind ihr euch jetzund? **Fr. Wöchn.** Ich bedancke mich euers Nachfragens: Gott Lob! noch gar wol: Ich habe alleweile ein wenig geschlummert. **Fr. Justin:** Ich wünsche euch einen

an empty stomach] I spread a little spittle thrice crosswise over their bodies;[53] I know for certain that this will help you." **Muhme**: "Well, if people ever had an empty stomach!" The young mother: "Well, I know for sure it would not be you! You have already devoured a bowl of soup." **Frau Judith**: "So let's try the first remedy. Notice, *Muhme*, the little mouse is already a bit better. Swaddle it gently, pull back the corner of the swaddling cloth so that the demon does not swaddle it again, and gently put it into the cradle.[54] And now we two had better take our leave so that the little sweetheart and Frau *Magisterin* can get some rest. Good day, Frau *Magisterin*; sleep well and look after yourself. Have the *Muhme* fix you a nice wine soup and a bit of chicken." The young mother: "Many thanks, dear lady; please say hello to your husband and come back soon." **Frau Anna**: "I wish you well, and a good rest for you and your little one. I will return in a few days." The young mother: "Thank you very much! Please do come back soon; don't forget to visit me before I am done with my confinement." [The visitors:] "Good day, *Muhme*, here is something for you" (they give her something [presumably a tip] as she stands by the cradle). *Muhme*: "Thank you very much; this really isn't necessary." The *Muhme* begins to sing a lullaby:

"Sleep, little child, close your little eyes.
God will guard you now and evermore.
Sleep softly.
God is your guardian
Who gave you body and soul.
Through your parents
You were born into sin
Like all humankind.
You bore God's wrath
Through Adam's fall
When he gave his only Son, etc. . . ."

The Third Chapter or Discussion.

The young mother; Frau Christina; Frau Justina; Frau Regina; Friedrich; *Muhme*

Frau Christina: "Good day, Frau *Magisterin*! How are you today?" The young mother: "Thank you very much for asking; thank God, I am doing well; I just took a little nap." **Frau Justina**: "I wish you a good day, Frau *Magisterin*. What are you doing? Are you and your little baby boy doing well?" The young

---

[53] "Nüchternen Speichel": saliva from a person who has not yet eaten anything, usually in the morning.

[54] "Alp": demon who sits on a person's chest, taking his or her breath away.

guten Tag Frau Mag. Was macht ihr guts? seyd ihr noch wol auff mit eurem
Jungen Söhnlein? **Fr. Wöchn.** Grossen Danck eures Nachfragens/ ich weiß nicht
anders/ als Gott Lob noch gar wol. **Fr. Regin:** Gott grüsse euch Fr.
Magisterin:
Und weil ich noch nicht so lange bin bey euch gewesen/ als jetzund zum er-
stenmahl/ so wünsche euch viel Glücks zu eurem jungen Erben: Der liebe Gott
stärcke euch sampt dem lieben Kinde; daß ihr gesunde Wochen möget halten/
und darnach frölichen Kirchgang habet. **Fr. Wöchn:** Habt fleissigen Danck liebe
Junge Frau/ daß ihr mir die Ehre auch anthut/ und auß guter Wohlmeynung zu
mir kommet: Setzt euch doch miteinander was nieder/ ihr lieben Weibrichen;
Muhme/ setzet ihnen die Stüle zu rechte! **Sie sprechen alle:** Ey Fr. Magisterin/
wir sind nicht müde. Muhme/ bemühet euch nur nicht so sehr/ daß das Kind
nicht auß der Ruhe verstöhret werde. **Muhme:** Ey/ ihr werdet euch jo was nieder
setzen/ daß ihr unsern Püppgen die Ruhe nicht weg traget.
   Das Kind fängt an zu schreyen: Fr Wöchn. Je Muhme was machet ihr denn/
daß ihr von dem Kinde lauffet? Ihr wisset ja wol daß es keine Minute schläffet/
wenn es nicht immer [19] geboyet wird. Seyd ihr doch wie eine Fotze/ und wolt
nicht einmal klug werden. **Fr. Christ:** Ey Fr. Magisterin eyfert euch doch nicht/
daß es euch nicht zur Milch schlage/ und dem lieben Kindgen Schaden bringe.
Fr. Wöchn: Ey was soll mir nicht kräncken? Ich sage es dem dummen Menschen
so vielmal als ich wil/ so hilffts doch einmal so viel als das ander. **Muhme:** Nun
muß ich es über mir ergehen lassen: Sehet ihr doch wol/ Junge Frau/ daß ich
keinen Tritt von der Wiegen fast gewichen bin. So wisset ihr auch so wol/ daß es
des lieben Kindes/ Gott gesegne es/ gewönliche Art ist; daß es ohn unterlaß im
Schlaff auffähret und schreyet. **Fr. Regin:** Das arme Würmichen ist gewiß be-
schryen: Gebet ihm doch alle Morgen nüchtern etwa ein bißgen Käse ein/ oder
henget ihm stilleschweigens über das Hembdgen und Hälßgen/ in ein Säcklein/
ein bißgen Brodt/ Salz/ und eine dreyhellers Pfennig; was gilts/ es wird für die
bösen Mäuler gut seyn. Doch stille/ es schläfft wieder ein: Muhme/ wieget es
nur ein wenig geschwinde. **Fr. Justin:** Ach wie lächelt das liebe Herzgen so im
Schlaffe. **Muhme:** Es spielet mit ihm. **Fr. Christ:** Lasset euch doch Wunder sa-
gen/ Fr. Regina/ was mir unser Magd heut bey der Wäsche für ein Fratze erzehlete: Als hette man in einen Schwibbogen auff dem Gottes Acker gestern früh ein
Kind gefunden/ welches balde vom Spittel-Pfarrn getaufft worden/ und Hans
Schwiebboge soll genannt worden seyn; weil es ein Fündling gewesen/ und niemand von seinem Vater was gewust: Doch wollen etlich sagen/ daß es Huren-
Jäckel soll gezimmert haben; der es auß Armuth allda habe hingeleget/ damit es
möchte erhalten werden. **Fr. Regin:** Ich habe auch was davon gehöret/ Aber mir
ward gesaget/ daß es Korb-Hans were getauffet worden/ weil es im Korbe gefunden. **Fr. Christ:** Nein/ Junge Frau gläubet mir; es heisset Hans Schwibbogen:

mother: "Thank you for asking; I can tell you that we are both doing fine." **Frau Regina:** "God's blessings, *Magisterin*; and since I am visiting you for the first time, let me wish you all the very best for your young heir. May the good Lord strengthen you and your sweet child, so that you have a good confinement and a happy churching when this is over." **The young mother:** "Thank you very much, dear lady, for honoring me with your visit. Please, won't you all sit down, dear ladies? *Muhme*, please move the chairs for them." **They all talk at once:** "Dear Frau *Magisterin*, we are not tired. *Muhme*, don't make such a fuss, the baby's sleep will be disturbed." *Muhme*: "Come now, you'd better sit down, otherwise you are going to upset the baby."[55]

The child begins to scream: **The young mother:** "Oh dear, *Muhme*, what are you doing leaving the child all by itself? You know that it won't sleep even a minute if it is not rocked. [19] What a bitch[56] you are, you never learn." **Frau Christina:** "Dear Frau *Magisterin*, don't get so upset; it will affect your milk, and that will hurt the little one." **The young mother:** "For heaven's sake, why wouldn't I be upset? It doesn't matter how often I tell this stupid fool: it still makes no difference whatsoever." **Muhme:** "What I have to put up with! Don't you see, young lady, that I have not moved even one step away from the cradle? You know yourself that this sweet baby, God bless him, always gets startled in his sleep and screams." **Frau Regina:** "The little worm must be under a spell.[57] You should give him a piece of cheese in the morning, first thing; or put a little bag with bread, salt, and a penny around his neck over his shirt, but don't tell anyone about it.[58] Who knows, it is said to help against evil talk. Let's be quiet now, the baby has gone to sleep again. *Muhme*, rock the cradle just a bit faster." **Frau Justina:** "Look how sweetly the little angel smiles in his sleep." **Muhme:** "It is playing!" **Frau Christina:** "Let me tell you an amazing story, Frau Regina, that our maid told today just for fun when we were doing our wash. It appears that a newborn was found under the arch[59] by the cemetery. The pastor from the Spital[60] came quickly to baptize it, naming it 'Hans Schwiebboge' because it is a foundling and nobody knows who the father might be—although gossip has it that the whoremonger Jäckel produced it [is the father]. He put it there in hopes that it might survive, because he is so poor." **Frau Regina:** "I too have heard talk about this. But I was told that it would be baptized 'Basket-Hans' because it was found in a basket." **Frau Christina:** "No, young woman, believe me, it will be called Hans Schwibbogen; for the maid heard it with her very own ears from

---

[55] "Die Ruhe wegtragen." Proverbial: you will carry away rest = you will get everyone upset, nervous.

[56] "Fotze": bitch, cunt.

[57] "Beschreyen": to put a curse on someone.

[58] These kinds of charms were forbidden by all Christian denominations.

[59] "Schwibbogen": flying buttress.

[60] "Spital": hospital: place for the sick, the old, and the poor.

Denn unser Magd hat es selber vom Spittelschen Küster gehöret/ der Gevatter hat stehen müssen mit seiner Frauen/ und noch einem andern Vorsteher. **Fr. Justin.** Ja/ es gehen wol seltzame Sachen für: Nächten erzehlte mir mein Mann auffm Bette/ daß man einen Ehemann abermahl bey [20] einer Concubinen ertappet habe; Der zur Straffe die umbgewehete und von Wasser verdorbene Vogelstange solle wieder machen lassen. **Frau Wöchn.** Ich wolte schier errahten wer er were. **Frau Christ:** Ja ich lasse es mir auch bedüncken: Der Krug gehet so lange zum Wasser/ biß er einmahl bricht: Er hat es lange genug getrieben mit seiner Köchin; Es schadet ihme nicht/ daß er einmahl in die Büchse blasen muß. **Das Kind erwachet: Die Muhme nimpt es auff. Frau Justin.** Ach das liebe Englichen/ wie fein munter ist es doch/ Gott gesegne es; hat es nicht so seine klare Kucklichen? Frau Magisterin/ ihr habet doch/ wie ihr schwanger damit gewesen/ viel Brandtewein getruncken; Denn die Leute sagen/ daß die Kindergen alsdenn helle Gesichtgen davon kriegen. **Frau Wöchn.** Je/ vergebe es euch Gott/ Jungfrau: Wie kommet ihr auff den Unraht? Ja/ ich hette ihn wol manchmahl trincken wollen/ wenn ich nicht so einen kargen Herrn hätte; Der mir lieber ungebrante Asche einer Ellen lange über den Buckel gibt/ als ein Nösel Brandtewein. **Frau Christ.** Ja Frau Magisterin/ wer es nicht wüste/ der solte wol meinen daß es wahr were. Habt ihr doch so einen lieben frommen Herrn/ der kein Wasser betrübet/ und wol kein Kind erzürnet; ich schweige denn/ daß er euch solchen Dampff solte anthun. Ach der liebe fromme Herr Magister. **Fr. Wöchn:** Liebe Jungfrau/ ihr wüst viel drümb wie mich der Schuch drücket: Ich erfahre es/ Gott erbarme es! gar zu offte. Ich wüste nicht/ wenn ich ein Zahren Brandtewein in mein Maul gebracht hette. **Das Kind schreyet: Fr. Wöchn:** Muhme/ gebet mir doch das Püppgen herein/ ich wills ein wenig anlegen: Es wird wol wiedrumb durstig seyn. **Muhme:** Melcket euch doch ein wenig erstlich auß/ daß es dem Kinde nicht ein reissen bringe/ weil ihr euch vorher erbosset habt. **Fr. Wöchn:** Wie gebt ihrs mir denn so ärschling her; Wisset ihr euch nicht zum Teuffel zu schicken. Geht ein weilgen hinauß und sehet wo die Jungen herumb jachtern/ ob sie auch abermal Schelmstücke thun. Doch gebt mir erst den Wochen Krug her/ daß ich ein wenig trincke: denn ich bin ganz matt; das liebe Kind zopffet mich Tag und Nacht/ und sauget [21] mir das Marck auß den Beinen. Hoho/ umbspannet auch den Krug nicht/ wie ewer alte Manier ist. **Fr. Christ:** Fr. Magisterin/ rucket ihr das Kind nicht ein wenig ab von der Brust: Sie sagen es soll nicht gut seyn/ daß man das Kindgen zutschen lässet/ wenn die Mutter trincket. **Fr. Wöchn:** Muhme/ da setzt den Krug wieder hin: Geht ein

the Spital's sexton, who had to stand as godparent together with his wife and another trustee." **Frau Justina**: "Well, strange things happen; the other night, in bed, my husband told me [20] that a certain husband had been found once again with his mistress.[61] As punishment, he had to repair the maypole,[62] which had been damaged by wind and rain." **The young mother**: "I can guess pretty well who that might be." **Frau Christina**: "Yes, me too. The jar goes to the water until it breaks.[63] He has whored around long enough with his cook. It serves him right that he has had his comeuppance." **The child wakes up.** The *Muhme* picks it up. **Frau Justina**: "The sweet little angel; see how cheerful he is; God bless him! Look at the pretty, clear little eyes! Surely, Frau *Magisterin*, this comes from your drinking brandy[64] while you were pregnant. People say that this gives babies a pretty and fair skin." **The young mother**: "May God forgive you, dear young woman! Where do you get such ideas? I would have loved to have a nip or two, if I did not have such a stingy husband. He would rather hit me with piece of wood[65] than give me a dram of liquor." **Frau Christina**: "Dear Frau *Magister*, if one did not know better one might believe you. You have such a sweet and devout husband, who would not hurt a fly[66] or upset a child, let alone give you such grief. Oh, the sweet devout *Herr Magister*!" **The young mother**: "My dear damsel, if only you knew how much I have to put up with.[67] I am sorry to have to tell you that I experience it [the pain of married life] all too frequently. I don't know when a swig of brandy ever crossed my lips." **The child cries.** The young mother: "*Muhme*, please hand me the little doll, I want to nurse him a bit. He might be hungry again." *Muhme*: "Why don't you first press out a little bit of milk, so the baby won't get a stomach ache since you got so upset just a minute ago." **The young mother**: "Why do you hand it to me ass-backwards? For Christ's sake, can't you do anything right? Just leave the room for a little while and see what the boys are doing, what mischief they're getting into. But before you leave, hand me the confinement pitcher so I can take a swallow; I'm completely exhausted. The baby nurses day and night, practically [21] sucking the marrow from my bones. Wait a minute, don't grab the pitcher the way you always do." **Frau Christina**: "Frau *Magisterin*, move the baby away from the breast a bit; they say it is not good if the baby nurses while the mother drinks." **The young mother**: "Here, *Muhme*, put the pitcher back and take a break, as I told you. Afterwards, come back here

---

[61] "Concubine": mistress, also woman who lived in sexual union with Catholic clergyman.

[62] "Vogelstange."

[63] Proverbial: a person does wrong until he is finally caught.

[64] "Brantwein": hard liquor usually made from rye; also brandy, made from grapes.

[65] "Ungebrannte Asche": unburned ashes, piece of wood.

[66] "Nicht ein Wasser (Wässerchen) trüben": not disturb the water = not hurt a fly.

[67] "Wo mich der Schuh drückt": how much the shoe hurts (pinches) me = how much I have to put up with.

weiligen hinauß/ wie ich euch gesaget habe; und kompt darnach wieder/ daß ihr
das Kind zu rechte leget: und bleibet mir ja nicht zu lange/ daß ich euch muß
ruffen lassen. **Die Muhme gehet weg**: **Fr. Wöchn**: Je das ist ein Schind-Weib/
ich habe wol mein liebe Noth mit sie: Ich muß ihr alles wol zehenmal sagen/
ehe sie ein Ding recht außrichtet. Sie kan doch den Teuffel nichtes: Sie gehet so
dumm als ein blind Pferd hinein/ aber auff ihre Art ist sie klug genug/ und hat
den Schelm hinter den Ohren Daumens dicke. Mit dem Kerl mag das geile Thier
gerne rantzen; sie wird doch noch einmal wieder zur Hure gemachet; man sihets
dem leichtfertigen Sack bald an den Augen an: Unser Praeceptor muste ihr vergangen in die Hand sehen/ da hat er es ihr auch prophezeyet: Es ist eine freche
wilde Hummel/ und man kan wenig guts mit ihr außrichten. Wenn ich meyne/
sie soll wiegen/ so schläfft sie wie ein Ratz/ wie sie denn vergangen als ein Ochs
vom Stuhl herunter fiel/ daß ich und das liebe Kind drüber erschracken/ und
hoch in die Höhe fuhren. **Fr. Christ:** Was will man machen/ liebe Frau Magis-
terin/ man muß doch noch Gott dancken/ daß man Gesinde haben kan: Wird
doch die Welt so böse/ als sie noch nie gewesen ist. Ich hatte vergangen auch
solch Teuffels-Gesichte; das mit unserm Laden-Jungen hüpsch kunte löffeln: wie
sie denn der Diener drüber ertappet hat/ ließ ich die Hur/ beym Borg-Keller ins
Narren Häußgen einsperren; gab ihr ihren Lohn/ und ließ sie lauffen. **Fr. Reg:**
So höre ich nun/ daß ich nicht allein hierüber klagen kan. Ich hatte vorm halben Jahre auch ein solch Kräutgen; das hielte gar mit unserm Schreiber zu/ stahl
wie ein Rabe/ und hatte ein Gosche zu plaudern wie nichts guts. Es hat mir die
Schurmutz ein Possen gerissen/ den ich mein Leben nicht vergessen will. Denn
wie ich vergangen mit meinem Jeremießgen in Wochen lag/ da hat mir das [22]
Gottlosen Stück alle Reden auffgeschnappet/ welche die Weibrichen in meiner
Stuben fürm Kindelbett gehalten: Und hat solche Heimlichkeiten hernach dem
Schreiber offenbahret/ der es auff Herr Licentiatens Hochzeit mit in ein Carmen
gebracht. Ach wie hat mich das Ding gekräncket/ wie ich es hernach zu lesen
bekam. Ich ließ auch die Hur dessentwegen gehen/ und zwar zur Stadt hinauß/
daß sie mir in einem Jahr allhier nicht mehr dienen soll. **Fr. Wöchn:** Je/ das wird
ja nicht die Braut- Suppe seyn/ drüber sich mein Herr vergangen sich zu lachen
kunte. Er hat das Ding noch unlängst in seinen Händen gehabt/ und legete es/
meines Erachtens/ auff jenen Sims. **Fr. Christin:** Wo denn/ **Fr. Magisterin/** ist es
etwa da und dieses? **Fr. Wöchn.** Gar recht Junge Frau; hette ich es so bald nicht
sollen finden. **Fr. Reg:** Ja/ ja/ gar recht/ das ist das Teuffels Ding. **Fr. Christ:**
Ey lasset es mir doch ein wenig; Ich muß es auch lesen was denn drinne stehet:

and look after the baby; don't stay away too long, so that I have to send for you again." The *Muhme* leaves. The young mother: "Oh, she's is a real piece of work; I have nothing but trouble with her. I have to repeat everything ten times before she does one thing right. She knows not a whit. She stumbles around as stupid as a blind horse, but in her way she's pretty smart; actually quite sly, much more than one might suspect.[68] The randy bitch loves to fuck the guy[s]; she will definitely end up a whore again, you can see it in her eyes. This is what our tutor predicted when he recently had occasion to read her palms. She is a wild, cheeky creature,[69] a little good-for-nothing. When I think she is rocking the cradle, she sleeps like a log. The other day she even fell off her chair like an ox, scaring the baby and me to death." Frau Christina: "There is little we can do, Frau *Magisterin*! We actually should be grateful even to have servants; the world is getting more corrupt than it has ever been. Recently I, too, had such a devil's whore working for me. She carried on with our store clerk. When our servant surprised her in the act, I had the whore locked up in the cellar of the crazyhouse with the debtors. I paid her what I owed and threw her out." Frau Regina: "Well, I hear that I'm not the only one that complains about this. A year ago I, too, had one of those jewels who actually had something going with our tutor. She stole like a magpie, and had a gossipy mouth like you would not believe. In fact, this little piece played a trick on me that I will never forget as long as I live. Recently, when I was lying in with my little Jeremiah, [22] the godless cunt listened to all the confidences that my women friends and I exchanged. And then she blabbed about it to the tutor, who made a song of it, which he brought along to the recent wedding of one of the lawyers. I cannot tell you how offended I was when I later read a copy of it. I fired the whore because of it; in fact, chased her out of town so that she will never again find employment here." The young mother: "Oh, I hope that was not the wedding gossip that recently made my husband laugh so hard. Just the other day he had it in his hands. If I am not mistaken, he put it on the mantel." Frau Christina: "Where would that be, Frau *Magisterin*, is it this or is it that over here?" The young mother: "That's it, young woman, I could not have found it so quickly." Frau Regina: "Yes, yes, that's right, that is the devil's tract." Frau Christina: "Please let me look at it; I really am dying to see what it says."

---

[68] "Es faustdick hinter den Ohren haben." Proverbial: to be clever in a conniving, underhanded, tricky sort of way.

[69] "Eine freche wilde Hummel": a wild, impudent bumblebee.

Geheimer Wochen=Stul/ welchen der Jungfrau
Braut in künfftige Haußhaltung zum freundlichen
Angedencken/ verehret Matz-Steiff

Ihr Jungfern windet mir den schönsten Krantz von Blumen/
Die auß *Sanchaja* schickt das prächtige Idumen/
    Deß Sommers Vaterland/ fürwahr ein sanffter Kuß/
    Der were kaum genug für diß/ daß ich mich muß
Zu retten eure Lob/ den plauderhafften Frauen   5
Und in der ganzen Stadt den Wochen-Stülen trauen;
    Ich habe mir jetzund die Feder umbgewand/
    Und mache mich/ Gott lob/ den Weibern auch bekand/
Und zwar ich muß es thun/ verzeiht mir doch ihr Weiber/
Verzeiht mir/ denn ich bin auch ein geheimer Schreiber/   10
    In euer Cantzeley/ und hoffe mit der Zeit
    Noch mehr Beförderung von Euer Freudigkeit.
Mich traumte diese Nacht/ ich säß in meiner Stube/
Und schrieb das Carmen ab/ da kam der kleine Bube/
    Der kleine Schaden-froh/ und stieß das Dinten-Faß   15
    Für Muthwilln umb und umb/ das Carmen wurde naß/
[23]Daß ich/ wie schlecht es war/ der Jungfer Braut zu Ehren
Von Jungfern außgesetzt. Du Schelm ich will dich lehren/
    Fuhr ich Cupiden an. Ich/ sagt er/ thus mit Fleiß:
    Doch schmiß ich ihn dafür wol dreymal für den Steiß/   20
Er schreye Mortio/ ich muste drüber lachen/
Schweig sagt ich/ schweig doch nur/ und halte doch den Rachen/
    Ich hab mehr zu thun/ mein laß mir doch nur Ruh/
    Ich kan ja jetzund nicht dem Heulen hören zu/
Wer heist dirs/ daß du mir die Dinte solst verschütten?   25
Drauff gab er mir die Hand mir dieses abzubitten/
    Doch muxt er gleichwol noch/ und sagte ganz gebückt:

[The Tutor's Poem]

The Secret Birthing Stool Dedicated to the Virgin Bride in Honor of Her Future Household; by Matz Steiff.[70]

You virgins, braid me a pretty wreath of flowers,
From *Sanchaja* sent by the lovely Idumen;[71]
    Summer's fatherland, a truly gentle kiss
    Would scarcely be enough for this; so,
In order to secure your praise, I must entrust myself   5
To the gossipy ladies and the birthing stools of the whole town.
    Now I must turn my quill
    And, praise the Lord, introduce myself to the women.
I have to do it, you ladies forgive me;
Forgive me, because I am only a privy councillor[72]   10
    In your chancellery; and, in time,
    I hope to gain more advancement through your enjoyment.
Last night I dreamt that I was sitting in my room
Copying the poem when a little boy
    Entered, the little trickster [Cupid], and intentionally   15
    Upset my inkwell, pouring ink all over my poem,
[23] Which, as bad as it was, I had dedicated
To the bride. "You rascal, I'll teach you,"
    I chided Cupid. "I," he started hastily—but I [the writer] thrice kicked his
        butt.
    He screamed bloody murder,[73] which just made me laugh.   20
"Quiet," I told him, "just shut your trap.
I have much to do, so leave me be.
    I cannot waste my time listening to your whining.
    Who told you to spill my ink?"
Whereupon he offered his hand, asking my pardon.   25
But he still muttered and said under his breath,
    "My mother [Venus] has not sent me here for this reason.

---

[70] The poem is written by a male (the tutor, husband) who calls himself Matz Steiff, which is possibly a sexual innuendo alluding to the wedding night.

[71] Probably an allusion to the ancestry of Herod in the New Testament, whose stepdaughter Salome performed her famous dance (Matthew 14:6–11; Mark 6:21–28).

[72] "Geheimer Schreiber": personal confidential secretary (administrator) at court.

[73] "Zeter und Mordio."

Die Mutter hat mich nicht deswegen hergeschickt.
Als hettstu in geheim von ihrem stillen Lieben/
(Was thut der Argwohn nit?) was schimpfflich nachgeschrieben
Vulcan, ihr lahmer Schmid/ der sah sie flämmisch an/
Und hat ihr noch kein gut darsieder [sic] nicht gethan.   5
Stell' doch die Sachen ein/ bald diß bald das zu sagen;
Daß Venus, wie du sih'st/ so übel kan vertragen:
 Du machst sie und ihr Volck dir endlich spinnen feind;
 Da sie dir doch zuvor nicht gar zu grüne seynd/
Wirstu ins künfftige nichts mehr davon gedencken   10
So wird sie ihre Gunst schon wieder zu dir lencken:
 Den Recompans dafür der ist geringe zwar
 Du sollst hinführo seyn geheimter Secretar/
Der Weiber ingesambt/ doch soltu höher steigen/
Wo ferne du nur kanst für allen Dingen schweigen: 15
 Ich gieng den Handel ein; da führte mich geschwind
 Ich weiß kaum selbst wohin/ der Venus kleines Kind;
Und ist mir anders recht/ so war es gar der Spittel
Ein Weib saß für der Thür und flöhte ihren Küttel/
 Es schrie/ ich weiß nicht wo/ dort einer ans der Wand: 20
 Komm du mir nicht zu nah/ ich weich dir nicht vom stand:
Ich gieng zur Stub hinein/ da küff ein alte Mutter
Mit einer andern sich umb ihr alt Brillenfutter
 Die flickte dort den Stumpff/ die schmierte gleich den grind
 [24] Mit Butter/ die ihr selbst auß beyden Augen rinnt.   25
Die rieb die Pflaster aus/ die spunn an ihren Rocken/
Die dritte lage kranck an grossen Weiber Bocken;
 Die kraute hinten sich und stund am Ofen dort
 Und sah so niedlich aus/ dieweil sie halb verdort.
Die saß und hatte so ein Wärtzgen auff den Rücken   30
Wie Klausens Hüner Korb/ die ging an halben Kricken/
 Und was dergleichen mehr/ da fragte mich der Dieb/
 Ob mir ein Dienst vielleicht bey diesen Damen lieb.
Was/ sagt ich/ hälstu mich dann gar für einen Narren?
Was solt ich dann wol thun bey diesen alten Scharren   35
 Ich bin noch lange nicht ein alter Löffelknecht.

As if you had secretly written something funny about her private life
(What won't suspicion do?).
Vulcan, her limping blacksmith lover, stared at her in anger [because of it],
    And to this day he has not forgiven her.[74]
    So stop writing stuff like this or that,   5
For it really annoys Venus, as you can see.
You will ultimately turn her and her people [women] into enemies
    Especially considering that she didn't like you all that much even before this.[75]
    If you write no more poems about her love affairs in the future,
She will surely return you to her favor.   10
Your recompense, however, is modest:
    In future you will be her privy councillor.
    All women will henceforth hold you in high esteem,
As long as you are able to keep your mouth shut about certain things."
I agreed, and right away   15
    Venus's little boy carried me in a flash to I-don't-know-where.
    I noticed right away that it was the *Spital*.[76]
[I saw] a woman sitting at the door checking her dress for fleas.
I heard someone screaming from behind the wall, I don't know from where:
        "Don't come near me, I will not leave this place!"   20
        I entered the room, and I saw an old woman
Fighting with another over a glasses-case.
One was darning socks, another salved her scabs[77]
    [24] With butter that was running from both her eyes.
    One worked with bandages, another spun at her spinning wheel.   25
A third lay sick with great women's cramps.[78]
This one scratched her backside by the stove
    And looked really cute all shriveled up.
    That one sat with a little wart on her back
Like Claus's chicken basket; another walked on her short crutches.   30
And there was more of the like. The little thief asked me
    If I would like to serve these ladies.
    "What," I replied, "do you think me a fool?
What do I want with these old bags?
I am not yet an old codger, not by a long shot."   35

---

[74] Myth of the cuckolded husband of Venus. See Brumble, *Classical Myths and Legends*, 207–10, 349–51.

[75] "Jemandem grün sein": to like somebody.

[76] The secretary is carried in his dream to the *Spital*, where he observes unnoticed what is going on.

[77] "Grind": scabs; usually associated with poverty and filth.

[78] "An grossen weiber Bocken": menstrual cramps.

Gut/ sagt er/ ist dir das/ ich such es wol zu schlecht/
So komm du nur mit mir/ ich wil dich weiters führen/
Wir kamen in ein Hauß/ da war ein Jubiliren/
    Ein trefflich groß Geschrey/ ich hörte kaum mein Wort
    Und war schon an der Thür und wolte wieder fort/   5
Da kriegte mich der Schalck gleich wieder bey dem Leibe.
Hilff Gott! Was sturm war da/ ich kam zu einem Weibe
    Die brachte mir ein Glaß vom allerbesten Wein
    Sauff/ sprach sie/ siehstu nicht/ daß wir zur Tauffe seyn.
Sauff auff Gesundheit aus des Badgens und Gefattern/   10
Ich kont es hören kaum für ihrem grossen schnattern/
    Die sah ein roht umbn Kamm und lag an einer Wand/
    Die Geister waren ihr vom Weine ganz entbrand:
Frau Urschel schmälte dort/ und wolte lieber fluchen/
Daß man jetzunder gibt nur einen kahlen Kuchen;   15
    Sonst waren doch noch zwo: Die tadelte den Wein/
    Und trunck ihn gleichsehr noch so immer sachte nein.
Die hat man gar versehn; Drumb fing sie an zu brummen;
Und were gleichwol noch nicht ungebeten kommen:
    Die hatte sich noch nicht/ sonst gieng sie wol/ bedanckt;   20
    Und warte/ biß man ihr noch einmahl erst geschanckt.
Was/ sagt ich/ soll ich denn in diesen Lermen schreiben;
Man kan ja selbsten kaum für dem Getümmel bleiben?
[25] Es hat/ du siehst es selbst/ jo keine mehr Verstand
    Drauff lachte dieser Schalck/ und nam mich bey der Hand/   25
Und führte mich getrost gleich in die Wochen Stube.
Ich schrey: Verzieh/ verzieh/ verzieh [sic] du loser Bube:
    Ich geh dir nicht hinein: Ich schwer dir auff mein Blut/
    Ich geh dir nicht hinein: es kostet meinen Hut.
Die Amm ist gar zu schlimm/ die Muhme bald noch ärger: 30
Fürwahr es kostet mich den besten Schreckenberger.
    Doch gleichwol must ich fort/ da halffe nichts dafür/
    Halt/ halt einandermahl/ so gehe mehr mit mir/
Fieng Amor zu mir an: Nun brauche deine Feder;
Hier gibt es/ siehstu wol/ das allerbeste Leder: 35
    Wir kamen unvermerckt biß in die Helle hin/
    Kein Mensch sah uns nicht/ auch nicht die Wöchnerin.
Ich juckte hier bald da/ dieweil ich mich verschlichen;
Die Zügen waren hüpsch mit klaren Klöppel-Strichen: 40
    Der Fürhang war span new/ und nocht nicht abgenützt;

"OK," he said, "I see that I chose badly.
Follow me, I will lead you further."
We came to a house where there was a great celebration,
So much merriment that I could hardly hear myself think.
    I had barely reached the door when I wanted to leave again.   5
    But this little imp caught hold of me again.
Heavens, what commotion broke out! I met a woman
Who offered me a glass of the very best wine.
    "Drink," she said, "don't you see that we are celebrating a baptism?
    Drink to the health of the baby and the godparents!"   10
I could barely hear for all the people talking.
I saw one [woman] red in the face lying by the wall,
    Her head made empty from all the wine.
    Frau Ursel mumbled something, although she'd rather curse,
That nowadays only bare cakes [without filling, sauce, fruit, or cream] were served. 15
Then there were another two [women]:
    One criticized the wine,
    All the while drinking as she kept on saying no.
Another felt ignored; and she began to complain that she had not come uninvited.
Another went to leave, without expressing thanks,   20
    But waited nonetheless for yet another drink.
    "What," said I, "am I supposed to write in this chaos [of the birthing chamber]?
You cannot stand it, the chaos is almost unbearable.
[25] All women here are crazy, you can see it yourself."
    Whereupon the little fool laughed and took my hand   25
    And confidently led me into the birthing chamber.
I screamed: "Get away, get away, get away, you nut.
I am not entering here: I swear by my blood
    I won't enter here: Even if it costs me my hat.
    The nursemaid is a terror, the *Muhme* even worse.   30
My word, it scares me half to death."
However, I had to go in, there was no way around it.
    "Stop, stop, another time, but now come with me,"
    Amor said to me. "Now, go and use your pen,
As you can see, the best [stuff] to write about is here."   35
Unnoticed we entered the very hell;
    Unseen by anyone, even by the young mother.
    I had an itch, now here, now there, as I was hiding.
The window dressing was pretty with airy lace.[79]   40
The bed curtains were brand new, not yet used at all;

---

[79] "Klöppel": lace produced in rural areas in eastern Germany (Spreewald).

Das Bette halb vergült/ und zierlich außgeschnitzt.
Hilff Gott/ was waren da/ für Pulster und für Pfiele/
Doch schöner waren doch die grünen Wochen-Stüle.
Die Wiege wie der Tisch/ der Tisch gleich wie die Banck/
Die Windel-Lade war gleich wie der Bade-Schranck.   5
Wie fünckelte doch nur der Küpfferling und Wanne;
Noch sehrer fünckelte die breite Wochen-Kanne:
In Summa/ was man sah/ das ware nett und schön/
Und must ein jegliches/ an seinem Orte stehn.
Die Weiber saßen dort man kriegte gar ein Lüstgen/   10
Und wusten sich so viel mit den geklarten Brüstgen:
Es war das Erbars gleich so gar verzumpffen thut:
Wie/ fieng die eine an: Ists nun bald wieder gut/
Frau Schwester könnt ihr denn noch gleichwol selber stillen?
Ich halt' ihr müst es thun auch wider euren Willen.   15
Je habt ihr doch bald nichts; wo nembt ihr doch nur her?
Ja siht euch doch so roth die Wartzke wie ein Schwer:
Es hat gewiß das Kind an euch nicht viel gesogen;
[26] Drümb ist sie noch nicht recht/ man sichts wol/ außgezogen/
Versuchtes und legt doch nur das liebe Hertzgen an/   20
Es lernet kaum den Zug; es hats mir auch gethan/
Mein kleiner Strompel Sohn. Ach langt uns Mutter Marte
Doch dort den Kühstrich her/ wie ist er doch so harte!
Eßt doch das Süppgen auß/ es schlägt euch fein zur Milch.
Ach/ mein Gevatter/ sagt was kost't euch doch der Zwilch/   25
Den ihr hier unter habt zu euren Wochen-Betten?
Wie beugt sich doch das Kind/ ich wolte mich verwetten
Es kriegt das Herzgespan: Gebt doch ein Wachs Liecht her/
(Wie steht ihr Muhme doch?) ein Gläßgen ohngefehr:
Ich wills ihm bald erziehn: es mag auch immer bleiben/   30
Der Doctor mag dafür ein Haus Clißtirgen schreiben;
Recht geht doch Muhme/ geht; sprecht daß mans haben muß;

The bed was partly gilded and delicately carved.
Good God, what fluffy cushions, what luxurious bedstuff!
But even prettier than that was the green birthing stool.
The cradle like the table, the table like the bench;
    The changing table like an armoire.   5
    How the copper basin and the bathtub sparkled!
And even more sparkly was the broad confinement pitcher.
In sum, all that one could see was pleasing and beautiful,
    And everything was where it belonged.
    The women sat around,   10
And showed off those beautiful little breasts
So that one could get quite excited.
    In spite of all this, everything was honorable.
    "What," one began to say, "is everything all right now?
Frau Sister? Are you now able to nurse?   15
I think you have to do it, even if you don't want to.
    Soon you will have no milk at all, and then where will you get it?
    See how red your nipple, like a boil.
It must be that the baby has not yet suckled much.
[26] That's why it [the breast] is not yet emptied sufficiently.   20
    Go and try once more to nurse the dear little heart.
    It has barely learned to suck; that is the same
As my little wiggly son. Oh, please, Mother Marte
Hand me the cow rope, [80] how awfully tight it is.
    Come now, eat a bit of the soup, it will help your milk;   25
    Oh, dear godparent, how much did you pay for this blanket
On your confinement bed?
Look at the baby, how it writhes, I bet it suffers
    From colic. Hand me the wax candle
    (*Muhme*, what are you standing around for?), a little glass.   30
I will teach him for good.
The doctor would give him a laxative for it.
    Indeed, go, *Muhme*, go, and tell him we need it.

---

[80] "Kühstrick": cow rope; proverbial: someone is cunning, crafty.

Gebt doch das Käppgen her/ es fällt ihm gar der Fluß.
Wie/ Wöchnern/ wills mit euch? steigt euch nit auff die Mutter.
Ach Amme zünd doch an ein bißgen altes Futter:
    Rebhüner Federn her; doch nein/ ihr eignes Haar
    Das ist bald besser noch: Nun hats nicht mehr Gefahr/   5
Es ist schon über hin seht doch die alte Hure/
Wie windelt sie das Kind/ macht mit der Windel Schnure
    Kein Creutze nicht zuvor; schlagt einen Zipffel auff;
    Sonst Windelts noch einmal der Alb: Geh Görge/ lauff/
Und hole Bibelöhl in schwarzen Mohrs Aptecken;   10
Das Kindgen bricht sich dort/ es fängt schon an zu köcken:
    Wo ist das Rindgen Brodt/ das ihr mit habt getaufft?
    Hat niemand nennerley von Kräutig eingekaufft/
Das in die Wiege soll? Geht liebes Jungfer Ließgen/
Und macht der Mutter doch ein feines Mandel-Müßgen: 15
    Sie eß zur Noth noch wol von einem jungen Hun:
    Ach eßt/ Gevatter/ doch wie könt ihrs doch nur thun.
Last euch doch rösten nur ein Häuptgen von dem Lamme.
Die ander sitzt dabey/ und schwatzt von ihrer Amme;
    Wie sie mit ihr geplagt. Die dritte fäht auch an: 20
    Erzehl was neulich nur die Muhme hat gethan;
[27] Wie sie die Kinder schilt/ und hengt sich an den Schreiber;
Wie sie ansich gewehnt ein hauffen alte Weiber:
    Sie macht nichts mehr recht/ sie rollte gar nicht glatt.
    In dem die dritte fragt/ was man guts neues hat.   25
Wer ist zur Hochzeit doch gewesen hier darneben;
Hats nichts possierlichs sonst von Carmen dar gegeben?
    Ich habe neulich nur auch gar zu sehr gelacht/
    Als ich ins Carmen laß: Wer hats doch nur gemacht?
Ach Gott! wie wurden da die Jungfern auffgezogen: 30
Es ist/ ich muß gestehn/ fürwar nichts dran erlogen:
    Wie weiß der Kerl es doch/ wie weiß ers doch so fein?
    Er muß/ ich sehs ihm an/ wol gar ein rechter seyn.
Die lobte sonst die Frau/ die ihr die Hauben machte:
Die gieng zu albern her/ und jene gar zu sachte: 35
    Die gienge zugemacht/ die andre gar zu bloß;
    Und die wer ihren Mann auch gar zu gerne loß.
Der ware kranck und alt/ und jener gar ein Henger;
Der soff und spielte nur/ und wer ein Müssiggänger:

Hand me his little cap, he is constipated.
How are you, young mother? Don't upset your womb. [81]
Please, nurse, burn a little old lining,
    And pheasant feathers; her [the mother's] own hair,
    That is even better. Now the worst is over.   5
It is past. Look at the old whore [*Muhme*],
How she swaddles the baby; neglects
    To tie the diaper crosswise; go, and turn up one of the diaper's corners
    Or else the demon will swaddle the baby a second time. [82] Go, Görge, go
And fetch Bible oil from the Black Moor's apothecary.   10
The baby is spitting up, it is starting to hiccup.
    Where is the piece of bread that we had blessed?
    Has no one bought even a few herbs
To put into the cradle? Hurry, dear Lieschen,
And cook a bit of almond porridge for the mother.   15
    She should also eat a bit of meat from a young chicken.
    Oh, please eat, dear friend! But how could you?
Please, have them roast a bit of lamb for you."
The other visitor sits and gossips about her nurse;
    How much trouble she has with her. The third, in turn, begins,   20
    Tells what the *Muhme* has recently done.
[27] How she yells at the children and goes hanging around the tutor.
How she hangs out with a bunch of old women;
    She doesn't do anything right; she doesn't get anything straight.
    Then the third [woman] asks, "What's new?   25
Who went to the wedding next door?
Has there ever been anything more amusing than this charming little poem?
    Recently I really had to laugh
    When I read this little ditty. Who wrote it?
Oh dear, how it made fun of the young women.   30
I have to agree, it was a hoot.
    How does this fellow know it all [what goes on in the birthing room]?
    Really, how does he?
    He must be a real joker; I can tell in his face."
One of the [women] began to sing the praises of her milliner.   35
One acted really silly; the other very shy;
    One was too buttoned up, another one let it all hang out.
    And this one would just as soon get rid of her husband.
This one's [husband] was sick and old; another was a devil.
One was a lush and a gambler, a no-good loafer.   40

---

[81] "Mother": uterus, believed to cause bad moods in the mother.
[82] See note 54.

Die were noch zu jung/ und freyte gleichwol schon;
Der seh das Geld nur an; die were von Person
Annoch ein lauter Kind: Die hette andre lieber/
Die hülff gemeiniglich Soldaten immer über:
    Die hat der Mann ertappt/ nur neulich wers geschehn/   5
    Und hat doch müssen thun/ als hett ers nicht gesehn:
Die hett' des Kerrels dort im Hause wol genossen;
Da hat hie außgelegt so einen grossen bossen/
    Die gar was eingestopfft sie were jo so klein/
    Und hette doch so viel / es könte bald nicht seyn.   10
Sie wüste selbsten bald so viel nicht herzunehmen/
Da sie noch halb so starck; sie müste sich doch schämen/
    Und was dergleichen mehr. Die saß darbey und lacht/
    Und hört wie viel die hat zum Manne mitgebracht.
Die schneidet tapffer auff/ wie sie bey ihrem Leben/   15
Nur als zu dutzenden den Töchtern mitgegeben;
    In Summa was nur ist; das kame damals für:
    [28] Mir mangelts noch zu letzt an Dinten und Pappier.
Fast eine gantzen Rieß den hat ich voll geschrieben;
Das Schreiben wolte mir nicht länger mehr belieben: 20
    Der Ofen war zu warm; ich wurde matt und kranck/
    Biß daß ich gar zu letzt fiel von der Ofen Banck.
Was Sturm/ was Lerm war da! Die wolte mich drumb schmeissen!
Die andre wolte mir/ die Stuben-Thüre weisen:
    Da hett' ich dort das Kind im Schlaffe so erschreckt/   25
    Daß ich vor ängsten bald die Hosen voll gek—
Die gab mir eine Filtz/ daß ich mich da verkrochen/
Und hörte fein was hier die Weiber für den Wochen
    Ganz in geheim geredt: Ein jede sah mich an/
    Und fragte/ wo ich denn das Hertze hingethan?   30
Ob ich die Wöchnerin jetzunder solt erschrecken?
Und lieff/ und holte stracks des Mannes Kammerbecken;
    Die gab ihr Pulver ein: Der Hader ward gestillt/
    Die Muhme ware noch mein bestes Frieden Schild:
Ich durfft auch mein Hut/ wie sonsten nicht bezahlen;   35
Diß macht/ ich kunte mich ein wenig mit ihr tahlen.
    Sie führte da mein Wort; ich wer ihr was verwandt/
    Sie hette mich auch sonst vor diesen wol gekandt.
Zu letzte must ich hin fürs grosse Wochen-Bette/

This woman was judged too young although she seemed so eager [to marry].
This man only saw the money. This woman was still
A child. This one would rather have a different lover.
This woman is always ready for the soldiers.
    This one was caught just recently by her husband in the act,   5
    And yet he has to act as if nothing is amiss.
This one enjoys the guys in her very own house.
This one enjoyed a really big one,
    Filled her right up, as small as she was,[83]
    And still took it all in; hard as it is to imagine.   10
She was almost overwhelmed by it all;
Even if she were half as strong, she really should be ashamed.
    And so on and so on. Another one sat right there and laughed,
    And heard how much [money] this one had brought into the marriage.
This one boasts about how much [money]   15
She had given for her daughters' dowries.
    In short, whatever there is to talk about, here it was said.
    [28] In the end I ran out of ink and paper:
I almost filled a whole ream,
And I got pretty tired of writing.   20
    The stove was much too warm; I became sick and tired
    Until, in the end, I fell off the stove bench.
What a ruckus that caused! One of them wanted to hit me.
Another wanted to throw me out.
    I woke the baby from its sleep   25
    And was so afraid that I practically wet my pants.
One woman gave me a bunch of crap because I had been hiding
And listening to what the women secretly talked about in their birthing room.
    Each one looked at me and
    Asked why I was so heartless,   30
Whether I meant to frighten the young mother.
She hurried off to fetch the husband's chamberpot;
    One of them gave her a bit of medicine. The tumult calmed down.
    In all this, the *Muhme* was my best protector.
And I didn't even have to pay like I usually have to when I am hiding.   35
Because I talked with her a bit.
    She talked to me, told me that I owed her:
    If not, she would have given me away.
Finally, I had to step before the huge birthing bed

---

[83] Sexual innuendo.

Und muste/ weil ich mich so viel erkühnet hette/
   Geloben treulich an: daß keinem ich hinfort
   Davon nicht sagen soll/ nicht das geringste Wort.
Ich schwure hart und fest bey allen Wochen-Stühlen/
Bey dessen Heiligthumb/ und den geweihten Pfühlen   5
   Darauff sie sich gesetzt/ daß ich von solchen Thun
   Nicht leichte sagen würd/ drümb schreib ichs jetzund nun.
Hiermit so wacht ich auff; Was dieses wird bedeuten/
Erfahren wir vielleicht/ in kurtzen kurtzen Zeiten.
   Was meint ihr/ Jungfer Braut/ das wol der Traum vermag/   10
   Dieweil er gleich geschehn auff Euren Hochzeit Tag.
[29] Und treffen anders ein die schöne Wochen-Träume:
Eh' noch ein Jahr vergeht/ so denckt an meine Reime:
   Das Traum Buch ist gewiß/ es trifft gewißlich ein/
   Diß wird der Wochen-Stuhl mein Zeuge müssen seyn.   15

Ein ander Gemüse
Vermischung der Rede/ und Verse
Nach der Weise und Melodey der klatzschichten Weiber   20
Vor dem Wochen=Bette/
Im Jahr nach Anfang der plaprichten Weiber=Zungen nach 5663
durch [Χψ Ζε]

Dem Leser   25

Nach dem ein jedes ist/so ist sein Kleid und Sitten/
Dem groben Bauers-Mann wird nicht ein Kleid geschnitten/
Von Sammt und gülden Stück/ so er wer angethan
Mit Königlicher Pracht/ diß were (sag mir an)   30
Ein rechter Unverstand/ von liederlichen Sachen/
Auch liederliche Vers und leichte Worte machen/
Diß will die Redner Kunst. Denn wie ein jedes ist/
So ist das Kleid und Art. Hiermit sey sehr gegrüßt.

     35

Stille/ stille mit der Fiedel
Macht doch an daß ein groß Getiedel
Das Brummen
Und Summen/
Das Gänse nach Dattern/   40

And, because I had been so very foolish and daring,
    I had to faithfully swear that I would never
    Talk about what I had heard, not even a single word.
I swore as honorably and steadfastly as I was able by the world's birthing stools;
And by this sacred place, and the blessed bedding   5
    On which she was sitting, that I would not say a single word
    Of all those goings-on. Therefore I write[84] it now.
At which point I awoke. What all this is to mean,
We might know soon, maybe even sooner.
    What do you think, Damsel Bride, what might the   10
    Dream mean, since it happened on your wedding day?
[29] And we know that dreams at lying-in time
Come true before the year is out. So remember my rhymes.
    The Book of Dreams[85] tells the truth, will come true:
    For this the birthing-stool will be my witness.   15

Some more stuff.
A Mixture of Prose and Verse
According to the Tune and Melody   20
Of the Gossipy Ladies in the Birthing Room.
A Year since
The Beginning of the Chatty Women's Tongues

To the Reader   25

To each his own in clothes and manners:
The crude farmer does not go around in clothes
Cut from velvet or golden cloth, or dressed
In kingly garb. This would be true foolishness.   30
To make silly poems
From foolish things and asinine rhymes:
This is the writer's art. As is the nature of each thing,
So is its dress and art. With this I greet you.
      35
Quiet, quiet with your fiddle:
Go start a great noise
The humming
And strumming,
The chattering like geese   40

---

[84] He writes because he promised not to "speak"!

[85] In several of his writings Praetorius refers to a *Traumbuch* (Book of Dreams) that he wrote. No copy has ever been found.

Und Hattern/ und Schnattern/
Das Schlichten und Dichten und Richten der Weiber.
So sagte mir es unser Schreiber
Der es selbst gehört
[30] An einem gar heimlichen Ort/   5
Daß sie umb die Wette/
Bey dem Wochen-Bette/
Bewimmerten
Und sich bekümmerten
Sehr umb die Menschliche Notdurfft und Ding   10
Er nam kein Blat vors Maul/ er sagte wie es gieng;
Plappern/ hattern/ schnattern/ da/ da/ da
Wie sonst das Weibische ut, re, mi, fa, sol, la,
Ein weit bekandter *Componiste*,
Und Zischsiste/   15
Gänserich gebracht in Noten/
Jetzund kompts durch eignen Boten
Dann es ist wol werth
Eigne Post und eignes Pferd/
Man hat lang genug gefraget   20
Jederman der hat gesaget:
Kompt denn nichts von dem Bocks-Beutel herauß/
Damit ich vexier die Frau zu Hauß.
Euer Verlangen das ist nun gestillet
Und gäntzlich erfüllet   25
Nun wird man es hören singen/
Und in allen Gassen klingen
Wo eine Frau in Wochen lieget/
Und eine Amme Kinder wieget/
Mutter Krutze und Lutze die werden halten den Tact/   30
Damit unter/ unter/ unter/untereinander es werde gehackt/
Die Saue mit Jungen und Alten/
Werden nicht länger sich können enthalten/
Sie werden mit quicken und singen
Und immer/ und immer im Hause rumb springen/   35
Sie werden machen Capriolen
Ohne Tantz Schuh und Sohlen.
Ich wil es erzehlen/
[31] Ihr möget das beste rauß wehlen/

And the smacking and clacking
And talking, bitching, and gossiping of women.
That's what our tutor told me[86]
Who had heard it himself
[30] From a hidden place. 5
How the women compete
Around the birthing bed.
Much whining
And worrying
About other people's needs and wants. 10
He did not hold back,[87] he told it like it is.
Chattering, stammering, gossiping, here, there, and everywhere.
As women usually do: do, re, mi, fa, so, la.
A well-known composer
And music maker, 15
  Set it to silly music.
And now the song comes by special messenger.
For it is well worth
Its own horse and wagon.
We have asked long enough 20
Everyone who has said
Is there nothing coming from the billy-goat's bag[88]
With which I can vex the wife at home?
Now your desire is satisfied
And completely satiated. 25
Now we will hear it sung
And echo through all the lanes
Wherever a woman is lying in
And a nurse is rocking the children.
Mother Krutze and Lutze, they will keep the rhythm, 30
So that all to, to, to, together they keep the beat.
The sows with the young ones and the old
Won't be able to contain themselves any longer:
Joyfully squealing and singing along
They will dance 'round and 'round in the house, 35
They will playfully leap
Without dancing shoes and soles.
I want to tell the story—
[31] You can choose what you like best.

---

[86] The second tutor (male voice), who talks about women in their private domains.
[87] "Kein Blatt vor den Mund nehmen": to tell it like it is.
[88] "Bocks-Beutel": a popular German white wine.

Was ich behalten/
Und Mutter Plonen der Alten
Meistentheils wieder vernommen
Je liebe Frau Schwester sie sey mir willkommen/
Wir reden gleich von ihr   5
Wenn fasset das neue Bier?
Sie stehet auff gar frühe.
Was macht sie ihr viel Mühe?
Ach ja/ Frau Schwester/ ja wann ichs ihr sollte sagen/
Und mein Elende klagen   10
Wie ich wimre/
Wie ich mich bekümre/
Denn mein Mann
Vor nichts sorgen kan
Den Bauch zu versorgen/   15
Geh ich offt borgen/
Wer ich auch vergessen/
Müssen wir nichts essen/
Dieses ist der Schmertz
Der mir krabelt umb das Hertz   20
O wackere tapffere That
Die redt frisch umb Salat/
Und jen' umb Kohl und Kraut
Mein sagt mir? Ist die eine Braut.
Drümb wurd sie nechsten wol vexieret/   25
Seht doch wie der stets schoßiret/
Wie er schertzet
Wie er hertzet/
Dencket er doch nur
Meine Magd die lose Hur   30
Lieff geschwind/
Wie der Wind/
Zu den Soldaten/
Gleich da ich wolte braten.
[32] Frau Schwester/ ach höret! Ach höret doch nur!   35
Was mir neulich wiederfuhr;
Meine Magd der Klunckermutz/
Die mir alles thät zu trutz/
Kaufft mir am nechsten Schollen/
Da sie mir hat bringen sollen   40

What I remember
And Mother's stories of yore
I heard once again.
Dear Madam Sister, I bid you welcome.
We will speak soon of her.   5
When is the new beer ready?
She gets up very early.
How many pains she takes with it!
Oh, dear Madam Sister, what can I tell you
And complain about my suffering.   10
How I whimper,
How I fret,
Because my husband
Cannot provide for anything
To fill the belly.   15
I often borrow money;
Were I to forget
We would have nothing to eat.
This the pain
That gnaws at my heart.   20
Oh, brave and earnest deed:
This one [woman] talks fresh around the lettuce,[89]
And that one around the cabbage and *Kraut*.
Well, tell me, is this one a bride?
Soon she will be vexed.   25
See how he courts her,
See how he makes jokes
And how he hugs her.
He only thinks:
My maid, this loose chick,   30
Will run as
Fast as the wind
To the soldiers.
I would have liked to kill her.
[32] Madam Sister! Listen, please, listen!   35
What happened to me the other day.
My maid, the little tart
Who does everything to annoy me,
Bought a sole
Since she was to bring home   40

---

[89] Gossip.

Einen guten Fisch
Auff den Tisch.
Sie wuste daß ich keine aße/
Und keines das am Tische saße/
Sie fraße sie alleine.   5
Ach meine
Frau Schwester glaube sie mir
Ist auch ein lose Thier/
Gut Gesind
Man fast nirgends find/   10
Aber was machet das kleine!
Kompts auff die Beine?
Hält sichs auch reine?
Ist es/ wie meine.
Kan es auch ruhen   15
Nein? Frau Schwester wie soll ich thun?
Ey mein legt ihm unters Küßgen
Nur ein rauches Hasen-Füßgen/
Oder last die Krüpern kommen
Die ich nechsten hab genommen/   20
Sie benam dem Kind den Schmerz
Als sie griff zum hintern Herz.
Ja! Frau Schwester/ was ihr sagt
Tag und Nacht michs greulich plagt/
Ich singe/ ich sage/   25
Ich schelte/ ich klage/
Es hilfft lauter nichts;
Habt wegen des Berichts
Grossen Danck
[33] Frau Schwester geht sie schon/ sie setze sich auff die Banck/   30
Ach wißt ihr nicht ich bin kranck/
Ich braucht zwar den Tranck
Doch ist mirs nicht vergangen
Ich trage groß Verlangen
Nach eurem rathen/   35
Ob ich soll baden!
Es ist ein Aufflauff in dem Leibe/
Ich weiß nicht wo ich bleibe/

A nice fish
For the table.
She knew full well
That neither I
Nor anyone at the table   5
Would eat it.
So she ate it all by herself.
Oh, dear Madam Sister,
Believe me,
She is a real bitch.   10
Good servants
Cannot be found anywhere.
But how is the little one?
Is it walking nicely?
Is it potty-trained?   15
Is it like mine?
Is it sleeping well?
No? Madam Sister, what should I do?
Well, just put a little
Rabbit's foot under its pillow.   20
Or call the midwife[90]
Whom I recently employed.
She made the child's pain go away
When she touched it near the heart.
Madam Sister, what do you say?   25
Day and night I am suffering terribly.
I sing, I talk,
I bitch, I complain;
All is for naught;
But thank you most warmly   30
For the good gossip.
[33] Madam Sister, are you leaving already? Go sit on the bench.
Don't you know how sick I am?
I need a little refreshment
But I cannot decide.   35
I really need
Your advice,
Whether I should take a bath.
My stomach feels all bloated,
I don't know what to do.   40

---

[90] Wise woman: midwife.

Und krümbt und reißt mich auch
In dem Bauch
Jensmals war mir eben so
Daß es umb den Nabel da
Mich so plagte   5
Und nagte/
Biß ich etwa brauchte was/
Drauff ich mich befunde baß.
So lustige/ werckliche/ artige Händel
Brachten sie vor/ als wie jener zu Stendel/   10
Welcher verblümt vorbracht
Wie zu Nacht
Angeschrieben worden
Daß der Cantor in den Orden
Sie befinde/   15
Da sonst stünde
Mancher guter Mann
Der nichts kan.
Wie sauer? wie sauer ihr lieblichen Weiber?
Mein Ernst ist es nicht/ daß ich bin der Schreiber   20
Der Thaten und Rathen; das Loben und Schelten
Will ich nicht mehr vermelden
Ich möcht bey euch allen
In Ungunst fallen.

Mit nechster Post ein außführlichers

[34] **Fr. Just**: Das ist fürwar schnackisch genug gemacht. **Fr. Reg**: Ja/ er würde
es wol nicht so getroffen haben/ wenn er nit mit meiner Muhmen ihrem Kalb
gepflüget hette. **Fr. Wöchn.** Es ist wol ein schlimm Thun/ umb ein untreues und
waschhafftiges Gesind. Meine solte es wol nicht viel anders machen: Sie hat ein
Maul wie ein Breche/ und verschweigt mir kein Wort. Es ist noch nicht lange/
da hat sie mir auch ein Stückgen bewiesen mit ihrer Pläpper/ das ich noch diese
Stunde nicht vergessen kan: Dessentwegen ich sie denn ingemein/ als jetzund
geschehn/ fortschicke; damit sie mir nicht alles anhorche/ und für andere Leute
Ohren bringe. **Die Muhme kömpt wieder:** Nu/ ihr seyd fein lange aussen: Wo
habt ihr wieder herumb gejachtert? man solte euch noch dem Tode schicken/ da
weret ihr ein feiner Bote zu/ weil ihr fein lange außbleiben würdet; Was machen

And it tears and pulls
In my belly.
I have had this before,
It hurt just around the navel
And gnawed   5
Until I got something
Which made me feel better.
Such funny and cute chatting
They engaged in freely.
Just as the one in Stendhal[91]   10
Who described without being shy
How at night
It was recorded
That the cantor in the order
Took care of her   15
In the way that
Many a good man
Was unable [to do].[92]
How bitter, how bitter, my dear sweet ladies.
I am not serious, I am [only] the author   20
Of all acts and advice; praise and blame
I don't want to expose any more
For I do not want to incur
Your general disfavor.

The next delivery will bring you more about this topic.

[34] Frau Justina: "This is truly very funny." Frau Regina: "Yes, he [the writer]
would never have hit on all this, had he not kissed up to my *Muhme*."[93] The young
mother: "It really is a bad situation to have an unreliable and gossipy bunch of
servants. My maid would not have done any differently. She has a mouth like a
latrine; she does not keep anything from me. Not long ago, she showed her true
self, telling me a tale that I cannot forget to this very day: That is why, when I
have guests, I always send her away; so that she does not eavesdrop and then go
telling tales to other people." The *Muhme* returns: "Well, you have been gone
a good while! Where have you been hanging out? I should send you to fetch
Death. You would be the perfect messenger because it would take you forever.

---

[91] Stendhal: town close to Leipzig.
[92] A pun on the sexual appetites of women and priests.
[93] "Mit eines anderen Kalb pflügen": proverbial, succeeding with someone else's
(unwitting) help; also with sexual connotations.

die Kinder? **Muhme.** Sie waren droben beym Praeceptor/ und schriech alle-
weile einer greulich sehr: Da mir es denn dauchte daß es Friederich seyn müste.
Fr. Wöchn. Der Teufflische Kerl hat ihn gewiß wieder eine Schilling gegeben:
Kan doch der Flegel nichts anders als nur immer schlagen. Gehet mir hinauff
Muhme/ ruffet mir die Kinder herauß und saget/ daß ich es haben wolle; weil ich
sie zu verschicken benöthiget bin: Und lasset mir Friedrichen herein kommen.
Die Muhme gehet: Fr. Just. Ja es sind die Praceptor wol Blut-Aeser: Ich hatte
vergangen auch einen Schindhund/ der machte es mir nicht besser. Ich nam den
Hungerleider Pennalsweise an/ gab ihm zu Fressen/ so gut als es mein Gesinde
selber frißt: Und warff ihme auch hernach etliche Lümpgen zu: weil er ganz
nackicht war/ und ihn die Läuse bald hetten fressen mögen; Wie er sich hernach
außkleidete und ein Pursche ward/ da verhalff ich ihm auch fast zum hübschen
neuen Kleide: In deme ich auß Fürbitte bey meinem Mann erhielte/ daß er noch
ein paar andere Knaben auß der Nachbarschafft durffte zu sich gehenlassen.
Aber hernach wuste es mir der Flegel Danck/ er wurd so hochmütig in seinem
Sinn/ daß er den Tisch nicht mehr decken/ und bißweilen meinem Manne die
Leuchte nicht nachtragen wolte. [35] Darzu schmiß er mir die Jungens unerhört
sehr/ daß sie manchmal Beulen wie Hüner-Eyer groß auff den Köpffen hatten:
Biß ich ihme endlich die Schüppe gab. **Die Magd kompt mit dem Knaben: Die
Wöchn.** Je was thate dir denn der Praeceptor wieder? **Friederich:** Er schmiß
mich wie dem Catechismus-Buch an den Kopff/ daß ich die *Vocabeln* nicht außwendig gelernet hatte. **Fr. Wöchn.** Ist das nun keine Sache? Das Kind umb solche
kahle Ursache zu schmeissen! Da Muhme/ legt das liebe Kindgen/ Gott gesegne
es/ wieder in die Wiege: Es hat nunmehr wol eine halbe Stunde an meiner Brust
gelegen/ und sich gantz satt getruncken. Legts fein sachte in die Wiege: segnet
es hüpsch ein/ und schlaget Creutze drüber; und langets mir jo nicht über die
Wiege/ daß es nicht das Herzgespan kriege! **Die Muhme thut es: Fried.** Liebes
Mütterigen/ ich will mein Brüderigen helffen wiegen. **Fr. Wöchn.** Ey du Schel-
michen laß es bleiben/ und laß es der Muhme allein: sitze du auff deinem Arsch
stille/ daß die Mäuse keine Holzäpffel hinein tragen: Denn es ist nicht gut/
wenn ihr zwey ein Kind wiegen. **Fr. Christin:** Ihr Frauen Schwestern/ es wird
Zeit seyn/ daß wir auffbrechen/ und nach Hause gehen. Guten Tag also/ Frau
Magisterin: Der liebe Gott spare euch gesund/ und beschere euch eine gute Mit-
tags-Ruh sampt dem lieben Kinde. Grüsset doch euren Herrn meinetwegen. **Fr.
Wöchn.** Habt fleissigen Danck liebe Junge Frau/ daß ihr mich wieder besucht/
und nicht gelassen habet: Ich will künfftig schon gewisse Abrechnungen halten;
ihr habt doch allbereit was wieder für euch: Ich sehe es leichte an der Schürze:
Möget ihr doch bald umb die Helffte seyn. **Fr. Christin:** Ja liebe Fr. Magisterin/
nach meiner Rechnung/ mochte es wol den ersten Augusti auß seyn; da ich also
noch fünff und zwanzig Wochen hin habe. **Fr. Juste.** Nun Fr. Mag. der liebe
Gott behüte euch auch/ samt allen den eurigen: Ich will euch schon noch einmal
besuchen etwan auffm Sontag wills Gott. **Fr. Wöchn.** Habt doch Danck liebe
Nachbarin/ [36] daß ihr mir die Ehre angethan/ und bey meinem Kindelbett

What are the children doing?" *Muhme*: "They were still upstairs with the tutor; one of them screamed horribly all the while. I thought it might be Friedrich." **The young mother**: "This monster, he must have beaten him again; this guy does nothing but hit the kids. Go upstairs, *Muhme*, call the children and tell them that I want to see them, because I need to send them to fetch something. And have Friedrich come to my room." **The *Muhme* leaves. Frau Justina**: "These tutors, they're real bloodsuckers. I recently had one, a true son of a bitch, who was not much better. I took this starving pauper in as tutor, gave him food to eat[94] that was as good as what I feed my servants. And I threw him a few rags because he was almost naked; the lice had all but devoured him. Once he was dressed he looked more like a strapping young man; I even gave him money for a nice outfit. What is more, I asked my husband for permission for him to tutor a few more boys from the neighborhood. And after all that, the good-for-nothing's gratitude was only arrogance; he did not want to lay the table any more, nor did he want to carry the candle for my husband. [35] And he incessantly kept hitting the boys, so that often they had bumps on their heads as big as hens' eggs. Until I finally fired him."[95] **The maid enters with the young boy. The young mother**: "Oh, dear, what has the tutor done to you?" **Friedrich**: "He threw the catechism at me because I hadn't learned the vocabulary by heart." **The young mother**: "Isn't this awful? To hit the poor child for something this minor? Here, *Muhme*, put the little one, God bless it, back into the cradle. I have nursed it for at least half an hour, and it seems quite satisfied. Put it gently into the cradle, say a blessing over it, and make the sign of the cross. And don't reach across the cradle in this way, it will get colic." **The *Muhme* does as she is told. Friedrich**: "Dearest Mother, I want to help rock my little brother." **The young mother**: "You little fool, let the *Muhme* do that. Sit quietly on your ass, so that the mice won't stuff it with pinecones. It's not good for two to rock a baby."[96] **Frau Christina**: "My dear ladies, it is time for us to leave and go home. So therefore, good day, Frau *Magisterin*. May the Lord keep you well and grant a nice nap to you and your baby. And please say hello to your husband from me." **The young mother**: "Many thanks, dear young woman, that you have come to visit, and that you did not hold a grudge. In future, I will be sure to take a careful accounting. It looks to me like you are expecting. I can see it looking at your waistline. For your sake, I hope half the time has passed." **Frau Christina**: "Yes, dear Frau *Magisterin*, according to my calculations I will be due early August; I still have twenty-five weeks." **Frau Justina**: "God bless you and yours. I will come back and visit, maybe around Sunday, God willing." **The young mother**: "Many thanks, dear neighbor, [36] for doing me

---

[94] As earlier in the conversation, she uses "fressen," a very coarse synonym for "to eat." Animals "fressen," devour their food.

[95] "Die Schüppe gab": give him the heave-ho.

[96] Superstition associated with baby care.

zugesprochen habet. **Fr. Reg.** Guten Tag Fr. Mag; tragt doch kein Ungefallen/ daß ich zu euch gekommen bin. **Fr. Wöchn.** Je/ was sagt ihr doch liebe Junge Frau davon? Habt ihr vielmehr Danck/ daß ihr mit eurem Geschwätze mir die Zeit habt helffen verkürtzen. **Fr. Christin:** Nun behüte euch Gott miteinander/ Muhme; nehmet eure Wöchnerin als die Fr. Magisterin wol in acht: Es wird auff der Stund Mittag und umb 12. seyn; lasset sie nicht allein in der Stuben/ und bleibet bey ihr zur Gesellschaft/ daß der Nickert nicht komme. Liebe Fr. Mag. ihr könnet euch ein wenig zur Ruhe gegeben/ und schlaffen: Sehet aber zu/ daß euch die Füsse nicht bloß ans Bettebret kommen. **Die Muhme singet:** Schlaff Kindgen gerne/ wie leuchten dir die Sterne/ wie schön leucht dir der Mondenschein; Mein Kindlein du solst fromme seyn: Schlaff balde.

Schlaff Kindgen wolgemuth/ daß man dich in die Schule thut; Was lernestu darinnen/ Schreiben/ lesen und singen: Schreiben/ lesen und alles guts; daß man dich in die Schule thut: Schlaff balde.

Schlaff Kindgen balde/ die Vögelein fliegen im Walde: sie fliegen wol über Laub und Graß/ und bringen meinem Kingen einen süßen Schlaff: Schlaff balde.

Die vierdte Abhandlung/ oder plauderung/..

Frau Wöchnerinne. Fr. Liese. Fr. Draute.
Frau Barbara. Matthias: Praeceptor. Muhme/
Kindermägdgen.

Fr. Liese. Glückseligen guten Tag Fr. Magisterin/ was machet ihr mit eurem jungen Söhngen? **Fr. Wöchn:** Ich bedancke mich eures Nachfragens liebe Jungefrau/ seyd doch auch willkommen. **Fr. Draute:** Gott grüsse euch Fr. [37] Magisterin/ ich muß euch auch einmal besuchen. **Fr. Wöchn.** Ihr thut gar recht dran/ seyd doch auch willkommen. **Fr. Barbara:** Guten Tag Fr. Magisterin/ finde ich

the honor of visiting me during my confinement." **Frau Regina:** "Good day, Frau *Magisterin*, please don't hold it against me that I came along to visit you." The young mother: "What are you saying, dear young woman? Quite the contrary, I am grateful for your visit; your chatter made the time pass more quickly." **Frau Christina:** "May God bless you and keep you altogether; *Muhme*, take good care of the new mother. It is just about twelve noon; don't leave her alone in her chamber, stay with her and keep her company, so that no demon comes to visit her.[97] Dear Frau *Magisterin*, you should rest a bit and maybe sleep some. But take care that you don't touch the bedframe with your bare feet." **The *Muhme* begins to sing the baby to sleep:**

> Sleep, little child!
> How lovely the stars shine above,
> How beautiful glows the moon!
> My little child, be quiet. Go to sleep.
> Sweet little child, sleep well
> So that you might go to school
> Where you will learn
> Writing, reading, and singing,
> Writing, reading, and other good things—
> So that you will go to school.
> Sleep well,
> Sleep, little child, go to sleep now.
> The little birds fly in the wood
> Flying over meadow and glen
> Bringing sweet slumber to my baby.
> Sleep well.

The fourth Chapter or Chat.

The young mother; Frau Liese; Frau Draute; Frau Barbara; Mathias: Tutor; *Muhme*; children's maid (nurse)

Frau Liese: "A beautiful, wonderful day to you, Frau *Magisterin*! How is your sweet little son?" The young mother: "Thank you much for asking, dear damsel, everything is fine." **Frau Draute:** "God's greetings, Frau *Magisterin*! [37] It is time that I, too, paid you a visit." The young mother: "You are doing the right thing; you are certainly a welcome sight." **Frau Barbara:** "Hello, Frau *Magisterin*! Do I

---

[97] Allusion to Psalm 91:6, the "noonday demon."

euch in solchem guten Stande? Das hette ich vor drey Wochen nicht gedencken sollen/ daß ihr so bald würd einkommen. **Fr. Wöchn**: Ja ich habe selber meine Rechnung weiter hinauß gemacht gehabt; es ist nicht ohne; Seyd auch willkommen: Setzet euch doch miteinander was nieder ihr lieben Weibrigen. **Fr. Liese**: Wir sind nicht sehr müde/ und kommen miteinander gleich von sitzen her. **Muhme**: Ey lasset euch doch was nieder/ ihr habt ja eben so viel vom Sitzen als vom Stehen. **Fr. Barbara**: Wie thut es denn Fr. Magisterin/ habt ihr denn auch noch was zu stillen? **Fr. Wöchn**: O ja/ Gott lob/ so lange weiß ich noch keinen Mangel: Ohne daß es sich gestern ein wenig anliesse/ als wenn sich die Milch hette verlieren wollen. **Fr. Draute**: Das ist nicht gut Fr. Mag: ihr müst ein wenig schwartz Kümmel anhengen/ so wird sich die Milch häuffig finden. **Draussen schreyet ein Knabe. Fr. Wöchn**. Muhme laufft geschwinde nauß/ und sehet zu was Matthießgen fehlet: Denn ich höre es an seiner Stimme/ daß es der lose Bube ist. **Die Muhme kompt mit ihme**: Was fehlt dir denn du armes Kind? **Matth**. Liebe Mutter/ ich wolt mit Friedrichen spielen/ und fiel von der Treppen herunter. **Fr. Wöchn**. Das Gott im hohen Himmel erbarm! bistu denn etwa auff dein Köpffgen gefallen? Was machet denn der Teufflische Kerl der Praeceptor: daß er die Kinder nicht zu sich nauff nimbt und bey sich behelt? **Muhme**: Er ist ins Collegium gangen. **Fr. Wöchn**. Habe ich denn den Schind Kerl dessentwegen/ und gebe ihm Brod und Stube/ daß er nach seinem Gefallen soll außgehen/ wohin er will? Muhme/ sehet flugs darnach ob er ein Loch im Kopff gefallen habe? **Muhme**: Es ist freylich ein wenig auffgelauffen. **Fr. Barb**: Ey gebt euch zu frieden Fr. Mag: Es hat nicht viel zu bedeuten; Muhme/ ziehet nur seinen rechten Schuh auß/ und haltet solchen ein weilgen auff den Kopffe/ es wird bald besser werden. **Fr. Liese**: Nein/ nehme nur ein Creutzmesser/ und leget solches etlichmal Creutzweise [38] auff die Stelle: Das habe ich immer bey meinen Kindern gethan. **Fr. Wöchn**. Muhme/ sucht doch das Heilholtz auß meinem Schiebesacke hervor; es wird vielleicht in der Geldbüchse stecken: und haltet solches Creutzweise drauff/ und bestreicht es damit. **Muhme**: Hele/ Kätzgen hele: Das Kätzgen hat vier Beine: Das Kätzgen lieff den Berg hinan/ und ehe das Kätzgen wieder kam/ da war es schon gehelet. **Fr. Wöchn**. Muhme/ Schert zur Wiege her: Hört ihr denn nicht/ daß sich das Kind reget? Gebet mir das kleine Mäußgen her ich will es schencken: Und geht mit Matthießgen ein Bißgen hinauß auff den Saal/ und spielet mit ihm so lange biß der Praeceptor wieder kompt. Ja du liebes Kind/ wie beißestu in die Wartze hinein/ möcht ich doch immer schreyen: Ziehe doch die Milch herauß/ daß dirs Gott gesegnet. Ich weiß/ daß du noch genug drinnen finden wirst. **Fr. Draute**. Das liebe Kind/ Gott behüt es; mag wol Mangel leiden an der Milch/ daß es nicht ins Mäulgen fliessen will. **Fr. Liese**: Ja es schmertzet sehr/ wenn die lieben Würmgen die Brust so feste halten: Ich habe mich dessentwegen allezeit für Stillen gescheuet/ und eine Amme darzu gehalten. **Fr. Barb**. Ja/ wol dem der es thun kan! Die meisten müssen es auß Noth thun weil sie kein Geschirr darzu haben. Wolte Gott/ daß

find you in very good spirits? Three weeks ago I would not have expected you to give birth so soon." **The young mother:** "Yes, I, too had miscalculated, and had expected the baby a bit later. Welcome to you! Please, all of you dear ladies, won't you sit down." **Frau Liese:** "We are not very tired, and we are just now coming from having sat around awhile." *Muhme*: "Oh, please do sit down; sitting does you as much good as standing." **Frau Barbara:** "How is it going, Frau *Magisterin*? Do you still have enough milk?" **The young mother:** "Oh yes, praise the Lord, in that department nothing is amiss, even though yesterday it felt as if there were a bit less milk." **Frau Draute:** "That is not good, Frau *Magisterin*, you need to put a bit of black caraway seed around your neck; that will help the milk to flow more steadily." **Outside a boy is screaming. The young mother:** "*Muhme*, please hurry and see what is the matter with little Matthew. I can tell by the voice that it is the little rascal." **The *Muhme* returns with him.** "What is the matter, poor little child?" **Matthew:** "Dear Mother, I wanted to play with Friedrich and I fell down the stairs." **The young mother:** "May the Lord have mercy! Have you fallen on your little head? What is that devil of a tutor doing that he does not watch the kids and keep them by his side?" *Muhme*: "He went to the university [*Collegium*]." **The young mother:** "Is that why I keep this useless jerk around, giving him room and board, so that he can come and go as he pleases? *Muhme*, please, check quickly if the boy has a hole in his head." *Muhme*: "Well, yes, it is a bit black and blue." **Frau Barbara:** "Oh, just let it be, Frau *Magister*; it doesn't mean much; *Muhme*, just take off his right shoe and press it against the bump on his head; that will help right away." **Frau Liese:** "No, take a knife and put it crosswise [38] on the spot. This is what I have always done with my children." **The young mother:** "*Muhme*, go and fetch the healing wood from my drawer; it is probably in the money chest. Hold it crosswise on his head and stroke it." *Muhme*:

"Heal, little kitten, heal.
The kitten has four legs.
The kitten ran up the hill
And before it came back
It was already well again."

The young mother: "*Muhme*, get over here by the cradle; can't you hear that the baby is stirring? Give me the little one so I can feed him. And take little Matthew outside for a while, and play with him until the tutor returns. Oh, you sweet little baby, how you bite my nipples! I'm about to scream. Just draw the milk out, God bless you. I know that you will find enough to eat." **Frau Draute:** "The sweet child, may God bless it. Maybe it's not getting enough milk; it doesn't seem to want to flow into his mouth." **Frau Liese:** "Yes, it is very painful when the little dears hold onto the breast so tightly. That's why I always avoid nursing and hire a nursemaid instead." **Frau Barbara:** "Well, good for those who can afford it; most women have to [take a nurse] because their equipment is faulty. By God, I wish I

ich etwas Zeug darzu hette/ ich wolte meine Lebelang kein Kind einer Ammen
anvertrauen. Die lieben Kinder saugen manchmal/ ich weiß nicht was/ von den
Vetteln hinein. So muß ich es leider geschehen lassen. Ich sage immer/ daß ich
in dem Fall schlimmer bin als ein Hund/ denn solcher kan ja noch allezeit seine
Jungen selber ernehren; aber ich nicht. Wie mag es doch kommen; daß man bey
den Bauers Weibern von dergleichen Mangel nicht höret? **Fr. Liese:** Dessentwegen hat uns Gott mehr Geld bescheret/ als die Dorffleutgen haben/ daß wir
Ammen halten können. **Fr. Draute:** Ja wenn nur die Huren darbey gut thäten/
und nicht so frech und stoltz würden: Ich war gestern für die Wochen bey der
Fr. Doctorin N. die wuste sich auch höchlich zu beklagen wegen ihres Musters.
Die Schelmpetze war vom Born hierher gelauffen/ daß sie möchte Schutz fin-
den/ und droben nicht dürffte Kirchen-Buße thun: [39] weil sie als eine Frauen
Magd von Schirr Meister war beschlaffen worden: Da war die Grund Hure gar
armselig zu sie gekommen/ und hatte umb Gottes willen gebeten/ daß sie doch
ihr nur die Herberge vergönnen möchte/ und bey ihrem Gesinde das bloße bißgen Essen. So wolte sie gerne gutes thun/ und der Frau Doctorin ihr saugendes
Kindgen stillen. Jetzund aber ist die Schelmische Balch so hönisch und schnip-
pisch/ daß sie nicht weiß / wie sie die Fr. Doctorin anfahren soll: Bald ist ihr
das Essen nicht gut genug; Bald will sie täglich so und so viel Torgisch Bier zu
sauffen haben/ und was der Schlapp Keten sonsten mag mehr mangeln. Ja/ die
Fr. Doctorin gedachte wol gar/ daß sie in ihrem Hause zu den Studenten auff die
Stube giengt/ und allerhand leichtfertige Händel triebe. **Fr. Barb:** Das muß ein
recht Rabenstücke seyn/ die nicht ein wenig zurücke dencket. **Fr. Wöchn.** Kin-
dermägdgen gehe doch ganz leise an die Stuben-Thüre hin und mercke doch/
wer da horcht; denn ich verspühre/ daß etwas russelt/ es ist gewisse meine du-
rchtriebene Hure/ die Muhme: daß sie etwas will erschnappen/ was man von ihr
schwatze. **Fr. Draute:** Vielleicht kan es ein Kerl seyn/ der unser Geschwätze will
auffzeichnen: Wie vergangen zu Nürnberg ein Grämeling. **Fr. Wöchn:** Hui/ daß
noch ein anders herauß kömpt/ als wir Vormittage hatten an der Fr. Licentiaten
ihrer Braut Suppe. **Fr. Draute:** Das kan leichte seyn/ daß es euch noch was neues
ist: Ich kriegte es gestern von meinem Schwager verehret; der sich ja drüber zu
kichern kunte. **Fr. Liese:** Ey lasset es doch einmal lesen/ habt ihrs bey euch? **Fr.
Draute:** Ich weiß es nicht anders/ ich habe es zu mir gesteckt: Ich denck es soll
dieses seyn:

had the tools [milk] to nurse. In that case, I would never in a million years entrust
my baby to a nurse. I don't know somehow what the sweet children are sucking
along with the milk from these bitches. But I have no choice. I always say that in
this case I am worse than a she-dog; they can always feed their young. But not
me. How is it that peasant women never have any shortage of milk?" **Frau Liese:**
"That is why God has given us more money than the peasants, so we can hire
nursemaids." **Frau Draute:** "Well, yes, if only these whores would be nice about
it and not always act so uppity and proud. Yesterday I went and visited Frau *Dok-
tor*[98] N., who also complained much about her nursemaid. The plague of a woman had come over from Born [another town] so that she might find shelter and
would not have to do church penance [39] because, as a lady's maid, she had been
sleeping with the master. So this little whore came to her in pretty bad shape and
pleaded that for God's sake would they take her in and give her a little food. She
wanted to make up for it by nursing Frau Doctor's young one. Now, however, this
foolish cunt is so godawful, so sarcastic and tart, that she does not know how best
to annoy the doctor's wife. Sometimes the food is not good enough, sometimes
she demands a quantity of Torgau beer to swill, whatever this bitch thinks she is
lacking. Yes, and Frau Doctor suspects that at her house she goes up to the rooms
of their student boarders for all kinds of unsavory dealings." **Frau Barbara:** "She
must be a real piece of work, who so quickly forgets what she had been through."
The young mother: "Nanny, please go very quietly to the door and check who
is listening outside. I hear something rustling; I am sure that it is the good-for-
nothing whore *Muhme* who is trying to catch what we are saying." **Frau Draute:**
"Maybe it's a man who wants to write down what we are discussing as I heard
another one did most recently in Nuremberg." **The young mother:** "Oh boy, so
that we hear another poem like we did this morning about the bridal soup [wed-
ding night] of the *Licentiaten* wife." **Frau Draute:** "That may well be; it may still
be new to you; but my brother-in-law gave it to me yesterday; he couldn't stop
chuckling about it." **Frau Liese:** "Oh, let me read it. Do you have it with you?"
Frau Draute: "I couldn't help myself, I brought it with me. I think this is it:

---

[98] The wife of the physician.

[40] Der holdseligen Frauenzimmers
Kindbet=Gespräch*

Als jüngsten eine Frau/ war in die Wochen kommen/
Und ihre Kindbett-Zeit ein Ende schier genommen/
    Geschah es alle Tag/ daß sie bald da/ bald dort/
    Von Frauen ward besucht; Wann eine gienge fort/
So kam die ander an. Der Diener wolte wissen/   5
Was ihr Gespräch beysam/ und war einmal beflissen/
    Stund bey der Kammer Thür/ doch daß ihn niemand wust/
    Und hört was jede sagt/ drey Stund mit grossem Lust/
Und was er hat gemerckt/ das hat er auffgeschrieben/
Und theilt es jetzund mit/ zu jedermans Belieben/   10
    Doch was Geheimniß sind/ die einer nicht versteht/
    Der noch ein Jung Gesell/ er wissend übergeht.
Zwo Schwestern kamen erst/ als niemand noch verhanden/
Und da sie vor dem Bett geraume Zeit gestanden
    Und ihren GlückesWunsch mit vieler Wörter Zier/   15
    Nach Allemode weiß Kunstschicklich brachten für/
Hat man mit grossen Muh sie können sitzend machen/
Darauff war ihr Gespräch von sehr beliebten Sachen/
    Was macht der Frauen Herr? Das war die erste Frag/
    Der Diener hette bald gethan die Antworts Sag;   20
Allein er muste stehn/ und sich nicht mercken lassen
Die Frau Sechswöchnerin bedanckt sich bester massen/
    Und sagte/ daß er zwar gesund wer/ und wol auff/
    Doch fürchtet sie sich nur/ der Arbeit grossen hauff/
Das Reisen hin und her dörfft ihn in Kranckheit bringen/   25
Er wer ein Mann/ der stets wolt alles selbst erringen/
    Und meint es könte nichts geschehen recht im Hauß
    Als was/ durch seine Hand er selber richtet auß.
Ach! Wolte Gott/ daß ich / das Glück von Gott solt haben
So fieng die Ander an/ wie wolt ich mich erlaben/   30
    Wann sich mein Mann einmal zur Arbeit bringen ließ/
    Der je/ weil ich ihn hab/ ich sag es für gewiß/
[41] Nicht einen Nagel hat nur in die Wand geschlagen/

---

* This is a copy of a broadsheet with the same title (Nürnberg, Germanisches Nationalmuseum 2099/1293). I thank Professor Schilling, Magdeburg for a copy.

[40] A Conversation of the Lovely Ladies in the Birthing Chamber.

Recently, when a woman had given birth
And her time in the birthing room had nearly come to an end,
    It so happened that she had women
    Coming and going, in and out, to visit her every day.
When one left, the other came. The servant[99] wanted to know   5
What they were talking about, and he carefully tried
    To get close to the chamber door without anyone noticing.
    He listened with delight for three hours to what each woman said.
And all that he heard he wrote down,
And he shares it with us now to everyone's delight.   10
    However, he deliberately passes over the many secrets
    That someone who is still a bachelor might not understand.
Two sisters enter first, before anyone else;
And after they had been standing by the bed for a while
    And politely had expressed their congratulations   15
    With many artful, *allemode*[100] words,
They were finally urged, with much ado, to sit down.
They continued their conversation about many popular subjects.
    How is the lady's husband? That was the first question.
    The servant could have easily answered this one.   20
However, he had to remain quiet and keep from being noticed.
The "Lady Six-Weeks" graciously thanked them
    And said that he was hale and hearty,
    Although she feared he worked too hard,
And that all his travel hither and yon would make him sick.   25
He was a man always striving to do everything himself,
    One who believed that nothing in the house could be done right
    Except what he arranged and did with his own hands.
"Dear God, I should be so lucky!"
The other [visitor] began, "How relieved I would be   30
    If my husband only once could bring himself to work,
    Who never, as long as I have known him,
[41] Has ever so much as put a nail into the wall.

---

[99] Now the servant is the eavesdropper.

[100] Expression for being always up on the latest, usually overdone, fashion; used in much social criticism at the time.

Die faule Haußmagd.

Im Sommer erst vergangen hewr/
Kewm ich zu einer Abendtschewr/
Zn einem Hauß/darinn ich solt
Zu Abend essen/da man wolt/
Bevor geben ein jungen Han/
Die Fraw der Magd dem steckt an/
Da wir nun truncken auff kurtz Stund/
Das Hun nicht fertig werden kundt/
Die Fraw geht auß/schawt in die Kuchn
Vnd wider kam mit grossem Puchn/
Sprach/Kombt doch herauß alle bayd/
Beschawet mein häußliche Magd/
Beyd schleich wir hinauß mit der Frawen/
Der stolzen Köchin zu zuschawen/
Da saß die Magd beym Herr vnd schlieff/
Vnd schnarchend durch die Nasen pfiff/
Gleich wie ein alter Ackergaul/
Die Zotten hiengen ihr ins Maul/
Sie war im gantzen Gsicht besudelt/
Zn Kleidern beschmiert vnd verhudelt/
Jhr Hand weiß als der Ofen Herr/
Vnd in der Kuchn an der Erdt/
Lag Schüssel/Pfannen vngspület/
Als hett ein Saw darinn gewület/
Die Schüssel zerbochen vnd zerstossen/
Die Häfn zerbrochen/Bey dem allen
Der Hund auß einer Schüssel fraß/
Zu morgens kan mans nicht ermundern/
Dann kombt sie in die Stubn geloffen/
Der Wasen stehe ihr oben offen/
Jhr Har verwurglt vnd zerstrobelt/
Als ob sie hett der Rab gezobelt/

Wil ich dann Wasser ins Gießfaß hon/
Muß ich all morgens selbst drein thon/
Die Stuben kehres/das gröst letzt ligen/
Das Körich schütes vnder die Stigen/
Darnach geht sie nach Wasser auß/
Vnd trags gschochen ein ins Hauß/
Das brings zu Waren also warm/
Trags sie herauß ein Holz am Arm/
So würfft sies/daß sichs Hauß thut rühn/
Wann sie dann wil ein Fewr schüren/
Kaufft sie zum Nachbawrn mit dem Liecht/
Den Fewrzeug sie nicht zuricht/
Dann legt etwan sechs Scheuter an/
Zwey Köchlein köndtens auch wol thon/
Verbrennt das Holz/eh sie zusest/
Das Fleisch zugzaust/schon sie nicht letz/
Dann läst sies vngesaumte stehn/
Oder zulästs gar vberzagn/
Eins ist zerbrennt/das andr vngsalzen/
Das dritt vngseten/das viert vngschmalz/
Also wird durch ihr täglich Kochen/
Verwarlost vil verwüst/zerbrochen/
Wo sich nicht Herr oder Fraw/
So ist ihr Spinnen auch verlohren/
Eins zerdreht/das andr verwurgelt/
Hanff vnd Flachs sie schämlich verhudelt/
Gantz Schübel Werck sie mar verzettelt/
Verzwerte Spindel sie verlegt/
Mein Gsind ist vngebettet ligen/
Kein Arbeit thut ihr angestiegen/
Jch muß sie wie ein Esel treiben/
Es sey mit Fegen oder Reiben/
Nichts vn gilt sie auch mit dem Waschen/
Jens Körich schütet sie vnter den Aschen/
Verdrossen/Aller ding nachlässig/
Wie man spricht/Eintzückel vnd geträssig/
Jst sie/das Faust von Suppen naschet/
Vnd was Geschleckwercks sie erhascht/
Jst Wein vnd Vier/es ihr gleich gilt/
Ohn was sie mir sonsten abstilt/
Doch schleufft sie zu die Bubentänz/
Vnd macht den Jungen Gsellen Cränz/

Jst doch der aller gröst vnlust/
Der aller schandtlichst Suppenwust/
Wann wir Essen vnd sollen Tischen/
So thut sie nach den Flöhen fischen/
Sie schmeißt mir in Näsn vnd Scherben/
Der Wässer möchte sie verderben/
Jedoch die Zeit mir nie vermöchten/
Wie sie ihr magen hett vnd kochten/
Jhr Hembd/Goller/ist wie die Erde/
Sie ist in Summa gar nichts werth/
Dann mir zum Fressen vnd zum schlaffen/
Jch sprach/ich wolt die Lümpin straffen/
Sie sprach/ja wenn ich mit ihr schrey/
Gibt sie mir für ein Wort wol drey/
Jch sprach/so thut den Schlepsack nauß/
Was soll der Schawr in dem Hauß/
Weil sie kein Straff auffnemmen wil/
Endlicher Mägd findt ihr noch vil/
Die euch zu bette ligt vnd aufstohn/
Vnd ihr Hausarbeit embsig thon/
Nach Art/wie jedes thut gebühren/
Holz/Wasser tragen/Fewer schüren/
Waschen/Spinnen/Spüln vnd Kochn/
Zu rechter zeit auß die gantz Wochen/
Mit fleiß auffrichtig/recht vnd redlich/
Vnd euch auch sinst trew vnd vnschädlich/
Jn alln Sachen suchen ewer Nutz/
Mit einer solchen gschicht euch guts/
Sie sprach/Der Jahr Kirr soll der walth/
Jch wil sie noch nit lang behalten/
Dann Morgen ist S. Jacobs tag/
So hat sie gleich nach ihrer Saat/
Seyt Liechtmeß vierzehn Dienst gehabt/
Der Kirr hat mich mir ihr begabt/
Der Schwermet hub ich saur am lacht/
Jn dem sie faul Haußmagd erwacht/
Auffgiener weit/vnd sag vns an/
Da dacht ich in meim Herzen schon/
Wo Haut vnd Haar ist gar entweicht/
Da wird kein guter Vbel auß nicht/
Wer mit einer solchen Magd ist geschlagn/
Der weiß von groß Vnglück zu sagn/

Augspurg/bey Cunrad Roleder Brieffmaler/den Laden auff Barfüsser Bruck.

With Permission of the Herzog August Bibliothek, Wolfenbüttel, Germany

Nun achtet ich es nicht/ das wolt ich wol vertragen/
     Wann er sich nur enthielt/ vom Trincken/ und dabey
     Vom Spielen/ Ja ich sag/ es kräncken/ diese zwey
Mich darumd desto mehr/ dieweil er nach dem Trincken
Offt voller Zorn und Grimm nach Hause pflegt zu hincken/   5
     Da unser keines denn kan sicher für ihm seyn/
     Es glaubt es wol kein Mensch/ wie ich leyd Angst und Pein.
Ey! nein; Gott lob und Danck/ ich habe nicht zu klagen/
Ich kan von meinem Mann/ nichts/ als was rühmlich sagen/
     Sagt wiederümb die Erst/ er hält mich lieb und werth/   10
     Ich habe was ich will/ und was mein Herz begehrt.
Wir sind nunmehr zwey Jahr in lieber Eh beysammen
Und habe nie gespürt/ daß sich der Liebe Flammen/
     Solt haben abgezehrt/ er hat mir seit der Zeit
     Mit willigem Gemüth geschafft das vierdte Kleid/   15
Und wann die Weynacht kömpt/ hab ich mein Christbescheren/
Darauff mein Neues Jahr / mein Nahmens Tag verehren/
     O GOtt! ich litt es nicht/ daß er zum Zechen gieng
     Es käm mir greulich für/ wenn er sichs unterfieng/
Ich hette fast kein Creutz/ ich kan es je wol sagen/   20
Wann ich mich nicht so sehr mit Mägden müste plagen/
     Ich weiß nicht wie es kömpt/ die Mägde sind so schlimm/
     Sie machen/ daß ich fast mich alle Tag ergrimm.
Sie mögen nichts nicht thun/ und geben lose Reden/
Ich habe allererst gezanckt mit allen beeden/   25
     Die ich zu Hause hab/ der Kinds Magd thut es Zorn/
     Daß ich ihr eingeredt/ so hab ich hoch geschworn/
Wann sie noch sagt ein Wort/ so muß sie wieder wandern/
Mein Kind ist jetzt ein Jahr/ gewohnt bald einer andern
     Diß ist die sechste schon/ die ich hab gemiedt/   30
     Nach meiner Kellerin/ sie haben mich gebrüt/
Das Raben Schelmen Vieh/ ich kan es nicht erzehlen/
Ich muß die gantze Zeit mich nur mit Mägden quälen.
     Die neulich von mir weg/ war eine rechte Hur/
     [42] Ich hab es schon gemerckt/ es geht nicht wol die Uhr/   35
Sie wolte weiter noch von ihren Mägden sagen/
Wie manche Schläge sie bey ihr davon getragen/
     Allein es kam gleich jezt ein andre Frau hinein/
     Darauff gieng jene fort/ und ließen sie allein.

I would not even mind that and I would put up with it
    If he refrained from drinking and gambling.
    Yes, I say, these two [vices]
Bother me even more, because after he drinks
He often comes stumbling home filled with rage,   5
    So that none of us are safe from him.
    Surely no one understands how much fear and pain I suffer."
"Oh no, praise the Lord, I cannot complain.
I can only praise my husband,"
    The first woman replies, "He cherishes me.   10
    I have what I want and what my heart desires.
By now we have been together for two years in matrimony,
And I have not yet felt that love's flames
    Have abated. With generous spirit, he has given me
    A fourth dress since that time.   15
And on Christmas, he gives me presents;
As he does on New Year's and on my name day.
    Oh Lord, I would not tolerate him going out drinking;
    I would find it insufferable if he started.
I would have hardly anything to complain about, truly,   20
If I didn't have to trouble myself so with the maids.
    I don't know why it is that maids are such a bother.
    They incense me almost every day.
They don't want to work, and they talk back.
At first I yelled at both of them   25
    Who are working for me: the nurse was furious
    When I tried to instruct her. I swore that
If she said another word, I would make her take to the road again.
My child is a year old now, and has had to get used to one maid after the other.
    This is the sixth one that I have hired   30
    Since my kitchen maid; I really feel burned [by]
These dumb cows[101]—I cannot tell you
How much bother I have with these maids all the time.
    The one I most recently fired was truly a whore;
    [42] I noted right away that something wasn't right with her . . ."[102]   35
She wanted to go on and on about her maids,
How many blows she let them have.
    But just then another woman entered;
    Upon which this one [the previous speaker] departed, leaving the two alone.

---

[101] "Raben Schelmen Vieh": the horrible, foolish cows.
[102] "Es geht nicht wohl die Uhr": the clock is not set right.

Als nach vollbrachtem Gruß sich diese niedersetzet/
Hat sie mit Reden sich die ganze Zeit ergetzet/
    Von ihrem Sohn zu Hauß/ der ja so fleissig war/
    Daß einer het vermeint/ er wer schon zwantzig Jahr/.
Der doch nicht viere war/ sie kunte nicht gnug preisen/   5
Was Fleiß in seiner Schul er pflegte zu erweisen/
    Und lernet A.B.C. so bald der Tag entsteht/
    Sprach sie/ er mit dem Sinn schon in die Schule geht/
Mein Herr hat grosse Freud/ er soll ein Doctor werden/
Doch kein gemeiner nicht; der fähret mit sechs Pferden/   10
    Das trieb sie lange Zeit: In dem geht auff die Thür/
    Und kommen wiederumb auff einmal ihrer vier.
Die vor zugegen war/ thut nicht/ also ob sie merckte/
Daß jemand zu der Stell/ und da der Wein sie stärckte/
    So führ sie weiter fort/ von ihrem tapffern Sohn/   15
    In zwischen trug sich schier ein halbe Stund davon/
Zur letzte da sie meynt/ es wer nun Zeit zu gehen/
Enschuldigt sie sich erst/ se hette nicht gesehen
    Daß andre Frauen da/ und wünsche mit Höffligkeit/
    Der Frau Sechswöchnerin/ gesunde Fürgangs Zeit/   20
Hiemit schied sie dahin. Da sie hinauß gegangen/
Hat alsobald der Hauff der Frauen angefangen/
    Wer ist die grosse Frau/ die sich so stoltz gemacht
    Und unsre keine nicht hat ihrer werth gemacht?
Wir sind so gut/ als sie/ wir können auch wol prangen/   25
Und uns so wol als sie mit dem Geschmeid behangen.
    Wer weiß wer mehrer Geld? wer weiß ob noch ihr Kleid
    Dem Kramer ist bezahlt? Wer weiß/ ob ihr Geschmeid
Gemacht von gutem Zeug? und dieses ihr Beschweren/
Must eine halbe Stund und fast noch länger währen/   30
    [43] Nach dem fieng eine an/ und sagt sie käme her/
    Von einem Kindbett Hauß/ da sie gewesen wer/
Da hette sie gesehen/ was sie nicht konte sagen
Der gleichen sey ihr nicht/ bey allen ihren Tagen
    Gelanget zu Gesicht/ die Frau prangt wie ein Bild/   35
    Sprach sie/ die Stuben ist mit grossem Pracht erfüllt/
Das ganze Bett ist neu/ von Nußbaum Holz gezimmert/
Der Himmel überall von schönen Farben schimmert/
    Von Atlas das Gebräm/ leucht trefflich schön herfür/
    Der Um- und Fürhang ist vermengt mit Silber Zier/   40
Die Spiegel in der Mitt/ darinn man sich kan sehen/
Und alles hin und her/ was im Gemach geschehen/

When, after having said hello, the newcomer sat down,
She entertained herself the whole time by talking
    About her son who was so industrious
    That one would have thought he was already twenty years old,
Though he was not quite four; she could not praise enough   5
The diligence he showed at school
    And how well he studied his ABCs.
    "Already at daybreak," she said, "he thinks only of school.
My husband is delighted that he will become a medical doctor.
Not just an ordinary one, but one who would ride in a carriage drawn by six horses."10
    She had continued like this for a long time when the door opened,
    And in came four [women] all at once.
The one who had come earlier acted as if she did not notice
That anyone was there; since the wine had strengthened her,
    She just went on for another half hour
    About her amazing son.   15
Only when she thought it was time to leave
Did she excuse herself, saying that she had not noticed
    The other women there; and politely wished
    The "Six-Week Lady" a healthy churching
And thereupon left. As soon as she was gone,   20
The group of women began to ask:
    "Who is this great lady, who acts so proud
    That she did not think any of us worthy of her notice?
We are as good as she; we surely can show off, too,
And bedeck ourselves with jewelry as she does.   25
    Who knows who has the most money? Who knows if the merchant
    Has been paid for her dress? Who knows if her jewelry
Is of good quality?" And all of this complaining
Must have gone on for half an hour, if not longer.
    [43] After this, one of [the women] began by saying   30
    That she had just come from another lying-in;
There she had seen something which she could not possibly put into words;
Something the likes of which she had never seen in all her days.
    "The woman sat in bed resplendent as a picture," she said.
    "The chamber was sumptuously appointed.   35
The bed was brand-new, crafted from walnut;
The canopy above shimmered all over with beautiful colors;
    Decorated with atlas silk, immaculate and marvelous.
    The hangings were embroidered with silver thread.
The mirror in the middle of the room brilliantly reflecting   40
All that happened in the chamber,

Dz gleichwol ziemlich groß: Das Kind ist auch geschmückt/
Mit überschöner Zier/ es hat mich recht erquickt.
Ich weiß wol/ wo es war/ ich werd auch zu ihr kommen/
So fieng die ander an/ ich hab mirs fürgenommen/
    Nur daß ich auch einmal beschaue solchen Pracht   5
    Darvon mir schon so viel Erzehlens ward gemacht/
Ich wundre gleichwol sehr/ ich weiß wol wen ihr meinet
So sprach die dritt hernach/ daß solcher Pracht erscheinet/
    Sie dürfftens je wol nicht/ sie sind noch junge Leut/
    Der Kinder werden viel/ das Gut reicht nicht so weit/   10
Sie hat zwar ihrem Mann zehn in (sic) zwölf tausend Gülden
An Wahren zugebracht/ und theils auch böse Schulden/
    Er selber hat auch was von Eltern angeerbt/
    Allein/ durch solchen Pracht/ wird bald das Gut verderbt/
Ich habe wol mehr gesehen ihres gleichen   15
Sie musten aber bald von ihren Gütern weichen;
    Ich halte mehr darauff wenn Gold im Kasten stecket
    Als wann es hin und her an Wänden ist gekleckt/
Ich könte mir auch wol viel schöne neue Sachen/
Ring/ Ketten/ und was mehr/ auch Kleider lassen machen/   20
    Ich wüste wol wie man ein Haus beziehren soll/
    Allein ich hab nicht Lust/ und mir gefällts nicht wol:
Ich sage noch einmal/ das Geld in meinem Kasten/
[44] Das lieb ich zehnmal mehr/ so kan ich sicher rasten
    Geb ichs für solche Wahr/ die reysen mit der Zeit/   25
    So hab ich nichts hernach/ als langes HertzenLeid.
Was diese hat gesagt/ ward ihr bald widerleget/
Von einer in der Rey. Allein in dem sich reget
    Das kleine Wiegen Kind/ mit hefftigem Geschrey/
    So wolten dem nicht mehr/ die Reden kommen bey/   30
Der an der Kammer Thür sich zwar mit grossen Sorgen
Biß in die dritte Stund gehalten hat verborgen/
    Drümb/ machet er sich fort/ und zeichnet fleissig auff/
    Deß lieben Weiber-Volcks Kindbett-Gesprächs-Verlauff.

Frau Barbara: Das mag wol ein tausend Gast gewesen seyn/ der diesen Saalpat-
er gereimet hat; Man hat sich traun wol fürzusehen/ daß einen die arglistigen
Haußgenossen nicht außtragen/ und mit der Warheit ins Geschrey bringen. **Das
Kinder-Mägden sagt:** Hertzen Junge Frau/ es war der Praeceptor/ und hatte
eine Schreibe-Tafel in der Hand/ und horchte so leise mit der Muhmen zu/ was

Which was quite large.
The child was gorgeously adorned, which truly delighted me."
The other [woman] spoke: "I know who this is. I, too, plan to visit her,
If only so I can see the luxury about which I have heard so much."
"Still, I am amazed, I know whom you mean,"   5
Said the third. "Such sumptuous display . . .
They really shouldn't have done it; they are still such a young couple.
There will be many children, and the estate won't go that far!
    Although she brought twelve thousand gulden
    In goods, she also brought some bad debts.   10
    He himself inherited a little from his parents;
    But the estate will soon be ruined by such splendor.
I have seen the likes of them before,
Who before long had to leave their estates.
    I think it is wiser to keep one's gold in the coffers   15
    Than to hang it here and there all over the walls.
I, too, could buy many beautiful new things,
Rings, necklaces, and what not; I could have dresses made;
    I certainly know how to decorate a home.
    But I neither want to nor does it please me when others do so.   20
Still, I say it again, I love having gold in my coffers ten times more.
Then I have peace of mind.
    [44] If I were to spend it for [such] wares—they have no lasting value;
    And thus I would have nothing afterwards but a long heartache."
Whatever this [last one] had said was soon contradicted   25
By one of the other [women]. But at this moment the baby stirred
    With a loud wail.
    So it was impossible for any more remarks to be overheard by
The man who had been hiding behind the bedroom door
In great discomfort for more than three hours.   30
    So he took off and diligently wrote down
    The course of the dear womenfolk's confinement conversation.

Frau Barbara: "That must have been an eavesdropper[103] who rhymed this cutting nonsense; you really need to be watchful that no mean-spirited member of the household gossips about you and, by telling the truth, brings you into ill repute."
The nursemaid says: "Oh, dear me, dear young woman, it was the tutor who did it; he was carrying a little slate tablet in his hand. With the *Muhme* he listened

---

[103] "Tausend Gast, " "Tausendsassa": a wild person.

ihr hie schwatzet: Wie ich aber die Thüre anfieng auffzumachen/ da sprungen sie
gantz sachte in die Küche hinein/ und machten solche hinter sich zu. **Fr. Wöchn.**
Ich gedacht es ihm wol/ daß was dran seyn müste. Und nun soll mir der Diebi-
sche Praeceptor von Stund zum Hause hinauß. Mägdgen gehe/ und laß ihn
herein kommen/ ich will ihn so außfenstern/ daß kein Hund ein Stück Brot von
ihm nehmen soll. **Der Praeceptor kömpt und hat den Hut in die Hand:** Was
macht ihr Flegel draussen/ könt ihr nicht auff ewre Stuben hinscheren/ da ihr
was verlohren habt? Warumb last ihr meine Kinder so herumlauffen/ und wartet
eures Thuns ab? Packet euch vor meinen Auge zum Hause hinauß! **Praecept.**
Ach Hertzen Fr. Magist: Ich bin jetzund allererst auß dem Collegio gekommen/
da ich eines und das andere in meine Schreib-Tafel annotiret gehabt/ welches ich
im spatziren auff dem Saale durchlaß: Ich kan ja nicht darwieder/ daß die Kinder von der Stube entlauffen seyn [45] ich nam sie flugs nach der Mahlzeit mit mir
hinauff/ und gab ihnen was für außwendig zu lernen: So sind/ Gott erbarm es!
sie heimlich außgerissen; da ich doch vermeynete / daß ich die Thüre feste zu-
geschlossen hatt. Ich will jetzund flugs mit hinauff nehmen/ und besser Achtung
auff sie han: Vergebet es mir doch dißmal. **Fr. Wöchn.** Wer hat euch Hundsfott
geheissen/ daß ihr ewers Beliebens nach in die Lection solt gehen? halte ich euch
darümb Tisch und Stuben frey? daß euch der Teuffel hole! Kan ich doch für den
Tisch alleine wol wöchentlich fünff Ordt kriegen/ so ferne ich nur Tisch-Bursche
halten wolte: Ingleichen müste mir auch ja die Stube wol Jährlich 24. Thaler
gelten/ die ich euch Lumpenhund ümbsonst eingeräumet habe. **Praecept.** Habe
ich doch die Stube nicht allein für mich zugebrauchen/ sondern die Kinder den
gantzen Tag über bey mir über den Halse: Darzu kan ich mich ja auch kaum über
den Tisch satt fressen/ weil ich immer den Kindern / einem nach dem andern
vorlegen muß/ discurs mit ihnen führen/ und allerhand Sachen unter Essens ex-
aminiren muß; nach dem ich vorher gedecket und zuletzte wiederumb auffheben
muß; So verdiene ich allein mein Brodt ja nicht mit Sünden/ sondern wird mir
sauer gnug das bißgen Essen zu erwerben: Solt ich nur gar miteinander kein Collegium darzu halten/ so were ich ja der elendeste Mensch: sonderlich/ weil der
Herr Hospes es nicht gestatten will/ daß ich noch etwa einen oder ein paar Knaben darneben informirete/ und also etwa eine kleine Zubuße am Gelde kriegte.
Fr. Wöchn: Halt das Maul/ du Galgendieb/ oder ich wil dir die Wochen Kanne
an den Schabe-Hals werffen/ daß du verzweiffeln solst: Hastu Schlingel nicht
vergangen Weynachten eine Reichstthaler/ ein neu Hembde/ und vier Hälßgen
zum Heiligen Christ gekriegt? Weiter meynestu auch etwan/ daß ich es nicht
wisse/ daß die junge Magd ümbsonst dein Geräth mit wasche? Wer gibt wol die
Seiffe und andere Sachen darzu/ als ich? Gehe auß meinem Angesicht: Ich will
es dem Herrn wacker sagen/ wenn er wird zu Hause kommen/ wie du mit mein-
en Kindern ümbgehest: Du hast heute früh einem bald den Kopff eingeschlagen/
daß er es wol in acht Tagen nicht überwinden wird. [46] Gedenckstu nicht / daß
ichs erfahre/ wie du so unbarmhertzig auff die armen Bübigen zuschmeist? Du
hast vergangen dem andern einen Schilling gegeben/ daß ihme/ bey meiner

behind the door to hear what you all said in here. However, when I started to open the door, they both stepped back and very softly stole into the kitchen and closed the door behind them." **The young mother:** "I suspected him, thinking he had to have something to do with it. And right now, immediately, this thieving tutor must leave the house. Maid, go and fetch him; I am going to dress him down so that no dog will take a piece of bread from him." **The tutor arrives, hat in hand:** "What are you doing out there, you lout? Can't you stay in your room where you belong? Why do you let my children run wild and mind only your own business? Get yourself out of my sight and out of my house!" **Tutor:** "Oh, dear Frau *Magister*, I just came back from the *Collegium*,[104] where I had to note some things down on my writing tablet, which I was reading as I was walking in the hall. I really cannot help it that the children ran from the room. **[45]** I had taken them up with me right after lunch, and I gave them something to memorize. God have mercy, they secretly stole away while I was sure that I had locked the door. I will take them up with me immediately and pay better attention to them. Please forgive me just one more time." **The young mother:** "Who told you, you son of a bitch, that you could go and read whenever you felt like it? Do I keep you and give you free room and board for this? Go to hell! I could make money[105] if I only needed someone to serve at table. Likewise, your room, which I let you have for free, you dog, would bring me twenty-four gold pieces a year." **Tutor:** "If only I had the room for my own use! But the children are on top of me all day long! What's more, I barely get enough to eat because I always have to serve the children their food and teach them and test them on all sorts of things. After this I have to lay the table, I have to serve them and clear the table after the meal. All this is to say, this is how I earn my bread, certainly not by sinning, but rather by trying in great misery to earn a little bit to eat. If, in addition to all of this, I cannot go the *Collegium*, I would be most wretched, doubly so because my master will not permit me to tutor a few more boys, which might get me a bit more money." **The young mother:** "Shut your trap, you scoundrel, or I'll throw the birthing pitcher at your scabby neck so that you'll despair over it. Last Christmas, didn't you, you good-for-nothing, get a whole gold piece, a new shirt, and four collars? And furthermore, don't think for a moment that I don't know that the young maid is washing your underwear for nothing along with the household laundry! Whose soap and whatever else do you think she is using, if not mine? Get out of my sight! When the master comes home, I'm going to tell him how you deal with my children. This morning you practically bashed in the head of one of them so that he will not get over it for at least a week! **[46]** Do you think I will not find out how pitilessly you have beaten the poor little boy? And recently you spanked the other one so hard that, by my soul, the welts on his ass were as big as a

---

[104] University.
[105] "Ordt": money.

Seel/ die Schmielen auff den Arsche Daumens-dicke lagen. **Praeceptor:** Je nun du lieber Gott/ der Herr will es haben/ daß ich soll wacker zuschmeissen; und ihr wollet es nicht haben? Nach weme soll ich mich denn nun richten? und weme soll ich es recht machen? Ich wüste ja nicht/ daß ich jemaln ein Kind so sehr geschmissen hette/ als ihr es groß machet. **Fr. Wöchn.** Hörstu nicht/ Kerl/ packe dich zur Stube hinauß/ und gehe mit den Kindern in die Schul: Und wirstu sie noch einmal so geißeln/ ich kan es wol hören/ ich will fürm Schlappermente zum Bette herauß springen/ und deine Kolbe zulausen/ daß du dein Lebe an ein Weib gedencken solst. **Praeceptor abit. Fr. Draute:** Hertze liebe Fr. Mag erzürnet euch doch nicht so sehr: Das Raben-Geschmeiß macht es nicht anders; Ich habe mich selber mit meinem Galgendiebe vorgestern so zumartert/ daß ich gezittert und gebebet habe. Der plumpe Dieb hatte meinem Gottfriedgen eine Maulschelle gegeben/ daß die rothe Suppe hernach gegangen war: welches ich gar wol verspürete/ weil dem Kinde die Backen über Tische noch sehr geschwollen waren: und das Hälßgen hin und wieder mit Blut besprenget war. Man thut fast nicht besser/ als daß man die Teuffels Kerl gehen lässet/ und die Kinder der Marter überhebet. **Fr. Liese:** Hievon weiß ich Gott Lob wenig zu sagen/ ich behalte die Unkosten ein/ die man so unnöthig auff die nachlässigen Tag-Diebe wendet/ daß ich meinen Kindern dermaleins ein mehrers mitgeben könne. Und was bringet die Teuffeley auch sonderlichs ein/ wenn man sie studiren lässet? Ich weiß mir keinen Nutzen drauß zu nehmen. **Fr. Barb.** Ja ihr habt gut zu sagen/ eure Kinder seynd nunmehr erwachsen: Ich höre/ daß eure älteste Tochter schon versprochen ist. **Fr. Liese:** Ja liebe Junge Frau/ sie ist jo noch ein Kind: Ich werde sie ja nicht so früh vergeben. Sie hat noch lange zu warten. Mit meines Nachbars Töchtern möchte es wol bald eher reiffe Zeit seyn: Es sind fürwar grosse Strutzen; und wachsen/ Gott gesegne sie/ daher wie ein Reh/ und sehen nur immer [47] wo der Freyer mag herkommen. **Fr. Draute:** Hingegen sind auch faule Mehren/ damit ein Mann übel wird versehen werden. Die kleinen Butter-Fischgen lassen sich fast besser an/ es sind doch so niedliche Dingergen/ daß einem das Hertz im Leibe lacht/ wenn man sie ansihet. **Fr. Barb.** Was will man von der Fr. Kleisterinne ihr älteste Tochter sagen? daß sie soll zu Fall kommen seyn/ und draussen auffm Dorffe in die Wochen liegen/ darzu sie ein paar Bauren zu Gevattern gebeten/ die sie vorher wol mit den Hindern nicht hette angesehen. **Fr. Liese.** So strafft der liebe Gott den Hochmuth: Das Ding hielte sich so knappe/ und kriegte bald da von den Kerln spendiret: **Fr. Barb.** Das muß jetzund alles wieder fort: Wie du kommest so gehestu: sie soll all ihr Geschmeide schon versetzt und vertrödelt haben: Ich kriegte vergangen ein wunderschönes Körbigen zu sehen/ das ein Weib herumb trug/ welches ich gar wol weiß/ daß sie es mit ihren eigenen Händen gekünstelt hat. **Fr. Liese:** Ja das Raben Aaß soll sich sehr wol haben können behelffen mit allerhand Hoffart. **Fr. Draute:** Habt ihr denn auch was davon gehöret/ daß die stoltze Knüppel-Magd Fuchsgrillgen/ oder Fiddelkatzgen soll von Studenten bekrochen seyn/ mit welchen sie reißauß genommen/ und nach Eulenburg hin soll margiret seyn? Ich kan es zwar für keine gewisse

thumb!" **Tutor:** "Well, for heaven's sake! The master told me to hit them hard, and you don't want me to? Whom should I obey? And whom can I please? Moreover, I really can't remember ever hitting a child as hard as you're complaining about." **The young mother:** "Are you deaf, you jerk? Get out of here and take the children to school. And if you torture them again like that . . . I assure you, I will hear about it. I swear I will jump out of bed so quickly[106] and let you have it that you will remember this woman forever!" **Tutor leaves. Frau Draute:** "Dearest Frau *Magister*, calm down. This riff-raff is always like that. The day before yesterday I had so much trouble with the rogue at my house that I was shaking all over. The good-for-nothing thieving brute hit my little Gottfried in the mouth so hard that he bled. I could feel it because the child's cheek was still swollen at dinnertime, and there was blood all over his little neck. You would almost do better to fire these devils and end the children's martyrdom." **Frau Liese:** "Praise the Lord, there is little I can say about this; I am saving the money otherwise spent on these lazy thieves so that I will be able to leave more to my children when the time comes. And what good is this foolishness if [the children] go to the university? I just cannot see any use in it." **Frau Barbara:** "Well, that's easy for you to say! Your children are all grown by now. And I hear that your oldest daughter is already promised." **Frau Liese:** "Yes, dear young lady, even though she is still a mere child. I won't let her go too early. She has quite a bit of time yet to wait. Unlike my neighbor's daughters, for whom it may well be high time. They are getting as big as horses and truly growing like weeds, always on the lookout for men coming courting." **[47] Frau Draute:** "Still, they are lazy creatures, whom no man would want to be saddled with. The younger girls[107] seem to do a bit better; they are so cute that it is a delight to look at them." **Frau Barbara:** "What can we say about Frau Kleister's oldest daughter? That she has gotten into trouble, and had to deliver somewhere out in a village not far from here. She asked some peasants to stand as godparents, people whom previously she would not have looked at with her ass." **Frau Liese:** "That is how the good Lord punishes arrogance: the young thing was so conceited that here and there she let men buy her drinks." **Frau Barbara:** "This will not last; what goes around comes around. Rumor has it that she has already hawked all of her jewels. The other day I saw a woman carrying a really beautiful little basket; I know Frau Kleister's daughter made it with her own hands." **Frau Liese:** "Yes, this stupid ass is said to know how to help herself in spite of her arrogance." **Frau Draute:** "Did you hear that the bitch of a foxy cat had students crawl all over her, and that she ran away to Eulenburg with them? I don't know this for certain, but I do know it as hearsay."

---

[106] "Schlapperment": speedily, quickly.
[107] "Butter" = "Fischgen, Backfische": teenagers, young girls.

Warheit außgeben/ doch habe ich es von Höresagen. **Fr. Wöchn.** Sie kommen doch alle einmal wieder in der Stadt herein/ wenn sie sich außgeschämet haben/ und sind darnach die redlichsten Weiber wieder/ welchen kein Henger was sagen darff. Denn wer darff es jener Nußbäumin wol vorwerffen/ daß sie in ihren Jungfer Stande draussen auff ihrem Gute einen Sohn gebohren/ der jetzund bey den Bauren ein Gänse-Hirte ist? **Fr. Liese:** Das beste ist hier/ daß man keine Kirchen-Buße thun darff/ sonst würde der Henger ein Schelm werden: Wenn man allen Leuten zu Schimpff und Spott unter eine ganze geschlagene Predigt für den Altar sitzen solte. **Frau Barb:** Ja/ wo wolte man zum Teuffel Ammen her kriegen/ wenn der Unrath auffkäme? Sollten doch wol alle unsere Kinder/ die wir allhier gebähren/ über der Kirchen-Buße drauff gehen. [48] Wer nicht will redlich bleiben/ mag immer hinhuren: Sie werden wol einmal müssen auffhören/ und satt werden/ wenn sie es lange genug getrieben haben. In unser Nachbarschafft ist auch so eine Historie neulich vorgegangen/ daß man ein Jungfer Kindgen bekommen hat/ wiewol es noch zur Zeit vertuschet wird/ weil sie das Kind heimlich zur Stadt hinauß gepartiret haben/ und es auffm Lande von einer Gärtnerin saugen und aufferziehen lassen. **Fr. Wöchn.** Wo denn? Die den Rastrum feile haben? **Fr. Barb.** Ich mag nicht viel sagen. **Fr. Liese:** Liebe Junge Frau/ was schwatzet man denn jetzund von dem Rastrum? Ich hör er soll eine Pfennig höher steigen/ und nach diesen sieben Pfennig gelten. **Fr. Barb.** Das will ich wol glauben: Geben sie doch die andere Biere so unerhört theuer/ die anderswo/ und zwar an geringern Oertern gemachet werden: Warumb sol denn Leipzig als eine vornehme Stadt ihr eigen Bier nicht hoch halten? Vielleichte wird es alsdenn auch von vornehmen Leuten getruncken; da es sonsten dem gemeinen Manne kaum gut genug gewesen. **Fr. Draute:** Je Fotze/ schlägt es doch schon drey: Ich muß traun gehn/ ehe ich einen Außputzer kriege: **Fr. Barb:** Wartet ein wenig/ wir wollen mit/ es ist nunmehr auch zeit. **Fr. Liese:** O fett Fleisch/ hette ich doch bald auff meine Schürtze getretten/ und wer in dem auff die Erde nidergeschlagen als ein Ochse. **Fr. Draute:** Nun behüt euch Gott/ liebe Fr. Magist: Lebet wol/ und werdet fein starck; **Fr. Wöchn.** Habt doch fleissigen Danck/ daß ihr mich nicht verlassen/ und jetzund besucht habt. Ihr hettet ja noch wol ein wenig können verziehen/ wenn ihr nur selber gewolt hettet. **Fr. Barb.** Ach nein; wir haben Fürwar Zeit: Guten Tag Muhme; Bleibt jo drinne beym Kinde; Ihr dörfft unsertwegen nicht mit herauß gehen. **Die Muhme.** Schlaff Kindgen hiere/ der Vater geht zum Biere/ vertrinckt ein Groschen oder viere/ Die Mutter geht zum Weine/ vertrinckt ein Groschen oder neune/ und läst mein Kindgen alleine. Schlaff Kindgen schlaff/ der Vater hüt die Schaaff: Die Mutter hüt die Lämmergen/ bringt dem Kind ein Semmelgen.

The young mother: "In the end they all come back to town, when they have gotten over being ashamed. Then they are the most virtuous women ever, whom no one is allowed to criticize. For who says anything now about the matron Nussbaum, who, in her youth, went and gave birth to a son out in the country, where he stayed and now works as a gooseherd?" **Frau Liese:** "The best thing around here is that you don't have to do public penance in church, otherwise the devil would look a fool when one would have to sit in front of the altar for the length of the sermon, ridiculed and mocked by everyone." **Frau Barbara:** "So where the devil would we get nursemaids if all this garbage became known? All of our children born would die without help because of [church] penance. **[48]** Whoever does not want to remain honorable can always go and whore around. At some point they will have to quit and be satisfied when they've done it long enough. In our neighborhood there was a story going around about a young woman who had a baby, even though it was covered up; she spirited the baby out of town to be nursed and raised by a gardener woman." **The young mother:** "Where? Was it the *Rastrum* [beer] seller?" **Frau Barbara:** "I really don't want to say." **Frau Liese:** "Dear young woman, what's that about *Rastrum*? I heard it's going up a penny, and after that it will cost seven cents." **Frau Barbara:** "I can believe it; they sell the other beers at such unheard-of high prices, even though they are actually brewed at inferior places. Why shouldn't the proud city of Leipzig support its own beer? Maybe then even the well-to-do would drink what used to be hardly good enough for the common folk." **Frau Draute:** "Well, my goodness, [108] it's already three o'clock! I really have to hurry home before I get into trouble." **Frau Barbara:** "Wait a minute, we'll leave with you; it is really time." **Frau Liese:** "Oh, I'm such a fat clod, I almost tripped over my apron and fell on my face like an ox." **Frau Draute:** "Now may the Lord keep you, Frau *Magisterin*. Farewell and get good and strong." **The young mother:** "Thank you all very much for not abandoning me, and coming to visit me now. You could have come at a later time, if you had wished." **Frau Barbara:** "Oh no, we truly had the time; Good-bye, *Muhme*. Be sure to stay with the baby; don't leave the room on our account. *Muhme* sings a lullaby:

> "Sleep, little child.
> Father goes drinking beer,
> Drinks away a penny or four.
> Mother goes drinking wine,
> Drinks away a penny or nine.
> Sleep, little child, sleep,
> Father guards the sheep.
> Mother guards the little lambs
> And bring the child a little bun."

---

[108] "Je Fotze": oh, my cunt!

[49] Die fünffte Abhandlung/ oder
Gänse=Geschnatter/

**Frau Wöchnerin. Fr. Pfarrnerin. Frau Secretarien. Fr.
Apotheckerinn. Muhme**

Fr. Pfarrnerin: Guten Tag herein liebe Fr. Gevatterin/ was macht ihr mit eurem
lieben Mäußgen? **Fr. Secretarien:** Gott grüsse Euch Fr. Gevattterin/ seyd jhr
auch noch wol auff mit meinem Patgen? **Fr. Apoteckerin:** Viel Glücks herein Fr.
Gevatterin/ seyd ihr auch noch fein wol auff? Vergebet mir doch/ daß ich euch so
späte besuche: Ich solte billich viel eher gekommen seyn; so hat sich zu Hause immer eines und das ander im Wege gefunden/ das mich verhindert hat. **Fr. Wöchn:**
Je/ je/ je/ Ihr Hertzlieben Fr. Gevatterinnen/ ich hette mich euer umb all die
Wunder jetzund wol nicht versehn/ sonsten hette ich ein wenig auffräumen lassen: es siehet so garstig auß in der Stube/ daß ich mich selber schämen muß: Ver-
zeihets mir doch jo umb Gottes willen; und messet mir doch die Schuld nicht zu/
sondern meiner faulen Muhmen: Ich will mich ein andermal besser auff euch
schicken. Seyd doch alle von Hertzen willkommen/ ihr lieben Fr. Gevatterinnen/
und setzt euch doch alle ein wenig bey mir nieder/ und schwatzet doch ein bißgen
mit mir. **Fr. Pfarrn.** Wir sind nicht müde/ und kommen von Sitzen erstlich her.
Fr. Wöchnerin: O ihr möget leichte so müde seyn/ daß ihr euch kaum außruhen
könnet. Liebe Frau Secret. Fr. Gevatterin wolt ich sagen/ ich verirre mich noch
immer/ setzet euch doch ein wenig besser heran. **Fr. Secret.** Bin ich doch nahe
gnug/ sonsten hindere ich die Fr. Apoteckerin: **Fr. Apotheck:** O nein/ rücket ja
ein wenig besser herzu/ ich will euch nicht schwartz machen. **Fr. Secr.** Das will
ich freylich nicht hoffen. [50] Nun/ wenn es denn ja so seyn soll/ so verdencket
mich doch nicht drümb. **Fr. Pfarrn.** Liebe Frau Gevatterin/ ist auch sonsten jemand bey euch gwesen/ der euch besuchet hätte? Ich selbst hette wol sollen eher
kommen/ so kan ich auch nicht alleweile abmüssigen. Ist auch die Bade-Mutter
bey euch gewesen/ und hat nach dem Kindgen gesehen? **Fr. Wöchn.** O Ja/ sie war
noch frühe da/ und wickelte es auff und ein/ und versprach/ sie wolte morgen
gewiß wiederkommen und es baden. **Fr. Secr.** Was habt iher füre eine Wehe-
Mutter gehabt/ **Fr. Gevatterin?** **Fr. Wöchn.** Mutter Dorthen: Es ist gar eine hüp-
sche Frau/ sie ist fein bethuelich und Diensthafftig/ und läßt sich nichts verdries-
sen/ ob es schon lange währet. **Fr. Apoteck:** Ja ich muß es selber bekennen; weil
ich sie nunmehr auch einmal oder neune gebraucht habe in meinen Nöthen: Sie
kan so fein schwatzen und trösten; so weiß sie auch sehr viel Mittel; ich halte sie
vor einen halben Doctor/ so gewisse helffen ihre Sachen. **Fr. Pfarrn.** Ich weiß
nicht anders/ als daß sie Fr. Justine auch gebraucht. Fr. Gevatterin; ist diese auch
bey euch gewesen/ und hat euch etwan besucht? **Fr. Wöchn.** Ja wol/ sie bleibet
nicht auß wo es was giebet: Das Muster hat mich ja durchgezogen mit ihren

[49] The Fifth Chapter, or
Cackling of Geese.

The young mother; Frau Pastor; Frau Secretary; Frau Apothecary;[109] *Muhme*

Frau Pastor: "Good day, dear *Gevatterin*. How is our little mouse?" **Frau Secretary:** "God greet you, dear *Gevatterin*. Are you and my godchild still well?" **Frau Apothecary:** "All best wishes to you, dear godmother! Are you feeling well? Please forgive me for being so late in paying my visit. I should have come much sooner, but at the house this and that always got in the way, which kept me from stopping by." **The young mother:** "Dear, dearest godmothers, I did not expect you at all at this time. Had I done so, I would have had the parlor picked up a bit. It looks so awful that I feel ashamed. Please forgive me, for goodness sake, and do not blame me for it but rather [blame] my lazy *Muhme*. Next time I will be better prepared to receive you. That said, a hearty welcome to all of you, dear lady godmothers; sit down a while by my side and gossip a bit with me." **Frau Pastor:** "We're not at all tired, coming as we do from having sat for a while." **The young mother:** "Oh, you might well be so tired, that you can rest a little anyway. Dear Frau Secretary, . . . I meant to say Frau Godmother . . . I just can't get used to it; sit down a little closer." **Frau Secretary:** "I'm close enough; otherwise I will get in the way of Frau Apothecary." **Frau Apothecary:** "Oh, no, not at all, move a bit closer together; I am not contagious."[110] **Frau Secretary:** [50] "I certainly hope not! Well, if it must be, don't think ill of me because of it." **Frau Pastor:** "Dear lady, has anyone else been here with you for a visit? I should have come earlier myself, but I simply could not make the time. Has the nurse[111] come to check on your baby?" **The young mother:** "Oh, yes, she came early and changed the diapers, and promised to come again tomorrow to give the baby a bath." **Frau Secretary:** "Who was your midwife, Lady Godmother?" **The young mother:** "Mother Dorthen; she is a pretty woman, industrious, calm, and eager to please. Nor is she easily annoyed no matter how long it [the delivery] takes." **Frau Apothecary:** "Yes, I have to agree. If I have used her once, I have used her nine times when I had to deliver. She has such a nice way of talking and offering comfort. And she knows many remedies; I consider her almost a physician; her preparations are always quite effective." **Frau Pastor:** "I only know that Frau Justine also uses her, Lady Godmother; has she come to see you already?" **The young mother:** "Yes, indeed; she always shows up if there is something happening. The biddy

---

[109] Also druggist, chemist.
[110] "Nicht schwarz machen": not blacken someone; rubbing off on them.
[111] "Bademutter": nurse, midwife.

spitzsinnigen Wörten: sie sagte ich müste viel Brandtwein getruncken haben/
weil das liebe Kindgen so ein hell Gesichte hette; und was sie sonsten mehr dahl-
ete. **Fr. Pfarrnerin:** Ich gedachte es wol/ drümb fragte ich: Die Kluncker-Mutze
mochte sich doch nur umb sich selbst bekümmern. Sie meynet/ weil sie immer
viel Brandtwein trincket/ daß es ein ander auch thun müste: Sie möchte ihre
Töchter in acht nehmen/ daß sie sich so mit den Kerlen nicht rissen: Sie kommen
mir wie rechte Raben-Huren vor/ und lauffen auff allen Ablaßen herumb/ und
zwingen fast die Kerl darzu/ daß sie ihnen Zeichen lösen müssen. Vergangen war
die eine auch auff die Pfingst-Wiese und hatte Maul-Affen feil: Von der andern
will man gar schwatzen/ daß sie eine Nacht über draussen geblieben sey/ und mit
einem Huren-Jäger in den Busch gekrochen: Da sie denn [51] zu Lohne wie sie
wieder umbgekehret/ und nach ihrem Zelt hat wandern wollen/ ein Racketgen
unter den Pelz soll bekommen haben/ davon der ganze Plunder versenget worden:
Drüber sie grausam angefangen zu schreyen/ daß die ganze Vogelstange/ wenns
nur wahr ist/ soll gezittert haben. **Fr. Secr.** So recht/ die Teuffels-Bälge werden ja
noch eine Vogel-Wiese drauß machen/ dencke ich; Aber das Schelmzeug bietet es
in der Stadt auß. **Fr. Apotheckerin.** O/ da ist der lange Pfeffer und ungestossene
Saffran wieder gut zu; da werden die Materialisten wieder was zu lösen kriegen;
immer ein paar dreyer nach den andern/ daß es pufft. Auff diese Art soll auch
Frau Annen ihr niedlichs Bißgen/ das rantzigte Muster/ ihre Frucht abgetrieben
haben. **Fr. Wöchn.** Fr. Annen ihre Tochter? Je so höre ich nun allererst/ daß die
Mutter wol nicht viel besser mag seyn. Die hönische Pätze/ ist auch heute bey mir
für die Wochen gewesen/ da sie ihr schnepsisches Maul über alles muste haben;
Sie kan ja die Leute durchziehen. Bald verwunderte sie sich über mein Wochen-
Geräthe; bald stach ihr dieses/ und ein anders in die Augen/ und bekümmerte
sich umb alle ungelegte Eyer. **Fr. Apoteckerin.** Das ist ihr alte Manier/ daß sie
nur derentwegen zu den Wöchnerinnen gehet/ damit sie nach was neues gaffe/
und hernach was außzutragen habe: Ich habe sie auch mit Schaden lernen können; Sie ist so ein tückisches und hoffärtiges Aaß/ daß sie nicht weiß/ ob sie eine
grüssen oder dancken soll. **Ein Knabe schreyet: Fr. Wöchn.** Das Gott in hohen
Himmel erbarm! was ist wieder da? es wird gewisse der Nickel droben meine
Kinder wieder was zu pantzerfegen. **Das Kinder-Mägdgen kömpt rein/ und sag-**
et: Ach nein/ es hat schon fünffe geschlagen/ die Kinder sind schon lange auß der
Schule kommen: Der Praeceptor kömpt jetzund gleich auß dem Post-Hause wieder; und hat Jungfer Sybillgen einen Brieff auß Berlin von ihrem Liebsten mitge-
bracht; Der Vater schlug jetzund Friederichen/ daß er so sehr schrie. **Fr. Wöchn.**
Was hat denn das [52] arme Kind gethan/ daß es so grosse Püffe kriegte? schlug
er doch/ Gott behüte uns/ wie auff einen Mehl-Sack loß; und mag ihm wol eine

really annoyed me with her sharp tongue. She suggested that I must have drunk a lot of brandy because my baby has such a fair face. And whatever else she had to say." **Frau Pastor:** "I thought so, that is why I asked. The silly goose should worry about herself. She thinks that because she always drinks a lot of brandy, everyone else does, too. She should watch that her daughters don't hang out too much with the guys. They strike me as real whores, practically forcing [young men] to buy them favors. Recently one of them was seen hanging out at the fair at Pentecost.[112] The other is said to have stayed out all night fooling around under the bushes with one of those whore-chasers. [51] Then, when she wanted to return to her tent, a firecracker supposedly got under her dress and singed the whole mess. Because of this, she began to scream so horribly that the whole bird pole[113]—if it is true—is supposed to have shaken." **Frau Secretary:** "Serves her right; this devil's brood will surely make a whorehouse out of it [the place of the bird pole];[114] these foolish girls offer themselves to the whole town." **Frau Apothecary:** "Oh, dear, and then the long pepper and unground saffron will be needed for that [to abort];[115] then the apothecaries will have something to sell; one little one after the other. It has been said that Frau Anna's sweet young thing, the spoiled little bitch, aborted her 'fruit' this way." **The young mother:** "Frau Anna's daughter? That's the first I've heard about it! They say the mother is not much better than the daughter. This mean gossip also was here today running off at the mouth about everything. She can really go on about people. First she wondered about the stuff on my changing table; then this, then that caught her fancy; she was sticking her nose into everything where it did not belong."[116] **Frau Apothecary:** "That's the way she is! That is the only reason why she visits new mothers; so that she can gape at anything new and afterwards have something to blab about all over town. She has been a pain to me in the past; she is such a mean-spirited, conniving ass, who never knows if she should say hello or thank you." **A boy screams. The young mother:** "God in heaven have mercy! What is it now? It must be the devil upstairs beating my children again." **The maid enters and says:** "Oh, no, it is already five o'clock; the children have been out of school for a long time. The tutor just returned from the post office, where he picked up a love letter for the maid, Sybil, from her sweetheart over in Berlin. It was the father who just hit Friedrich so hard that he screamed." **The young mother:** [52] "What did the poor child do to deserve such hard blows? He [the father] whaled at him as if

---

[112] "Maulaffen feil halten": to hang out, stand around gaping.

[113] "Vogelstange": high pole in the center of town to which a bird was fastened to be shot down at *Vogelschiessen*, an annual summer celebration.

[114] Play on the word "*vogeln, vögeln*": to screw.

[115] On abortion, see John M. Riddle, *Eve's Herbs: A History of Contraception and Abortion in the West* (Cambridge, MA: Harvard University Press, 1997).

[116] "Sich um ungelegte Eier kümmern": worry about unlaid eggs = none of one's business.

Rippen im Leibe zerschlagen haben: Denn wenn er kömpt so kömpt er gut. **Kind-er-Mägdgen:** Er lieff auff der Gasse herumb mit den Strassen-Jungen/ und hat einem Bauer Mägdgen einen Häring auß der Hand gerissen und lebendig gefressen. **Fr. Wöchn.** Je/ Gott verzeihe mirs! ist das keine Ursache/ daß er derentwegen das Kind so sehr schlägt? was ists nunmehr? die Kinder sind muthwillig/ weil sie noch jung und frisch seyn/ das weiß man wol. Vielleichte hats der Vater viel ärger in seiner Kindheit gemachet. **Fr. Secr.** Was hilfft es; mein Kerl verfährt auch so mit meinen Kindern/ und wenn ich ein Wort drümb rede/ so will es ihn noch wol verschnuppen. Sie gedencken nicht zu rücke/ daß sie durch uns zu Männer geworden seyn/ und ihr Auffnehmen von uns haben. Was hatte mein Mann/ wie er zu mir kam? Nicht einer Lauß werth: Er war ein kahler Studente: Ich halff ihm zum Ampte/ und nahm ihn hernach gar; wie es ja nicht seltsam bey uns ist. Dafür habe ich nun den Danck habt/ daß er mir zu widern ist/ in meinen Anordern. Ich fragte von ihm vergangen/ ob er mich denn gar für eine Mutze und Arßwisch hielte/ daß ich ihme alles nachgeben/ und nach seinem Kopffe thun solte: Da schwieg er Mause still: Sagte mir diese Thüre was/ so sagte er mir auch was drauff. Wenn die Männer ihres Thuns warteten/ und überliessen den Weibern die Kinder und Gesinde zu ziehen; so bliebe mancher Hauß Krieg nach. **Fr. Apotheckerni:** Ey lasset die Gedancken fahren/ und schlaget das Hauß-Creutze in den Wind! wir wollen jetzund von anmuthigern Sachen reden. Was gibt es guts neues von dem wunderlichen Beginnen der vornehmen Hoch-Zeitern? Wie/ hör ich doch/ daß sich auch nunmehr die grossen Hansen umb zehne trawen lassen. War es vorher nicht besser/ da man Reiche und Arme in dem Fall unterscheiden kunte? da sich die ärmsten/ die gar nichts von der Mahlzeit spendiren mögen/ oder Unkosten auff eine Gasterey wenden können/ [53] sich umb achte zusammen geben liessen. Die mittelmassigsten aber umb zehne ihren Kirchgang hatten; welche etwan noch eine Taffel speisen kunten. Die reichsten aber auffm Abend umb fünffe sich trawen liessen; und hernach drauff/ nach aller Lust/ ein köstliches Pancket von vielen Tischen anstelleten. Wie kömpts nun aber / daß sehr vermögene ansehnliche Leute/ welche sich sonsten auch wol zu Hause trawen liessen/ ihre Abendszeit verändern/ und sich früh nach zehne zur Trawung finden? **Fr. Secr.** Diese Frage fiel auch vergangen in unsern Kräntzgen für: Da antwortete einer drauff/ der etwan so viel Einfälle hatte als ein klein Scheißhäußgen. Er übergab aber sein Bedencken Schrifftlich also:

> Die Reichen machen Frühe=Hochzeiten weil
> Heller Tag ist/ da man keine Fackeln darff.
> Ohne Groß-Vater die Sache vollen-bracht wird.
> Costen drauff gehen so weniger sind als sonsten.
> Heulen und Brüllen auff den Gassen auffhöret.
> Zu Bette der Bräutgam früher gehen kan.

he were a punching bag! God protect us! He could have broken one of the child's ribs; when he gets going he really hits hard." **The nursemaid:** "He [the boy] was hanging out in the street with the street kids and snatched a herring right out of the hands of a peasant girl and ate it alive." **The young mother:** "Oh, God forgive me! Is that a reason to beat the kid so hard? What's the fuss? That's the way kids are, always up to mischief because they are still young and energetic. Everyone knows that the father probably did a lot worse [things] in his youth." **Frau Secretary:** "What's the use? My guy [husband] treats my kids the same way, and if I say a thing about it, he gets himself all riled up. They [the men] don't remember that they only became men because of us, when we took them in! What did my husband amount to when we got married? Not anything! He was a bald-assed student! I helped him to get a job and took him as my husband after that. Which is not at all unusual around here! And that's the thanks I get for it: that he refuses to do what I say. In fact, the other day I asked him if he thinks me a whore or a doormat[117] because I give in to him in all things, doing what he wishes? At that he was quiet as a mouse. Had this door spoken to me, he said as much! If men would just mind their own business and leave the children and servants to us women, many a household war would be avoided." **Frau Apothecary:** "Oh, for goodness sake, forget about the fights at home; we want to talk about more pleasant things. What is new in the high-society wedding department? I hear that now the hoity-toity[118] want to get married at ten in the morning. Wasn't it better in the past, when one could tell rich and poor apart in such matters because the poorest, who could not afford a banquet or the expenses of a celebration, got married at eight in the morning? **[53]** Those in the middle married at ten; they could afford a nice meal. But the wealthiest people married at five, arranging with great pleasure a sumptuous banquet of many, many tables. How is it that the well-to-do and respectable people, who in the past married at home, have changed their evening time to now getting married at ten in the morning?" **Frau Secretary:** "This question came up recently in our little circle. Which prompted one of us, who usually has as much imagination as a little privy,[119] to make some suggestions, which he did in writing thus:

The well-to-do wed early because:
In broad daylight no torches are needed;
The whole thing can be managed without grandfather,
because the cost will be lower than otherwise.
The screaming and howling in the streets will stop.
The bridegroom can go to bed sooner.

---

[117] "Arßwisch": arsewipe.
[118] "Grossen Hansen": also fat cats, rich bitches.
[119] Play on the synonyms of *Einfälle*: things that drop down; ideas: as many drops (= ideas) as (drop into) a small shithouse (latrine).

Einerley Würde allen Ständen zugeeignet wird.

Jungfern von den Jungen Gesellen nicht verführet werde.

Täntzer nach ihrer Gültigkeit können erkennet werden.

Ebener die *Carmina* können durchlesen werden.

Niemand sich groß beklecken darff.

Von diesen Stücken allen discurirete der Lepsch über alle massen wichtig/ und sprach: **War es erstlich** von diesem kein Gescher mit den Fackeln/ und sonderlich des Winters/ da es so zeitig Abend wird? Doch mochte es noch endlich in abgewichenen Zeiten hingehen/ weil man Pennäle hatte/ die sich außbündig zu das Fackel tragen verstunden: Nun aber weil das Hottig und Rabenzeug abgeschafft ist; wie solte man umb all die Wunder/ zu rechte kommen? Billich ist also die Veränderung mit der Zeit zu trawen getroffen/ und auff solche Zeit geleget/ da es hüpsch helle auff der Gassen zu gehen ist/ die Jungfern sich nicht besorgen dörffen/ daß sie den Pfützen die Augen außtretten/ [54] oder von dem Peche der Fackeln betröffet werden/ oder auch sonsten von den Gassenpacke die Mägde mit Graß-Kräntze beworffen werden. **Was das ander anlanget/** da war es auch ein seltzam gehudele/ umb die Groß-Väter/ oder vielmehr kleine Väter/ ja Pusenicklige Jungen/ die deß Abends zu den Mahlzeiten und den Täntzen sich hinauff drungen/ schlichen oder stohlen; fürgebende/ sie wollen ihr Herren und Frauen bedienen und abholen: und soffen unter dem Scheine viel Bier und Wein auß; frassen viel Schüßeln leer/ und schlepten hernach unter ihren Diebes-Mänteln/ das Zinnerne und Gläserne Geschirr/ sampt den Tellern und andern kleinen Möbilien hinweg/ verpartiereten es unter einander/ oder schmoltzens gar im Rosen-Thal/ oder bespickten gar ihre Simse auff den Stuben damit: Ja etliche sollen gar Laden vol gesammelt han/ und solche Außbeute hernach in ihre Heimat genommen han; Wie man denn solche Mauseköpffe auff den Collegien will ertappet haben. Aber/ nach diesem/ wird es/ Gott Lob/ mit solchem Verluste nicht viel zu bedeuten haben; sintemal man den müssigen und ungedungenen Auffwärtern bey hellem Tage/ prav auff die Finger wird sehen können/ wie sich denn auch nicht so vieles Geschleppe wird hinauff dringen können. **Zum Dritten** werden die angestellten Hochzeiten auch allerdings so viel nicht kosten können als vorher/ wegen vorgedachten Ursachen: Zu dem so wird auch sonsten ein jeder Gast nicht so viel fressen können/ weil kurz vorher erstlich auß den Federn gekrochen/ und noch halb satt ist von seiner vorigen Nacht Mahlzeit: Als auff den Abend/ da sich einer drauff hungrig gefastet/ wegen der bevorstehenden Mahlzeit deß Mittags zu Hause nicht gegessen hat; sondern wie der Henger auff die Seele/ auff die Hochzeit sich gespitzt hat; und alsdenn Schüsseln außfressen kan/ drüber mein Hauß-Knecht wol nicht mit einem Hebe-Baum springen könte. Und also wird die Sache sehr rathsam seyn/ was die vielfrässigen Männer betrifft. Aber wie wirds mit den Jungfern werden/ die desto ärger/ wie ein Scheundrescher fressen; [55] in dem sie vorher gezumpffet und gezüchtet auff den Abend haben/ wenn sie des Mittags zu Hause ihren Magen voll gepfropffet

All estates will be accorded the same dignity.
Virgins will not be seduced by bachelors.
The dancers' skills will be more readily appreciated.
Poems can be read more smoothly.
And people won't spill things all over themselves.

"This fellow, Lepsch, carried on about all these matters quite seriously, and he said, '**First,** wasn't it always a nuisance messing around with the torches, especially in the winter, when it gets dark so early? It was not so bad in times past, when we still had students who knew how to carry the torches properly. But now, when this rabble has been done away with, how can we manage, for heaven's sake? So it is right that the change coincide with the new wedding charges, and the time be set when it is still nicely light. This way the young women, when parading in the lanes, can avoid stepping into the puddles [54] or being soiled from the pitch from the torches. And, in addition, the young girls won't be pelted with grass wreaths by street gangs. **Second,** there is always so much to do about the grandfathers, or better, the little fathers, the pimply boys who always crept around and slunk or forced their way in the dark of night into the dances and meals, pretending they wanted to pick up or assist their masters and mistresses. Under this pretense they drank much wine and beer and emptied many bowls [of soup]; and then they carried away under their clothes pewter dishes, glasses, plates, and small furniture, dividing the loot among themselves or melting them down or even having the nerve to decorate their mantels at home with it. In fact, some of them are said to have "collected" whole chests full of [stuff] and taken this booty with them when they returned home; people have caught such pea-brains in the university dorms. But now, thank goodness, there won't be much loss since there will be many who have nothing to do the whole long day but to watch these sticky-fingers, the idle and indolent attendants. Which means less carrying off of stuff. **Third,** the weddings organized in this way will not cost as much as in the past for the following reasons: First of all, each guest won't be able to eat as much, because he will just have crawled out of bed and will still be full from dinner the night before. At evening weddings, people fast in anticipation of the coming meal and don't eat their noon dinner at home. But like the devil starving for a soul, they will wait for the wedding feast and empty so many bowls that, if piled high, my servant could jump over them only if using a vaulting pole. So it is certainly a good idea where it concerns these starving young men. But what about the damsels, who are even worse and eat like field hands[120] [55] since they starved and denied themselves in anticipation of the evening? Normally they stuff their bellies at noon, which they could not do now. But I'm convinced

---

[120] "Wie ein Scheunendrescher fressen": eat like a harvest worker, i.e., a lot.

gehabt; welches nunmehr vorher nicht hat können geschehen? Doch ich halte
dennoch daß sie ihre höffliche Art hierüber nicht auffgeben werden. Sie werden
desto früher auffstehen und bald drauff einen mächtigen Topff voll Supffe in den
Leib hinein jagen. Sehet/ lieben Leutgen/ auff diesen Schlag möchte es nicht
uneben oder böß gelungen seyn/ daß man die Hochzeit zu Mittage anstelle/ und
die gesättigten Gäste auffm Abend wieder nach Hause wandern lasse. Aber es
wird auch/ auff vor gewiesene Wege/ den Hochzeitern auff den andern Tag/
zuträglich seyn? Ich zweiffele gar sehr dran: Sintemal ich gedenke/ man werde
desto unbarmherziger mit der Braut Suppe umbgehen; Und was man am vorigen
Tage dem Bräutgam/ am Gebratens und andern Victualien habe ungefehr zu
gute müssen ergehen lassen/ das werde man den andern Tag der Braut an ihrer
Suppe abzwacken. Die arme Sack wird müssen büssen/ und die Zeche bezahlen.
Ey/ ey/ und noch hundertmal ey/ ey/ wie jammerts mich schon/ daß die hungri-
gen Wölffe mit der armen Braut-Suppen so Türckisch umbgehen werden/ daß
sie auch die Löffel schier für Heiß-Hungrigkeit verschlingen möchten; nach
dem sie die vorhergehende Nacht außgefastet und den Magen fast platzend
gemachet haben. Doch was hilffts? was der liebe Gott einem Theil gibt/ das
nimbt der Teuffel dem andern Theil wiederumb hinweg. So kömpt mir also
diesenen auffgebrachte Mode bald so für/ wie der Seeländer in Holland ihr beginnen; wenn sie können allezeit/ so es ihnen nur gefällt/ das Wasser wegmahl-
en und frisch Land entdecken: Allein/ was saget Lemnius darvon? Was das
Wasser einem gibt/ das benimbt es dem andern: In dem sie auch selber sprechen/
daß auff die Flandrische Lufft/ und Seeländische Rente nicht zu bauen sey. **Zum**
Vierdten/ wird jo das Gaßaten gehen/ Steineplätzen/ Hop hophe ruffen Nacht-
Musicke bringen/ [56] und Ständgen machen/ die Leute auß dem Schlaff zu
verstören/ den lüstrigen Jungfergen das Maul wäßrig zu machen/ mit den He-
schern zu scharmesiren/ die Wache Unmuths zu machen/ die Thüren in finstern
zu öffnen/ und allerhand nächtliche Unfüglichkeit nachtreiben; wenn die ab-
gefütterten Gäste sich des Abends wieder miteinander nach Hause werden ver-
fügen müssen/ von der Hochzeit/ wie von einem Magister-Schmause. O wird
man da hüpsch ruhen können/ und die Tages Grillen außträumen: Wiewol es
den Spielleuten nicht zu passe kommen dürffte/ die also weniger Geld prosperi-
ren und beystecken können/ als sonsten. **Zum fünften** wird sich auch der Bräut-
gam desto eher und früher zu seiner Braut/ als zu einem anmuthigen Schlaffge-
sellen (drumb es meistentheils zu thun ist/) finden können/ und seine reiffe Lust/
die gantze geschlagene Nacht über/ mit ihr haben/ und das Kälbgen außtreiben
können: Wie ich denn mir sagen lasse/ daß sich die Bräute nicht wenig erfreuen
sollen/ auff das gewünschte Vornehmen der Früh-Hochzeiten. **Zum sechsten**
wird auff diesem Schlag Reich und Arm in einem *aestim* seyn/ und sich der
Schuster so viel einbilden können als der Kauffmann/ der Schneider als der Raths
Herr/ der Becker als der Doctor. Und wiewol solches den Vornehmen verdries-
sen und verschnuppen dürffte; so lächelt und schmunzelt doch ein Handwercks-
mann gleichwol drüber. **Zum siebenden** werden die Jungfern destoweniger

that they will not change their "courtly" ways over this. They'll just get up earlier, and before long they'll devour a huge pot of soup. For you see, dear people, that this way it will work out easily and without much effort. When the wedding is held at noon, the satisfied guests will stroll back home in the evening. But will the described proceedings be good for the bridal couple the next day? I doubt that very much. For I am afraid people will be all the harder on the bridal soup. [121] What was saved on the roast and the victuals by the bridegroom the previous night will be ripped off by the bride['s guests] with impunity at the bride's meal. The poor thing will have to make up the difference and pay the tab. Oh, alas and a hundred times alas, how it pains me how these hungry wolves treat the bridal soup like rapacious Turks, nearly swallowing the spoons in their burning hunger after they have spent the night before "fasting" until their stomachs were turning inside out. But who cares? What the dear Lord gives, the devil takes away! It reminds me of the customs of the Dutch people, who are always taking land away from the sea, just as they please. But what does Lemnius say about this? What the water gives to the one, it will take from the other. As they say: you cannot build on Flanders air nor on Zealand's rent! And **fourth**: the streetwalking, lounging in the square, yoo-hooing around, making night music, and serenading, **[56]** waking people up from their sleep, making young women's mouths water with lustful thoughts, upsetting the watchmen, secretly opening doors in the pursuit of all kinds of nighttime nonsense [will stop] when the well-fed guests betake themselves home together from the wedding as evening comes, just like from a master's feast. [122] Oh, everyone will get a good night's rest and will dream away the day's foolishness. The only losers will be the musicians, who earn and save less money this way than usual. And **fifth**: The bridegroom will be able to join his bride much earlier in the bedroom (which is really what it is all about); he will have his eager way with her all night long. [123] As I have heard, brides look forward with pleasure to this desired institution of early weddings. **Sixth**: In one stroke, poor and rich will be equal; the cobbler will be as arrogant as the merchant, the tailor [as proud] as the counselor; the baker [will be like] the doctor. And even though the rich will be annoyed about this, the working men will chuckle and smile about it. **And seventh**: Fewer virgins will be led astray because the young men will not be able to escort them home at night! Oh, how many have lost their virginity in the streets at night. They will still keep their virgin's wreath, so that they do not have to pay good money to the wreath-repairer the next day. [124] And even if it cannot be avoided that the girls be escorted home, the eager guys cannot feel up the girls quite as easily as before, when they were in the dark

---

[121] A regionally varying type of light soup served at the bride's house.

[122] Celebration of the master's [*Magister*] degree, commencement.

[123] "Das Kälbchen austreiben": to have sex.

[124] "Ihr Kräntzgen verlieren": to lose one's bridal wreath (virginity). Midwives were often called upon to restore the semblance of virginity before a wedding.

verführet werden/ wenn sie die Junge Gesellen des Nachts nicht nach Hause führen können. O wie manche hat unter den Schein auff der Gassen ihr Kräntz-gen verlohren; daß sie nach diesen behalten wird/ und also der Kräntzmacherin den andern Tag kein frisches Geld schicken darff! Ja/ solte dannoch das Heim-führen auff allen Fall/ nicht aussen bleiben; so werden doch die naschigten Kerl nicht so sehr irre greiffen können/ als wenn sie vorhin in finstern mit ihrere Dame/ als wie der Frosch im Monden Schein/ nach Hause gehüpffet/ und sie drüber bald bey der Hand/ bald anderswohin gegriffen haben. **Zum achten** [57] wird man auch der rechtschuldigen Tantzer desto Augenscheinlicher erkennen können; ob sie auff dem Tantzboden ihre weisse Schuh vergebens getragen/ und dem Galiart Meister ihre Ducaten vergebens zugewandt haben; oder was recht-schaffens von Capriol schnitten/ und andern kunterbundten Gehüpffe/ gelernet haben. Besser wird man diese bey Tag erkundigen/ als deß Nachtes; sonderlich wenn man darzu die Gersten Brille auff der Nase gesetzt oder sich bezecht habe. **Zum neundten** wird man auch die possierliche *Carmina* und Schnack oder Schmackhaffen Braut-Suppen desto andächtiger durchstanckern können/ beym Sonnen- als beym Unschlit-Liechte. **Zum zehenden** wird man die Kleider mehr schonen können/ und sie nicht so ungeheuer beflecken dürffen/ damit der Töpffer für seinen Thon nicht so viel Pfennige mehr erübrige/ und die stoltzen Mägde nicht so viel außzukratzen bekommen. **Fr. Wöchn.** Ja fürwahr/ was dieses letzte betrifft/ da hat jener Kerl wol das Ding beym rechten Loche ertappet. Freylich muß man die Mägde jetzund/ leyder in Ehren halten/ und sie über alle massen der Arbeit überheben/ damit sie nicht brummen oder schellig werden. Verdreust es doch meiner Kluncker-Mutze/ daß sie alle vier Wochen das Hauß putzen/ und Stube/ Küche und Kammern außscheuren soll; ich geschweige/ wenn ich ihr noch was mehres heissen würde. Die Schindfaulen Mehren wollen jetzund gar Jungfer spielen/ und nicht auff ihre Weiber geben. Sie kommen mir nicht anders für/ als das Handwercks-pack auff den Collegien/ das läufft derentwegen auch auß der Stadt weg/ und zeucht den Kopff auß deß Raths Schlinge/ damit es nicht so viel Aufflage bekommen/ und droben desto freyer leben mögen: Aber ich meine/ man bezahle sie hernach/ wenn sie sterben; was sie im Leben verschuldet haben: Wenn die Obrigkeit hernach ihnen kein Sarg erstattet/ sondern sie durch einen Kerl auff den Leichen Karren hinauß schleppen/ und bloß in die Grübe stürtzen läst. **Fr. Pfarrnerin.** Ey/ das Ding kan ich gleichwol nicht billigen. **Fr. Wöchnerin:** [58] Frau Gevatterin vergesset euer Wort nicht: Ich meine es sey gar recht; Was hat das Schindpack auff den Collegien verlohren: kan es sich nicht in die Stadt hinunter scheren/ da es was verlohren hat? **Fr. Pfarrnerin:** Wir haben nicht alle gleich viel Geld/ daß wir theure Miete bezahlen können; es muß sich mancher nach der Decke strecken und seine Pfennige zu rathe halten/ die er sparsam einnimbt. Und halte ich also noch mehr von sie/ als hierunten von

with their ladies, [acting] like frogs in the light of the moon, grasping [their la-
dies] first by the hand and then somewhere else. **[57] And eighth:** And we will
be much better able to separate the bad dancers from the good; whether they
wear their white shoes in vain on the dance floor, if they paid the galliard master[125] their ducats for naught; or whether they really can execute an expert capri-
ole and other fancy maneuvers. All this is better seen in the daytime than at
night, especially when you are wearing "beer glasses" or have tied one on.[126] **And
ninth:** And it will be possible to reverently appreciate and to take apart the humorous wedding songs and spoofs and [enjoy] the tasty bridal soup by day than
by candlelight. **And tenth:** People will take better care of their clothes, and they
won't stain them so much. Then the potter won't make so many extra pennies on
his fuller's earth, and the proud maids won't have so much to scour." **The young
mother:** "Yes, indeed, with regard to the latter, the guy has really got it right;
these days, unfortunately, we have to treat our maids well and not overwork
them, lest they get to grumbling and become contrary. My foolish goose gets
pretty annoyed that every four weeks she has to clean the house and scrub the
parlor, kitchen, and bedroom; I'll leave aside what happens if I ask her to do a
little more! Now, these lazy horses' asses[127] play the damsels,[128] not wanting to
serve their mistress any more. They seem to me no different than this riffraff of
artisans at the university who run out of town pulling their heads out of the town
council's noose so that they won't have to pay their dues; and they live much freer
up there [at the university]. But mark my words: when they die, they will be paid
according to the debt they incurred.[129] And then the authorities won't grant them
a coffin but rather will have some guy throw them on a hearse, cart them off, and
drop them in the hole." **Frau Pastor:** "Oh, no, I cannot agree with this." **The
young mother: [58]** "Oh, my dear godmother, forgive me if I interrupt you![130] I
think it is absolutely right. What has this riff raff lost at the university? Can't they
go down into the town where they belong?" **Frau Pastor:** "Not all of us have the
money so that we can pay the expensive rent; many have to make do just scraping
by and pinch the pennies they earn. I have to say, I think more of them than of
these rich bastards who constantly go bankrupt while gallantly gambling away

---

[125] Galliard: fast, often raucous dance, originally from Italy.
[126] "Die Gersten Brille": literally, glasses made of beer; having one's vision affected
by drink ("beer goggles").
[127] "Schindfaulen Mehren": lazy female horse; "schind~": anything related to execution, a horse that carried the convicted to the place of execution, i.e., "Schindanger."
[128] "Jungfer" here means a well-to-do young woman (damsel).
[129] Tensions between the universities and the towns were a frequent problem during
this time ("town and gown"). In order to control the student population, towns instituted
rules for student conduct, such as prohibitions against bearing weapons.
[130] "Vergesset euer Wort nicht": don't forget what you wanted to say, i.e., pardon my
interrupting you.

denselben reichen Schindern/ welche ohn unterlaß panckerot machen/ und beym grossen Muthe muthwillig verspielen. Warümb solte man aber den armen Leuten auff den Collegien keinen Sarg lassen zukommen? Genössen es doch des Rats-Bürger und Tischler mehr als sonsten/ und hetten auch also stärckere Einnahme ihren Schoß und Tribut zu erlegen; drüber sich mancher beklaget/ daß ers nicht wisse woher zu nehmen. **Fr. Wöchn.** Sie mag mir vergeben Frau Gevatterin/ ich weiß dennoch nicht/ was ich von den Collegien hottig halten soll. Es kömpt mir vor/ ich weiß nicht wie/ verdächtig. Ja mir daucht/ daß sich eine ehrliche Frau schämen müsse ins Collegien zu gehen. **Frau Pfarrnerin:** Vergangen kam mir auch eine Dünckertin und hoffertiges Muster mit diesen ungebührlichen Worten auffgezogen; Da antwortete ich ihr; ob sie es denn für auffrichtig und löblich hielte/ daß in ihr Hauß ein redlicher Mann gienge? Das krizelte sie in der Nasen: Drümb fuhre sie mich mit ihrer Schneppe an/ und erfragete/ ob ich denn meinete/ daß sie eine leichtfertige Hure were? Ich antwortete: Das sage ich nicht/ sondern ihr: Meinet ihr denn aber im Gegen-Theil/ daß es Schelme und Dachdiebe seyn/ die auff den Collegien wohnen: daß man sie scheuen solte/ sie zuzusprechen? Hierüber erblaßete sie/ und ward wie ein weiß und stumm Tuch. Doch mag mir die Frau Gevatterin gute halten/ daß ich ihr dieses erzehlet habe: Dazu ich noch dieses hinzu thun muß/ daß ein ehrlicher Mensch so rein auff das Collegium hinauff gehen/ als herunter gehen könne. Item daß ein redliches Gemüthe auff einem Collegio so recht mässig leben und herunter ziehen/ als hinnauff ziehen könne. Ungeachtet/ und der Sachen nichts benehmende/ daß bißweilen ungerathene und liederliche Gesellen droben seyn/ [59] welche zum Zeiten die Hescher nicht allein außschreyen; sondern auch außpfeiffen/ ja wol gar mit Küh-hörner und Retorten sie unverschämt außblasen und außmachen/ daß ein Hund kein Stücke Brot von einem dergleichen außgefensterten Galgenschwengel nehme. **Fr. Secr.** Aber das Volck wird so greulich hochmütig droben/ wie ich denn ein schnipsch Ding kenne/ daß kaum von aussen herein gekommen ist/ und sich so Bärbösig unter die Lästerer machen kan/ wenn man sie ein wenig ungefehr anrühret/ oder nur das Fleisch in die quer ansiehet/ das sie bepfennigen will. **Fr. Pfarrn:** Ey dergleichen Schur-Mutzen/ die sich so pätzig machen können/ und so zutäppisch; (wie Katzen-Fleisch/ daß selber in die Töpffe kreucht;) gibt es noch vielmehr unten in der Stadt: Ich kenne etliche Fladder-Geister/ die so kurz angebunden seyn/ und solchen Nasenweisen Wind haben/ daß nichts drüber ist: Sie gehen auff den Bauer-Marckte die Reigen auff und nieder/ und kucken allen Weibern in die Körbe/ kosten sich auch schier satt an Käß und Butter/ eher sie einen Heller wagen. Kömpt nun eine geringere Frau/ und machet mit den Bauren umb Eyer und Quärge einen Kauff/ so fallen sie wie die Raben ein/ und nehmen es jener bald unter den Fäusten weg. So trefflich klug seyn sie/ daß sie erstlich den unverständigen und albern (nach ihrem Witz und Postille/) das beste müssen außsuchen lassen/ eher sie sich unter den schlimsten zu schicken wissen. Das beste ists/ daß geringe Leute früh auff seyn/ bald auff den Marckt gehen/ und das wichtigste bey Zeiten nehmen/ damit sie/ wenn daß langsame

their fortunes. So why not let the poor university people have coffins? Wouldn't the council members and carpenters profit even more this way, and thus due to the increased profit have to pay more taxes? And this when many [others] complain that they don't know where their next dime is coming from." **The young mother:** "Please forgive me, dear godmother, I really don't know what to think about these college boys. I cannot help but be suspicious of them. In fact, it appears to me that an honorable woman would be ashamed to go to the university." **Frau Pastor:** "Recently a bitch and arrogant piece of work came at me with some rude words; I asked her if she thought it appropriate and right that an honorable man would enter her house. She wrinkled her nose and came after me with her big mouth, asking me if I thought her a loose whore, I replied, I did not say that—you did. And likewise, didn't you say that only fools and bums live at the university, whom one should avoid and under no circumstances speak with? She blanched, as white and silent as a sheet. But dear lady, please don't hold it against me that I told you this; furthermore, I want to add that an honorable man can enter the university as clean as he leaves it. A virtuous man can live at the university as modestly and as frugally as anyone in spite of the fact, which I cannot deny, that occasionally some rough and slovenly fellows live there. [59] They not only yell at the police but make fun of them, even whistle at them with cow horns and glass vessels so that no dog would take a piece of bread from these gallows knaves." **Frau Secretary:** "But folks up there [at the university] get so arrogant; I know an uppity young thing that barely had come in out of the rain who would turn so mean and awful if, just by chance, one only slightly touched her, or even just glanced at the meat that she deigned to consider purchasing." **Frau Pastor:** "Oh, yes, but aren't there even more of these hissy, snotty creatures—like cats in a pot—in town? I know some of those harebrained fools; they act so curt and hold their noses so high up in the air that there is nothing above it. At the farmer's market they just parade up and down, checking out all the women's wares; before they risk spending even one penny they taste here and there, [consuming] enough cheese and butter to be full for the day. And if a poorer woman comes by and agrees with the farmer on the price of eggs or her cottage cheese, they descend upon her like ravens, practically grabbing stuff right out of her hands. They are so smart that they first allow the simple and the silly to check for the best wares (that's the way they see it!) before they take advantage of their station. It is good that poor people get up and go to market early to take care of their most important purchases, so that the slowpokes can get what is left, most likely cottage cheese. But who wants to stir this stuff, which already stinks to high

Geschleppe kömbt/ ihnen zum öfftern den Quarck hinterlassen. Aber wer will den Dreck viel rühren/ es stincket ohne das fast zu viel? **Fr. Sec. Stehet unmuths auff/ und saget:** Behüt euch Gott F. Gevatterin/ ich muß nunmehr wieder nach Hause gehen. **Fr. Wöchn.** Ey wie denn so geschwinde Fr. Gevatterin? Verziehet doch etwas; ihr habt ja unsertwegen nicht zu eylen. Ich kan euch noch nicht gehen lassen. **Fr. Secr.** Fürwahr/ glaubet mir/ Fr. Gevatterin/ ich muß trabends nach Hause lauffen: Es fällt mir jähligen was ein/ das ich bald über unser Geschwätze solte vergessen haben. Nun behüt euch Gott miteinander: Und redet mir nichts übel nach. [60] **Fr. Wöchn:** Je weil es nicht anders ist/ so habt doch fleissigen Danck Fr. Gevatt. daß ihr mich besucht/ und die grosse Ehre angethan habt. Und so ich es der Fr. Gevatt. weiter darff zumuthen; so sey sie doch fleissig gebeten/ und komme doch noch sonsten mehr zu mir: Ich will es gerne wiederumb verschulden; Grüsset unterdessen großgünstig den Herrn Gevatter unseretwegen. **Fr. Pfarrn:** Sie gehet vorwahr unseretwegen/ weil ich sie zu sehr vorher getroffen habe. O ich kenne sie schon/ was sie für ein Thiergen ist/ und weiß gar zu wol was sie im Schilde führet. Sie ist nicht weit her/ so hat sie auch nicht weit hin: Sie ist gar kurtz angebunden/ und wohl die recht schuldige Matrone. Hette sie bey ihren Eltern etwas Haußhalten dafür gelernet/ so könte es etwas besser umb sie stehen. Ich will meinen Kopff verlohren haben/ und die Füsse zu Pfande setzen/ so sie weiß/ wenn ein Wasser siedet. Sie hat ein alte Frauen Magd zu Hause/ die muß ihr alles kochen und kauffen verrichten: Wenn aber die nicht da ist/ so gibt es schlecht Gemüse: Und auffm Bauermarckt heisset es denn: Wenn man Narren zu Marckte schicket/ so kauffen kluge Leute Geld: Wie sie denn vergangen von einer Käse Mutter betrogen worden: Die ihr auß vermerckten Unverstand/ sechs Möhren umb einen Groschen verlassen hat. Hierauß kan man abnehmen und überschlagen/ was ihre alte Hauß Magd für eine Unterschlag am Gelde endlich machen muß. Denn die alberne Närrin weiß weder Kicks noch Kacks/ daß sie solte können nachdencken/ oder wissen genaue Rechnung von ihrer Köchinnen zu fo(r)dern: Was ihr die durchgetriebene Hummel vorschwatzet das glaubet sie. Ihr Mann wird es aber drüber/ leider! gewahr in dem er verarmet/ und schier panckerotiren möchte; die ungerecht Haußhalterin aber reich wird. Wenn es klug were/ so gienge es selber mit zu Marckte/ und lauerte ab/ was andere Leute für die Eßel-Waare geben: aber da fladdert es mit den Augen herümb/ und siehet wenig wo sie kriechen; sondern wo sie fliehen. So ferne es ja noch einmal kömmet/ daß sie für lange werle ihr Körbgen nimbt/ und vor die Muhme auff den Marck mit hin spatzieret: Die muß kauffen/ und sie hat hingegen Maulaffen feil; dafür ihr der Henger [61] nicht eine Bratwurst gebe. Das alte Weib kauffet nach ihrem Wolgefallen/ ein/ so viel sie will/ und setzt ihr hernach die Rechnung hoch genug an/ weil sie sicher weiß/ daß ihr Frau auff den Preiß nicht achtung gegeben hat; ob sie schon darbey

heaven?"[131] **Frau Secretary gets up quite agitated and says:** "God bless you, dear godmother, I really have to go home now!" **The young mother:** "But why so suddenly, dear godmother? Why don't you stay a little longer? You don't have to hurry on our account. I really cannot allow you to leave just yet." **Frau Secretary:** "Dear godmother, believe me—I have to get home on the double. I just now remembered something that I had almost forgotten with all our gabbing. Now God keep you all, and don't badmouth me." **[60] The young mother:** "Well, if it has to be, let me thank you, dear godmother, for the honor that you have extended me with your visit. And if I may entreat the Lady Godmother further, then let her be eagerly urged to visit me more often. I will be more than happy to return the favor. Please greet the Lord Godfather warmly on our behalf." **Frau Pastor:** "Surely she is leaving because of us, because I upset her too much earlier. Oh, I know her well, what kind of a creature she is. I know all too well what she's planning to do. She's not from far away, so she does not have to go far. She's always quite blunt, acting the matron in the know. Had she learned instead a bit about keeping house at her parents', things would be a bit better for her. I would bet my head and hock my feet if she knows how to boil water. At home she has an old maid who has to do all the cooking and shopping; but when she [the maid] is not there, things are bad in the household.[132] At the farmer's market they say: When you send a fool to market, smart people buy better money. For example, recently a cheese woman cheated her; by feigning ignorance she sold her six carrots for one *Groschen*. From this you can easily imagine how her old maid can underhandedly put aside money. Her old fool of a mistress knows shit [about money]; because, if she did, she would ask for an accounting of her cook. Whatever this sly fox[133] tells her, she accepts for gospel. But her husband—alas—will only become aware of this when he finds himself impoverished and bankrupt. The dishonest housekeeper, on the other hand, is getting rich. If the lady were smart, she would go alone to market and watch what other people are paying for food; but all she does there is let her eyes flit here and there, ignoring what is underfoot for what flies in the air.[134] Sometimes she even goes so far as to take the basket and carry it to market out of boredom, where she strolls in front of the maid, who does the shopping while she [the lady], by contrast, gawks about,[135] for which the devil will not give her as much as a sausage which does no one any good. **[61]** Meanwhile, the old woman buys what and as much as her heart desires and then inflates the bills, because she knows for certain that her lady, although she stood right by her with her eyes and ears wide open, hasn't paid any attention to

---

[131] "But who wants to talk about this any further? It is surely a disgrace."

[132] "So gibt es schlecht Gemüse": there will be bad (not fresh) vegetables = things are in bad shape.

[133] "Durchgetriebene Hummel": sly/crafty bumblebee = clever old girl, biddy.

[134] Not paying attention to the important things.

[135] "Maulaffen feilhalten": idly looking about, wasting time in useless observation.

gestanden/ und ihre Glotzen/ sampt den Horchern/ nicht eine Spanne davon
gehabt. Ja es ist so eine Wirthin/ als der Teuffel ein Apostel. Ich habe gar recht
gethan/ daß ich vorher ein wenig loß gezogen habe. Es gereuet mich noch diese
Stunde/ daß ichs nicht ärger gemacht habe: Denn es muß ja die Warheit unter
die Leute kommen. **Fr. Apot.** Will ich nicht ehrlicher seyn/ der Seyger schläget
schon sechse: Ich muß/ mein Schelm! geschwinde nach Hause springen; daß ich
zusehe was meine Köchin machet: Denn wie bald verläufft sich eine Stunde/ da
es wird Sieben schlagen/ und da Essen bereit auff dem Tischen stehen muß? **Fr.
Pfarrn.** Ich will gleich mit gehen. Guten Abend Fr. Gevatt. Verzeihet mir doch
mein unnützes Geschwätze. **Fr. Apot.** Auch zu guter Nacht Fr. Gevatterin/ und
du liebes Mäußgen du frommes Patgen; gesegne dich der liebe Gott! haltet uns
doch ja zu gute/ daß wir euch so lange verunruhiget haben. **Fr. Wöchn.** Ey wolt
ihr euch viel entschuldigen/ lieben Frauen Gevatterinnen? Ihr seyd mir gar nicht
beschwerlich gewesen: Wolte Gott/ daß ich euch hette können was zu guts thun/
und nach Würden empfangen. Habet doch sehr fleissigen Danck/ daß ihr meiner eingedenck gewesen seyd/ und von euren Haußgeschäfften euch so viel haben wollen abmüssigen; daß ihr mich und mein Kindgen/ jezt besuchet habt.
Habt doch nochmal grossen Danck/ und unterlasset es ferner nicht/ mich weiter
nach diesen zu zusprechen. Grüsset doch allemiteinander die Herrn Gevattern.
Fr. Apot. Es soll geschehn liebe Fr. Gevatt. Sehet da/ Muhme/ nehmet so ver-
lieb/ und wieget mein Patgen fein fleissig/ daß es hüpsch groß und starck werde.
Muhme. Ey was soll das seyn/ ich habe es ja nicht umb euch verschuldet. **Fr.
Apot.** Nun/ nun/ was nöthiget ihr euch lange? es ist ein wenig/ nehmt so verlieb/
und verschmähet es nicht. **Muhme:** Wenn es denn ja so seyn soll; so habet unerhört mächtigen grossen Danck. Tanz Kätzgen tantz/ wie schön steht dir der
Krantz. [62] Soll mir der Kranz nicht schöne stehn? Ich will zu meinem Liebsten
gehn: Schlaff balde. Schlaff Kindgen/ schlaff/ dein Vater hütet der Schaaf: Die
Mutter geht auff den Kerckhoff: Schlaff du grosser Plärrkopff.

Biß hieher die vorgenommene Wochen-Comoedie: Künfftig/ geliebt es Gott/
und beliebet es dem lustigen Leser/ so soll was wercklichers erfolgen: Nemlich
die Tröge Weiber-Wäsche/ die ich mit ehesten an der Liechten Sonnen bringen will/ oder auff den Bleech-Platz schleppen/ damit sie was weisser werde/
Solte es mir auch schon eilff Pfennige kosten. Ich will aber nicht hoffen/ daß ich
im gegenwertigen Geschnacke irgend einen beleidget habe: Solte aber jo einer sich offendirt befinden; der verfechte es mit den klatzschigten Weibern; von
welchen ich es/ als ein unwürdiger Wochen-Störer/ abgehorchet habe. Ingleichen
werden es mir auch die Autores, der angeführten dreyen Wochen-Stülen/ oder
Kinder-Betterinnen-Gesprächen/ freundlich zu gute halten/ daß ich wolmeynend

the price and is entirely without a clue. Yes, if she is a housewife, the devil was an apostle. I was quite right to run on a bit earlier about types like her. In fact, I only regret that I did not say worse, because people have to hear the truth." **Frau Apothecary:** "I, too, have to be honest, the clock is already striking six, and, son of a gun, I have to rush home to see what my cook is doing. How quickly an hour passes! It will be seven o'clock, when dinner must be on the table." **Frau Pastor:** "I'll come right along, too. Good night, dear Lady Godmother. Please forgive my useless gossip." **Frau Apothecary:** "Good night, dear godmother, and you sweet little mouse, my dear little godchild, may God bless you. Please don't think less of us for staying so long." **The young mother:** "Oh dear, why would you want to apologize? You haven't been any trouble at all. Would to God that I could have treated you better and received you with more ceremony. But thank you very much for having thought of me, and that you have been willing to abandon so many of your household chores to visit me and my little baby. Once again, thank you most warmly and please do come again. And all of you, please, greet the Lord Godfathers." **Frau Apothecary:** "It will be done, dear Lady Godmother. Here, dear *Muhme*, please take this small gift, and rock my little godchild carefully, so that he grows up big and strong." *Muhme*: "Dear me, what for? I haven't done anything special!" **Frau Apothecary:** "Please don't act so shy, it isn't much, please accept it." *Muhme*: "Very well, if it has to be. Thank you very, very much. [She sings a lullaby:]

> "Dance, little cat, dance.
> How lovely you look in your wreath. **[62]**
> I want to visit my lover.
> So sleep, little child, sleep.
> Your father guards the sheep,
> Your mother visits the graves.
> Sleep, you bawling baby."

Up this point [you have] the lying-in comedy [that I set out to present]. In the future, if it pleases the dear reader, I will follow up with something more pleasing: namely the washerwomen's laundry, which I will bring to the light of day or haul onto the bleaching lawn so that it [the laundry] will get whiter, even if it costs me dearly.[136] I do hope that I did not offend anyone with my present chatter. But if someone should be offended, I blame it on gossipy women from whom I, as an unworthy confinement eavesdropper, overheard [this stuff]. And I hope that, equally, the authors of the three birthing-chair poems, or lying-in-ladies' conversations, will kindly understand that my intentions in using their things

---

[136] Play on words about washing or hanging out the laundry, that is, making public what usually remains unsaid: airing dirty linen. The custom of putting linens out to bleach on bleaching lawns was widely practiced in early modern Germany.

mich jetzund ihrere Sachen gebrauchet habe. Ein Schelm in meinem Nahmen/ der es böse gemeint hat. *Valete & plaudite, fi merui: si non, date merum!* Wollet ihr es nicht; so lasset es bleiben/ und lasset mich Rastern und Kovent trincken.

Ende

[words] were good. Damned be who thinks ill of it. Farewell and praise me, if I deserve it; if not, give me hell. If you do not like it, let it be, and let me drink my beer or wine.

The End